# LAW & BANKING
## PRINCIPLES

KATHLYN L. FARRELL

*FOURTH EDITION*

The AMERICAN BANKERS ASSOCIATION is committed to providing innovative, high-quality products and services that are responsive to its members' critical needs.

To comment about this product, or to learn more about the AMERICAN BANKERS ASSOCIATION and the many products and services it offers, please call **1-800-Bankers.** You may also learn about ABA and its products and services by visiting our Web site: **www.aba.com.**

AMERICAN
**BANKERS**
ASSOCIATION ®

# CONTENTS

# LIST OF EXHIBITS

# Chapter 8

# Chapter 9

# Chapter 10

# LIST OF CASES FOR DISCUSSION

# TABLE OF LAWS AND REGULATIONS

Uniform Commercial Code, Article 3: Negotiable Instruments

Uniform Commercial Code, Article 4: Bank Deposits and Collections

Uniform Commercial Code, Article 4A: Funds Transfers,

Uniform Commercial Code, Article 5: Letters of Credit

Expedited Funds Availability Act (12 U.S.C. 4001)

Federal Reserve Board Regulation CC (Availability of Funds and Collection of Checks)

Electronic Funds Transfer Act (15 U.S.C. 1693)
    Federal Reserve Board Regulation E (Electronic Funds Transfers)

Bank Secrecy Act (31 U.S.C. 5311)
    31 C.F.R. Part 103 (Regulations governing currency transaction reporting)

Federal Reserve Board Regulation D (Reserve Requirements)

Federal Deposit Insurance Act (12 U.S.C. 1811)
    FDIC Regulation 12 C.F.R. 330 (Deposit Insurance Coverage)

# ABOUT THE AUTHOR

**Kathlyn Farrell** is an attorney practicing financial services law in Houston, Texas. She has more than 20 years of experience in banking in the fields of regulatory compliance, lending transactions, litigation management, contract negotiation, and bankruptcy. She has worked for large commercial banks and for the legal division of General Electric Capital Corporation. Currently she is the Director of Regulatory Compliance for The Bankers Advantage Group, Inc., a bank consulting company.

Ms. Farrell has been a lecturer and faculty advisor at the ABA National Compliance School and has written extensively about banking law issues, including co-authoring the *ABA Compliance Audit Manual* and authoring the *Reference Guide to Regulatory Compliance.* Her clients include small and medium size banks, including one based solely on the Internet.

# ACKNOWLEDGMENTS

The American Bankers Association and the author would like to thank Susan M. Siegel for helping to focus the instructional design of this course.

Susan M. Siegel, an education and training consultant, has been writing seminars, instructor's manuals, and correspondence courses for AIB/ABA for more than 20 years. She has contributed her instructional design expertise to many AIB textbooks, including *Principles of Banking, Marketing Financial Services,* and *Law & Banking: Applications.* Susan is the author of one of ABA's first Internet courses, based on the previous edition of *Law & Banking: Principles.*

Recently, Susan earned a Certificate in Distance Learning from the University of Wisconsin. In addition, she holds masters degrees in Educational Measurements and Instructional Design from the University of Pennsylvania.

As the instructional designer for *Law & Banking: Principles,* Susan made a significant contribution to the text's overall organizational structure and ensured that the content was well written and fully supported the learning objectives. For her considerable time and effort in working to improve the manuscript, Susan has my gratitude and respect.

The American Bankers Association and the author thank the following members of the review committee, whose suggestions, contributions, and critical reviews of the initial drafts helped to ensure the accuracy, thoroughness, and usefulness of *Law & Banking: Principles.*

John Baiocco
Vice President
SunTrust Bank
Norfolk, Virginia

Thomas P. Laskaris
Vice President
Wilmington Trust Company
Wilmington, Delaware

Michael F. Crotty
Deputy General Counsel
Office of the General Counsel
American Bankers Association
Washington, District of Columbia

Steve Rinaldi
Associate General Counsel
Office of the General Counsel
American Bankers Association
Washington, District of Columbia

Nessa E. Feddis
Senior Federal Counsel
Office of the General Counsel
American Bankers Association
Washington, District of Columbia

Peter Seitz
Senior Vice President and General Counsel
First National Bank
Christiansburg, Virginia

Craig W. Smith
Managing Director
VanCott Rowe & Smith, LLC
Hartford, Connecticut

Mathew H. Street
Associate General Counsel
Office of the General Counsel
American Bankers Association
Washington, District of Columbia

Konrad T. Tuchscherer
Partner
Tuchscherer, Eckert, Smith & Rudolph, S.C.
Wausau, Wisconsin

Irving D. Warden
Associate General Counsel
Office of the General Counsel
American Bankers Association
Washington, District of Columbia

L. H. Wilson
Associate General Counsel
Office of the General Counsel
American Bankers Association
Washington, District of Columbia

Finally, thanks go to Todd Skelton, Lending Product Expert, Concentrex, for the contribution of documents used as exhibits and visuals in this edition of *Law and Banking: Principles*.

# PREFACE

Nearly every banker wonders at one time or another why the bank follows certain procedures. Often the answer can be found in the laws that regulate the many facets of banking. Every part of the banking process, from taking deposits and making loans to operating safe deposit boxes and offering trust services, is governed by laws for the purpose of protecting consumers or maintaining the safety and soundness of the bank. Knowing the basics of banking law will enable every banker to grasp the requirements of his or her job and perform it with more understanding.

One way to learn more about the law as it relates to banking is by reading about some of the legal problems banks have experienced in dealing with their customers' accounts. Throughout this book you will find interesting stories illustrating the way various laws affect the outcome of banking decisions. These cases for discussion are brief accounts of legal situations that may help you to better understand the concepts described in the text. The questions at the conclusion of these stories can be used for group discussion or for individual reflection.

Keeping current with banking law changes is one of the challenges of a successful banking career. Every year old laws are modified or replaced by new ones and bank regulatory agencies make significant changes in the regulations that apply to the banking industry. This new edition of *Law & Banking: Principles* contains many changes to reflect the most current versions of banking laws and regulations.

This edition adds a chapter on the Uniform Commercial Code (UCC), highlighting some of the most important portions of that law as it applies to banking. The chapter includes sections on negotiable instruments, bank deposits, wire transfers, and the newly revised Article 5 covering letters of credit. A new chapter on consumer lending covers many of the consumer protection regulations that govern consumer lending. And the secured transactions chapter reflects the most current revision to UCC Article 9.

Since the last edition of *Law & Banking: Principles,* the legal issues surrounding Internet banking have become an important topic in banking law. These issues are considered in many of the chapters.

Bank employees need to understand and correctly use many legal words and phrases. Words like *beneficiary, assignment,* and *collateral* are examples of standard legal terms that are used constantly in the world of banking. *Law & Banking: Principles* contains illustrations of how legal terms should be used in banking, and as you make your way through the chapters of this book you will add many new words to your vocabulary. Important new words appear in **bold** where they are defined in the text. Each new word is defined, either explicitly or by context, in the text. For your convenience each bolded word also appears in the glossary at the back of the book. Some of these terms may be easily confused or may be best understood when they appear together with related terms.

To reinforce the definitions for these terms they also appear in special short lists of *critical terms* within the text.

At the end of each chapter you will find a set of questions you may use to review the legal concepts and rules that were presented in the chapter. Taking a few minutes to respond to these questions when you have finished reading the chapter will help you make certain that you have mastered the material before you move on to the next assigned chapter.

After you have completed your study of each chapter you should be able to answer the questions in the learning activities section with little difficulty. After successfully completing this course, you should be able to

- explain the regulatory system by which regulations are made and banks are governed
- identify the major laws that affect the business of banking today
- list the articles of the Uniform Commercial Code that pertain to bank deposits and letters of credit
- describe the difference between a crime and a tort and list crimes and torts that affect banking today
- explain the relationships between an agent and a principal and between a partner and a partnership
- identify the type of documentation a bank needs when dealing with an agent or a partnership
- explain how a corporation is formed and the differences between a corporation and a limited liability company
- identify the documentation a bank requires to do business with a corporation
- list the requirements for a contract and identify some types of contracts into which a bank enters
- list the types of property ownership and how banks obtain an interest in a customer's property
- identify the important laws that regulate consumer lending
- explain how a bank obtains a valid security interest in a borrower's property
- describe the requirements that Article 9 of the Uniform Commercial Code imposes on a bank when repossessing collateral
- list three types of bankruptcy filings and the purposes for each type

Federal and state laws have a profound effect on the business of banking. Learning how they affect your job is an important part of your personal professional development. This course will give you a broader frame of reference for your current job, and I hope it will encourage you to continue exploring other facets of banking.

# 1

# INTRODUCTION TO LAW AND BANKING

**LEARNING OBJECTIVES**

After studying this chapter, you should be able to

- explain how various historical banking and economic events have shaped the legal and regulatory evolution of the industry and list significant pieces of legislation
- describe the role of the legislative branch of federal and state governments in the regulation of banking and explain how a bill becomes a law
- list the federal and state agencies responsible for regulating banking and describe the role each agency plays in examining banks and writing implementing regulations
- describe the function of the judicial system and explain the hierarchy within the federal and state court systems
- Give examples of several categories of federal and state laws that affect banking
- define and use the legal and banking terms that appear in bold in the chapter text

## INTRODUCTION

Banks are vital to the life of all modern societies. Without banks most of the nation's business would grind to a halt. Nearly every business transaction conducted each day in this country requires the services of a bank to deposit cash, clear a check, or process a credit card or electronic payment. Banks provide security for payment systems and reliability for check processing. Banks help foster a healthy economy by providing a source of capital to businesses in the form of working capital and development loans. Banks also provide much of the credit consumers use to make major purchases and fund expensive endeavors such as college education.

One of the most important contributions banks make to society is to provide safe and secure places to retain money until it is needed. Individuals and businesses deposit money in bank accounts with confidence that it will be safe and available when needed. In the first quarter of 1999, more than $695 billion was deposited in checking accounts in U.S. commercial banks. More than a trillion dollars was deposited in savings accounts during the same time period. The banking industry is built on public trust and confidence.

Because banks are so important to the economic life of the country, the government has enacted many laws to regulate and protect the banking industry. The importance of maintaining the integrity and safety of the banking system cannot be understated. History has demonstrated that economic chaos results when the banking system is undermined, so the government takes seriously its responsibility to protect the banking system.

Many banking regulations also protect bank customers. Banking services are considered an essential part of life for most Americans; therefore, the government has enacted laws to protect consumers in their transactions with banks. Consumer protection regulations also protect the banking

system because they maintain public confidence in that system.

In this book you will learn about the laws and regulations that have been created to protect banks and their customers. These laws cover all facets of banking, from making loans to processing checks and payments. In this chapter you will be introduced to the types of laws that govern the banking industry. You also will learn how the laws and regulations are made and who enforces compliance with them.

## EVOLUTION OF BANKING LAWS AND REGULATIONS

Most of the laws and regulations that affect banking have been enacted in response to an economic climate or event in U.S. history. To understand today's banking laws and regulations, it is important to briefly review the history of banking in the United States. Banks were not always as safe and reliable as they are today. In fact, during much of the history of this country, banks were regarded with some suspicion. Laws in some jurisdictions actually prevented the establishment of banks until the latter part of the nineteenth century.

Before 1791, when Alexander Hamilton established the first central bank in the United States, banks were established and operated without much regulation or oversight. Each bank printed its own currency, and many banks refused to accept any currency other than their own. A poorly managed bank might fail, rendering its currency worthless. The first central bank of the United States was created in 1791 to solve these problems. However, opposition to centralized government was so strong during the first 30 years of U.S. history that Congress did not renew the charter of the First Bank of the United States, which, consequently, closed in 1811.

Confidence in the banking system plummeted again when the same problems recurred in the locally established banking institutions. Congress again chartered a central bank in 1816. However, in 1828 Andrew Jackson ran for the presidency on a platform that called for ending the central bank. Jackson was elected and the bank's charter was allowed to expire in 1836. After that time, bank owners obtained **bank charters**—official documents authorizing the opening and operation of the bank—from local governments.

Confidence in the banking system sank again to a low level. Nearly half the banks that opened during this time failed within their first 10 years. The public's opinion of banking was at an all-time low by 1852, when nine states prohibited banking. This patchwork-quilt system of banking quickly became unwieldy as the nation's economy grew and became more industrialized.

The congressional response over the past one and one-half centuries to the expanding economy and the growth of technology has been to enact more than 30 major banking laws (exhibit 1.1). Many of these laws were enacted as a reaction to the Great Depression that began following the stock market crash of 1929. The common purpose of these laws was to strengthen the banking system. Other laws have since been passed to provide consumer protections. Some of these laws provide the government with information it needs to conduct law enforcement investigations. More recently, Congress has begun to loosen the restrictions that were placed on banks during the era of the Great Depression. This effort culminated in 1999 with

---

### Exhibit 1.1    Banking Law Timeline

| Year | Law |
| --- | --- |
| 1862 | *National Bank Act* |
| | The National Bank Act established both a national banking system and a regulatory agency, the Comptroller of the Currency, to oversee it. The act instituted tighter capital requirements and management standards for banks and created reserve requirements to make the banking system safer. |
| 1913 | *Federal Reserve Act* |
| | This law created 12 Federal Reserve Districts, each containing a Federal Reserve Bank operating under the authority of the Federal Reserve Board in Washington, D.C. Each Federal Reserve Bank acts as a check-collecting clearing house for banks in its district. Because required reserves are kept in the Federal Reserve Banks, they are spread out throughout the country. The Federal Reserve issues the nation's basic form of currency—the Federal Reserve Note. |
| 1933 | *Glass-Steagall Act* |
| | This law created the Federal Deposit Insurance Corporation to provide insurance to depositors and restore confidence in the banking system during the Great Depression. The act strengthened banks by prohibiting the charging of interest on demand deposits and by raising the minimum capital requirements for national banks. It legally separated the securities industry and the banking industry by expressly prohibiting banks from participating in underwriting and selling securities. Some provisions of the Glass-Steagall Act have since been reversed by the Financial Modernization Act of 1999. |
| 1934 | *Securities Exchange Act* |
| | Another reaction to the Great Depression, this law limits the lending of funds to purchase stock. The Securities Exchange Act requires stock purchasers to have more equity in their holdings and prevents much dangerous speculation. |

*(continued)*

## Exhibit 1.1 Banking Law Timeline

**1935**   *Federal Deposit Insurance Corporation Act*
The Federal Deposit Insurance Corporation Act requires national banks to belong to the Federal Deposit Insurance Corporation and grants regulatory authority over insured banks to the FDIC. The act also gives the FDIC broad-reaching powers to take action if a bank is in danger of failing. (Membership in the FDIC was voluntary between 1933 and 1935.)

**1946**   *Administrative Procedure Act*
The Administrative Procedure Act specifies the procedures government agencies must follow in promulgating new regulations and provides guidelines for courts to follow in reviewing agency regulations. Many jurisdictions have enacted similar laws at the state level.

**1956**   *Bank Holding Company Act*
This law allows the formation of bank holding companies that can own banks and engage in a limited number of other types of business.

**1968**   *Truth in Lending Act*
*Fair Housing Act*
These laws were designed for consumer protection. The Truth in Lending Act requires that banks provide uniform disclosures on consumer loans to applicants and borrowers. The Fair Housing Act prohibits discrimination based on race, sex, color, religion, national origin, familial status, or handicap in housing-related transactions.

**1970**   *Bank Secrecy Act*
The Bank Secrecy Act strengthens federal law enforcement efforts to thwart money laundering by requiring banks to report suspicious activities and large currency transactions.

**1971**   *Fair Credit Reporting Act*
This law protects consumers from inaccurate credit reporting by placing standards on credit reporting agencies and users of such reports.

**1972**   *Flood Disaster Protection Act*
This law requires financial institutions to determine if property they take as collateral is located in a special flood hazard area and prohibits the making, extending, or renewing of any loan secured by property in a flood hazard area unless the borrower has purchased flood insurance.

**1974**   *Real Estate Settlement Procedures Act*
This law requires banks to disclose the closing costs in residential real estate transactions. RESPA also prohibits unearned referral fees or kickbacks in residential real estate transactions.

**1975**   *Equal Credit Opportunity Act*
This law prohibits discrimination in credit transactions based upon race, sex, age, marital status, religion, national origin, color, public assistance income, or exercise of rights under the Consumer Credit Protection Act. The law requires that banks send notices to applicants when loan applications are denied.

## Exhibit 1.1   Banking Law Timeline

1975    *Home Mortgage Disclosure Act*
This law requires banks to compile and report data on mortgage loans annually. The reports are made to regulatory agencies, and the information must be made available to the public.

1976    *Consumer Leasing Act*
This law requires Truth-in-Lending-type disclosures for consumer leases.

1977    *Fair Debt Collection Practices Act*
This law prohibits abusive debt-collection practices and requires that debt collectors send notices to consumers.

        *Community Reinvestment Act*
The Community Reinvestment Act encourages banks to lend within their own geographic communities and requires that certain loan and deposit information be maintained for public review. Large banks are required to compile data related to their lending practices. The act establishes various tests for examiners to use when assessing a bank's Community Reinvestment Act performance.

1978    *Electronic Funds Transfer Act*
This law establishes disclosures and protections for consumers against unauthorized electronic financial transactions, such as automated teller machine transactions, point-of-sale transactions, and automated clearing house payments.

1978    *Financial Institutions Regulatory and Interest Rate Control Act*
This law restricts lending transactions with bank directors and executive officers and requires disclosures of loans made to insiders. The law also prohibits the payment of overdrafts to insiders except under very restricted conditions.

1978    *Right to Financial Privacy Act*
This law limits the federal government's access to bank customers' financial information and specifies the methods by which such access may be acquired.

1980    *Depository Institutions Deregulation and Monetary Control Act*
A major law that began to undo some of the Great Depression restrictions on banking, this act began the deregulation of interest rates on deposits; required universal reserve requirements so that state and federal banks would be on an equal plane; and simplified Truth in Lending requirements.

1982    *Garn-St Germain Depository Institutions Act of 1982*
Garn-St Germain represents another significant loosening of bank restrictions. It permits banks to compete more effectively with the securities industry by allowing interest-paying transaction accounts.

1984    *Bank Bribery Act*
The Bank Bribery Act limits the types of gifts that can be accepted by bank officers and employees from customers and other persons with an interest in doing business with the bank.

1986    *Money Laundering Control Act*
This law expands the Bank Secrecy Act and requires that banks establish a compliance program to monitor BSA activities.

*(continued)*

**Exhibit 1.1    Banking Law Timeline**

1987    *Expedited Funds Availability Act*
This law restricts the amount of time a bank may place a deposit on hold. It requires disclosures of bank deposit hold policies and specific disclosures at the time a hold is placed.

1989    *Financial Institutions Reform, Recovery and Enforcement Act*
This law reformed the thrift regulatory system by replacing the Federal Savings and Loan Insurance Corporation with the Office of Thrift Supervision. The act set higher capital standards for thrift institutions, recapitalized the deposit insurance system, and established standards for property appraisals on large real estate loans. It also raises the civil money penalties for bank officers and directors who break the law.

1990    *Americans with Disabilities Act*
This law requires that public buildings and services, including banking services, be made accessible to persons with disabilities. The act also prohibits discrimination by employers against persons with disabilities.

1991    *Truth in Savings Act*
This law requires that financial institutions provide uniform disclosures of rates and terms on deposits.

1991    *Federal Deposit Insurance Corporation Improvement Act*
This law increased the power of the Federal Deposit Insurance Corporation and recapitalized the Bank Insurance Fund. It also requires a prompt resolution approach to handling failing institutions and restricts the use of brokered deposits. (Brokered deposits are generally certificates of deposit controlled by a deposit broker and placed with a bank according to the highest rate available.)

1994    *Riegle Community Development Act*
This law revamped the National Flood Insurance Program, reduced some paperwork and regulatory requirements, and prohibits reverse redlining.

1994    *Reigle-Neal Interstate Bank Act*
This law allowed interstate branch banking to begin in 1995 and interstate mergers to begin in 1997.

1999    *Financial Modernization Act (Gramm-Leach-Bliley Act)*
This law allows banks to affiliate with other companies to sell insurance and other financial products, effectively reversing the restrictions of the Glass-Steagall Act of 1933. The act also institutes requirements to protect customer privacy and lengthens the time between Community Reinvestment Act examinations.

the passage of the Financial Modernization Act, which effectively reversed many of the restrictions that the Glass-Steagall Act of 1933 had placed on banks regarding participation in underwriting and selling securities. The new Act permits commercial banks to affiliate with investment banks. It also permits companies that own commercial banks to engage in any type of financial activity. And it allows subsidiaries of banks to engage in a broad range of financial activities that are not permitted for banks themselves. As a result, banks of all sizes now can offer their customers a wide range of financial products and services without the costly restraints of outdated laws. Moreover, banking companies and other types of financial companies are now able to combine much more readily.

The laws designed to keep the banking system safe were put to the test during the 1980s when savings and loan institutions, originally chartered to provide credit to the building industry, began to lose money in record amounts. Savings and loan associations (also called S&Ls or thrifts) were insured and regulated much like commercial banks but by a different agency, the Federal Savings and Loan Insurance Corporation (FSLIC). The S&L crisis reached such major proportions that Congress had to fund a bailout of the industry's insurance fund. At the same time, Congress completely restructured the thrift regulatory structure, abolishing FSLIC and transferring its insurance functions to the **Federal Deposit Insurance Corporation (FDIC)** while transferring its regulatory functions to a new agency, the **Office of Thrift Supervision (OTS),** within the Department of the Treasury. Now the FDIC maintains two funds: the Bank Insurance Fund (BIF), which primarily insures the deposits of commercial banks, and the Savings Association Insurance Fund (SAIF), which insures the deposits of thrifts, most of which were formerly insured by FSLIC.

## HOW BANKING REGULATIONS ARE CREATED

All three branches of government—the legislative, executive, and judicial—play a part in governing the banking system. The rules that apply to banks and financial transactions can be divided into two categories—statutes and regulations. Rules in both categories are very important in the day-to-day activities of banks. **Statutes** are laws enacted by the legislative branch: the U.S. Congress and state **legislatures.** Once enacted, banking laws are implemented primarily through regulations. **Regulations** are written by federal or state agencies, which are representatives of the executive branch. Usually these agencies write regulations as directed by the legislature. In the case of a dispute or a challenge, both statutes and regulations are interpreted by courts—the judicial branch. Federal laws and regulations generally are interpreted by federal courts.

In making their interpretations, courts consider not only statutory laws and regulations but also **common law.** Common law is derived from the ancient, unwritten law of England and has been reflected in judges' rulings over the years, based in part on prevailing moral standards.

---

**Critical Terms**

*Statute* A statute is a law enacted by a legislature. Statutes specify actions that are not allowed or actions that must be taken. Some statutes apply to everyone. Other statutes apply only to certain types of people or organizations. For example, many laws apply only to banks.

*Legislature* A legislature is a group of elected officials with the authority to enact new laws. The U.S. Congress is an example of a legislature. All 50 states have state legislatures.

---

## LEGISLATIVE AUTHORITY

The U.S. Congress and the state legislatures are the primary source of banking laws. The members of these legislative bodies are elected by the people in their states or districts for the purpose of representing them in the lawmaking process. Banking laws written by the U.S. Congress apply to all banks within the country, unless the law itself limits its coverage. Laws written by a state legislature apply to banks only within that state.

### U.S. Congress

**Laws** begin life as bills (see exhibit 1.2). A *bill* is a proposed law that is introduced by a member of the House of Representatives or the Senate. Congressmen and senators introduce bills on subjects in which they or their constituencies have particular interest. For example, a congressman from

## Exhibit 1.2   How a Law Is Made in Congress

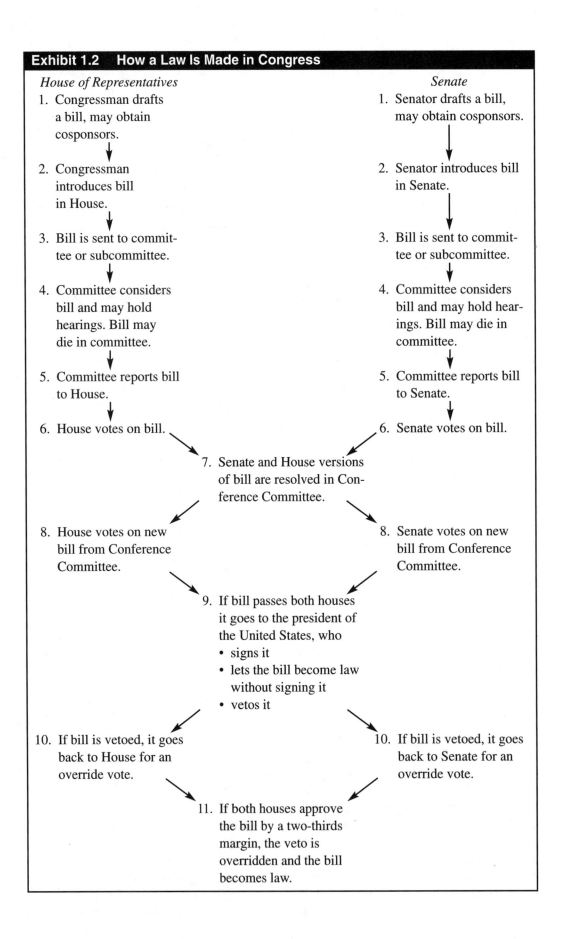

*House of Representatives*

1. Congressman drafts a bill, may obtain cosponsors.

2. Congressman introduces bill in House.

3. Bill is sent to committee or subcommittee.

4. Committee considers bill and may hold hearings. Bill may die in committee.

5. Committee reports bill to House.

6. House votes on bill.

*Senate*

1. Senator drafts a bill, may obtain cosponsors.

2. Senator introduces bill in Senate.

3. Bill is sent to committee or subcommittee.

4. Committee considers bill and may hold hearings. Bill may die in committee.

5. Committee reports bill to Senate.

6. Senate votes on bill.

7. Senate and House versions of bill are resolved in Conference Committee.

8. House votes on new bill from Conference Committee.

8. Senate votes on new bill from Conference Committee.

9. If bill passes both houses it goes to the president of the United States, who
   • signs it
   • lets the bill become law without signing it
   • vetos it

10. If bill is vetoed, it goes back to House for an override vote.

10. If bill is vetoed, it goes back to Senate for an override vote.

11. If both houses approve the bill by a two-thirds margin, the veto is overridden and the bill becomes law.

a district where the major employers are software developers may have a special interest in writing laws that protect this industry. Members of Congress also may receive proposals for laws from the president, federal agencies, industry trade groups, or other interest groups. A member may choose to sponsor one of these proposals as a bill.

The bill is drafted by the legislator's staff and the legislator introduces it into the House of Representatives or the Senate. The primary backer of the legislation is known as the *sponsor*. Other members may cosponsor the bill. Once introduced, the bill is given a number and assigned to a committee made up of members of both parties with a chairperson from the majority party. The bill generally is assigned to a committee with jurisdiction over the subject matter of the proposed law. For example, banking bills in the House usually are assigned to the Committee on Banking and Financial Services. In the Senate, banking bills generally are placed in the Banking, Housing, and Urban Affairs Committee.

The committee considers the bills sent to it and if a bill is significant may even hold public hearings. In some cases subcommittees may consider the bill. The committee or subcommittee can either vote to report the bill out of committee and back onto the floor of the House or Senate or postpone action on the bill. Action on a bill may be postponed indefinitely, effectively killing its chance to become a law.

If the bill is reported back to the House or Senate, the committee sends a report with it. The House or Senate then has an opportunity to vote on the bill. While the House or Senate may approve a bill, it cannot become law until both houses of the legislature approve it.

In most cases different versions of bills will pass the House and Senate, and these differences must be reconciled before the bill is sent to the president for signature. A conference committee made up of senators and congressmen completes the reconciliation process.

Once the reconciled bill is reported out of conference, it must be approved by a majority in both the House and the Senate. Then the bill is sent to the president for signature. The president can sign the bill, allow it to become law without his or her signature, or veto the bill. Congress can override a presidential veto if at least two-thirds of the representatives and senators subsequently vote to approve the vetoed bill.

## State Legislatures

Most state legislatures follow a legislative process similar to that of the U.S. Congress. All but one state have bicameral (*two-chambered*) legislatures; that is, legislatures with both a House of Representatives and a Senate. Some state legislatures do not meet every year, but most meet annually. In most states the governor must sign a bill before it becomes law.

## REGULATORY AUTHORITY

As with legislative bodies, regulatory authorities exist at both the federal level and the state level. Federal agencies regulate national banks, banks that are members of the Federal Reserve System (the Fed), and banks that have deposits insured by the FDIC. State agencies regulate state-chartered banks. **Bank examiners** from all these agencies review banks within their jurisdictions.

## Federal Banking Agencies

Banking oversight on the federal level is distributed among three agencies. Each agency is assigned to be the primary regulator of particular banks, but the authority is overlapping.

### Office of the Comptroller of the Currency

The **Office of the Comptroller of the Currency (OCC),** an agency of the U.S. Treasury Department, is responsible for chartering and supervising all national banks. If the owners of a bank choose to obtain a federal charter, they apply to the OCC. All federally chartered banks are chartered by this agency. Officials from the OCC conduct regular examinations of national banks to ensure that all banking regulations are being followed. Regulations issued by the OCC apply to all national banks.

### Federal Reserve System

The **Federal Reserve System (the Fed)** comprises 12 districts, each containing a Federal Reserve Bank known as a *regional bank.* State-chartered banks are not required to be members of the Fed. However, many state-chartered banks choose to affiliate themselves with the Fed to obtain direct access to the Fed's check-clearing system. If a state bank chooses to be a member it must maintain a certain amount of cash on deposit with the Fed and it becomes subject to the agency's regulations. Regulations written by the Federal Reserve Board apply to all banks that are members of the Fed.

### Federal Deposit Insurance Corporation

The **Federal Deposit Insurance Corporation (FDIC),** an agency of the federal government, insures accounts in commercial banks up to a certain amount. Currently this amount is $100,000. All commercial banks that are members of the Fed must also participate in the FDIC. Although most state-chartered banks participate in the FDIC, not all states have laws requiring them to do so. Banks that have their deposits insured by the FDIC are required to advertise that fact in the lobby of the bank and in most other bank advertising.

## State Banking Authorities

In every state a person (often called a superintendent of banks) or an agency (such as a state banking commission) gov-erns state-chartered banks and enforces the state banking laws.

Before a bank can open for business, the owners must first obtain a charter from a state or federal banking authority. If they choose to obtain one or more state charters, the owners will apply to the superintendent of banks in each state in which they plan to operate the bank. Approximately two-thirds of the banks in the United States have state charters. All other commercial banks are federally chartered. Only federally chartered banks are permitted to include the word *national* in their name. Indeed, all nationally chartered banks must use *national, national association,* or *N.A.* in the banks' official names. These banks are called **national banks.** The United States has more than 2,500 national banks.

## Bank Examinations

Officials from state and federal regulatory agencies conduct regular examinations of all commercial banks. Many bank functions are subject to examination. The most common type of bank examination is known as a *safety and soundness examination.* In this type of examination the bank's financial soundness is tested by

- reviewing the loans the bank has made to ensure that the loans will be repaid in a timely manner
- testing the bank's internal control procedures to make sure that the bank's business practices will prevent fraud and embezzlement

The state banking authorities conduct the safety and soundness examination if the bank has a state charter. The OCC conducts the safety and soundness examination if the bank has a national charter. The FDIC also conducts safety and soundness examinations of state-chartered banks that have insured deposits but are not members of the Federal Reserve. The Fed conducts safety and soundness examinations of state-chartered banks that are members (see exhibit 1.3).

| Exhibit 1.3 | Regulation of Financial Institutions | | |
|---|---|---|---|
| *Type of Bank* | *Deposits Insured by* | *Safety and Soundness Regulated by* | *Examined for Regulatory Compliance by* |
| 1. National banks | Federal Deposit Insurance Corporation; Bank Insurance Fund | Office of the Comptroller of the Currency | Office of the Comptroller of the Currency |
| 2. Thrift institutions: all federal charters and some state charters | Federal Deposit Insurance Corporation; Savings Association Insurance Fund | Office of Thrift Supervision | Office of Thrift Supervision |
| 3. State banks that are members of the Federal Reserve System | Federal Deposit Insurance Corporation; Bank Insurance Fund | State Banking Department; Federal Reserve Board | Federal Reserve Board |
| 4. State banks that are not members of the Federal Reserve System | Federal Deposit Insurance Corporation; Bank Insurance Fund | State Banking Department; Federal Deposit Insurance Corporation | Federal Deposit Insurance Corporation |

Banks are subject to other examinations of different functions, including regulatory compliance. A compliance examination tests whether the bank is in compliance with laws designed to protect consumers, such as the Truth in Lending Act (TILA), the Home Mortgage Disclosure Act (HMDA), the Fair Housing Act, and so forth. Compliance examinations are conducted by the bank's primary federal regulator. Other types of specialized examinations to which the bank may be subject are information system examinations and trust examinations. These examinations also are usually performed by the bank's primary federal regulator, although state banking authorities may include these types of examinations in their jurisdiction as well.

## Regulatory Rulemaking Process

When Congress passes a banking law, it often designates a federal banking regulatory agency to write a **regulation** imple-menting the requirements of the law. The regulation will be more specific and will contain more explanatory material than the law itself. Usually the Federal Reserve Board writes banking regulations that apply to all banks. In some cases, however, each agency writes regulations for the banks it governs. When a regulatory agency writes a regulation, the agency first studies the law and the legislative history behind the law to determine the intention of Congress. The agency then proposes a draft of the regulation and publishes it in the *Federal Register* for public comment. After the comment period passes, the agency takes the comments into consideration and publishes a final rule.

This process of regulatory rulemaking is governed by the **Administrative Procedure Act.** This law was enacted in 1946 for the purpose of bringing uniformity to federal rulemaking. The law also ensures that anyone with an interest in a new regulation has an opportunity to respond to proposals and specifies the steps government agencies must follow in promulgating new regulations. For example, the act requires agencies to publish all proposed rules in the *Federal Register* before they are made final. In most cases agencies must allow at least 90 days for public comment before finalizing a proposed regulation.

The Administrative Procedure Act was a compromise between lawmakers who wanted the regulatory agencies to have greater power and other lawmakers who favored a judicial review of every new regulation. The act includes guidelines for courts to follow in reviewing new regulations, including consideration of the following three questions:

- Is the new rule consistent with the law on which it is based?
- Was the agency's action in establishing the new rule arbitrary, capricious, or an abuse of its discretion?
- If the agency conducted a public hearing before establishing the new rule, is the rule supported by substantial evidence in the record of the hearing?

---

### Critical Terms

*Regulation* A regulation is a rule or set of rules having the force of law. Regulations are issued by government agencies and are based on, and designed to implement, laws enacted by legislatures. For example, the Federal Reserve Board's Regulation C is a set of rules based on the Home Mortgage Disclosure Act of 1975.

*Regulatory Agency* Government organizations responsible for issuing regulations and for enforcing those regulations are called regulatory agencies. The federal government and the state governments have many of these agencies. The Office of the Comptroller of the Currency and a state banking commission are examples of regulatory agencies.

---

## JUDICIAL AUTHORITY

The U.S. judicial system has the authority to interpret banking laws and regulations and to limit or expand their scope. Therefore, court rulings affect the way banks operate. Congress and federal agencies make the law, but the judicial system applies it.

The judicial system consists of the state and federal courts. Courts decide disputes between parties by interpreting the law and applying the law to the facts of a given situation. Once a court enters a final decision, called a *judgment,* that decision has the power of law itself and may be enforced.

To judge a matter in controversy, a court must first have **jurisdiction** to hear the case. Jurisdiction means that the court has the authority to interpret the law in relation to a particular matter. Courts (and their jurisdictional authority) may be established by a constitution or by statute. The U.S. Constitution and Congress establish the federal courts, and each state constitution and most state legislatures establish the state courts.

Both the federal and state court systems have trial courts and higher-level courts where parties may seek review of the trial courts' decisions (see exhibits 1.4 and 1.5). Courts that review trial court decisions are called courts of appeals, or **appellate courts.** Both the federal and state court systems also have a court of final appeal (or court of last resort). In the federal system, this is the **United States Supreme Court.** The highest courts in most, but not all, states generally are also called supreme courts. Banks generally are subject both to federal and state court jurisdiction.

### Federal Court System

Federal trial and appellate courts exist throughout the United States. The trial courts are known as U.S. district courts. The appellate courts are federal courts of appeals. The federal courts have jurisdic-

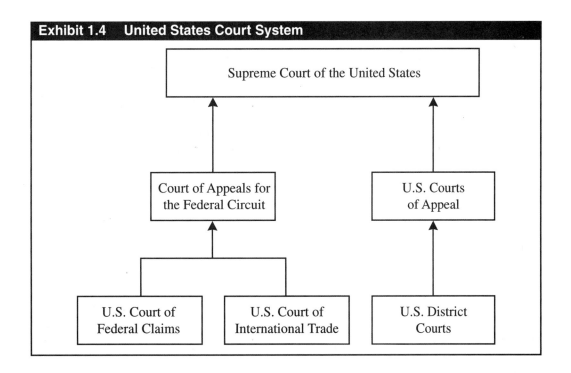

**Exhibit 1.4    United States Court System**

Supreme Court of the United States

Court of Appeals for the Federal Circuit

U.S. Courts of Appeal

U.S. Court of Federal Claims

U.S. Court of International Trade

U.S. District Courts

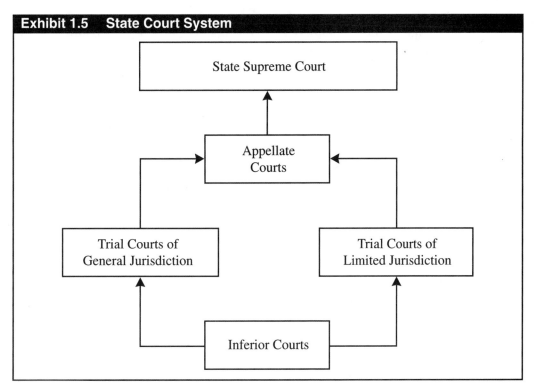

**Exhibit 1.5    State Court System**

State Supreme Court

Appellate Courts

Trial Courts of General Jurisdiction

Trial Courts of Limited Jurisdiction

Inferior Courts

tion in cases involving the Constitution, federal laws, treaties with other nations, controversies between states, and certain controversies between persons who live in different states.

**U.S. District Courts**

The United States currently has 91 federal districts—at least one in each state. Some states have two, three, or more federal districts, depending on the size of the state, its population, and other factors. Each district is served by a U.S. district court. These courts conduct trials in both criminal and civil (noncriminal) cases under their jurisdiction. Criminal trials in federal court involve crimes committed in violation of federal law. Robbery of a state bank insured by the FDIC is a crime that could be tried in U.S. district court because a federal law is involved in the case.

Because federal trial courts exist in each state along with the state courts, the federal and state courts often both have jurisdiction to hear a particular case. This can occur, for example, in a civil case involving federal law or involving parties who live in different states. Federal courts do have jurisdiction in such cases under the U.S. Constitution—but their jurisdiction is not exclusive. State courts also may hear cases involving the Constitution, federal laws, or a dispute between a state citizen and a party from another state. When either the federal or the state court can hear a case, the courts have **concurrent jurisdiction.**

In cases of concurrent jurisdiction, the party who initiates the lawsuit (the plaintiff) decides whether to file in the federal or the state trial court. If the state court is selected, the other party (the defendant) has the option for a limited time to try the case in the federal court. This process is called **removal.** Defendants are not required to exercise this option, and the courts have no authority to remove cases unless defendants request it. The purpose of removal is to allow defendants some control over where the claims against them will be heard, rather than leaving that choice solely to the plaintiffs.

### Courts of Appeals

Federal judicial districts are grouped geographically into federal circuits. Each circuit has a federal court of appeals whose main function is to review decisions of the district courts when a losing party asks the court to review the judgment. The courts of appeals also review the actions of various federal regulatory agencies when **judicial review** is requested. *Judicial review* is the term used when a party (such as a bank or association of banks) appeals an order or decision of a regulatory agency, seeking to have it reversed by a court.

The federal circuits throughout the country are called First Circuit, Second Circuit, and so forth, up to the Eleventh Circuit. There is also a Federal Circuit for the District of Columbia. In the 1980s Congress established the Court of Appeals for the Federal Circuit, which has jurisdiction to hear appeals in specialized types of cases (patents, trademarks, international trade, and government contracts, for example). Altogether there are 13 circuit courts of appeals in the federal system.

### United States Supreme Court

The authority and jurisdiction of the United States Supreme Court are established in the U.S. Constitution. The Supreme Court is given appellate jurisdiction in all cases that generally fall within the jurisdiction of federal courts, such as cases involving the Constitution or federal laws. The Supreme Court also has **original jurisdiction** to act as the trial court in a very limited class of cases. For example, the Supreme Court would have original jurisdiction for a case in which one state sues another state.

The Supreme Court is the final court of appeals in the federal system. The Court reviews decisions of the federal courts of appeals as well as state high-court decisions involving the U.S. Constitution or federal law. Two methods are used to obtain Supreme Court review of a case. The method used depends on the type of case for which review is sought. If the case is of a type that the Court has no option to reject (such as the constitutionality of a U.S. treaty), the parties file an appeal and the Court automatically allows the review. In all other cases the parties seeking the review petition the Court for a writ of certiorari, or re-examination of the case. In the latter situation the Court has complete discretion to grant or deny the review. The Court denies many more of these petitions than it grants, conserving its time and energy only for cases it considers significant to the development of the law.

## State Court Systems

Each state has a system of courts that usually includes inferior (petty) courts, trial courts, and one or more appellate courts.

### Inferior Courts

Inferior courts deal with cases involving small amounts of money or minor criminal penalties, such as traffic fines. Traffic courts and small claims courts are examples of inferior courts. The judge in an inferior court is usually called a *justice of the peace* or a *magistrate*. Court procedures generally are informal, often with no lawyers in attendance. The judge's decision can be automatically appealed to a higher level trial court, which often means conducting another trial under more formal procedures.

### Trial Courts

There are two types of state trial courts—those with general jurisdiction and those with jurisdiction limited to specific kinds of cases. Trial courts with general jurisdiction are authorized to hear most civil and criminal cases. Local trial courts are lower courts with limited jurisdiction. In some states these are called *municipal* or *district* courts. Their jurisdiction is limited to minor civil or criminal matters. However, these local trial courts often conduct hearings to decide whether there is sufficient evidence to justify a trial in very serious criminal cases. If the municipal or district court judge decides that there is sufficient evidence, the criminal case will go forward to trial in a court with general jurisdiction.

Specialized trial courts have jurisdiction limited to particular types of cases, such as those involving divorce, child custody, paternity, adoption, juvenile delinquency, probate, or other matters. Many states have a court of claims that deals with citizens' suits for monetary relief filed against the state or its agencies. These specialized courts, in addition to courts of claims, may be called *family, probate, surrogate,* or *orphans'* courts, depending on their jurisdiction.

### Appellate Courts

Appeals from the decisions of trial courts are made to the state's court of appeals. Some states have only one appeals court, which is the highest court in the state. Other states have appellate courts below the highest court. These intermediate courts of appeals review trial court decisions before they are allowed to be appealed to the state's highest court. Review of decisions by intermediate courts helps enable the state's highest court to review cases selectively.

## LAWS THAT AFFECT BANKING

Today a multitude of laws affect the banking industry. Laws that protect consumers who do business with banks include

- the Truth in Lending Act (TILA), which requires that uniform lending disclosures be made to consumers
- the Equal Credit Opportunity Act (ECOA), which prohibits discrimination in lending based on certain characteristics
- the Real Estate Settlement Procedures Act (RESPA), which requires disclosures in all phases of the mortgage lending process
- the Flood Disaster Protection Act, which requires that the bank determine if a borrower's property is in a special flood hazard area

Bank depositors also are protected by the Truth in Savings Act and the Expedited Funds Availability Act. The Truth in Savings Act requires that truthful disclosures be given regarding the interest rate and terms of an account. The Expedited Funds Availability Act limits the amount of time a bank can delay making the funds from a deposit available to the customer.

Other laws protect the safety and soundness of banking. Laws that require certain levels of capitalization for banks, laws that prohibit or restrict insider transactions, laws that require written appraisals for real property loans, and laws that prevent bribery of bank officers and employees all exist for the purpose of protecting the bank, its depositors, and its shareholders.

While many consumer protection laws are federal laws, state laws also have a major effect on banking. One of the most significant, written by the National Conference of Commissioners on Uniform State Laws, is the **Uniform Commercial Code (UCC).** The UCC is a complex set of provisions that covers many different kinds of business transactions, including those related to banking. The UCC was first adopted by a state in the early 1950s. The UCC has since been revised several times, and all states have adopted some form of the UCC. The UCC governs most bank deposit transactions. It establishes the rights and duties of the depositor, the payee, and the banks in the collection process. The UCC also governs letters of credit, wire transfers, and secured transactions. The UCC is covered in depth in chapter 2.

## CONCLUSION

Banks are a vital part of the American economy. The current structure of banking has its roots in the social and political development of the country, particularly during the Great Depression. The two most important activities of commercial banks are accepting deposits and making loans, and many different kinds of laws and regulations govern these activities. Most banking laws are designed to protect the banking system and to protect consumers in banking transactions.

All branches of government make rules that apply to banking. Laws originate in the U.S. Congress and state legislatures, while regulations are written by federal and state agencies. In the case of a challenge, the courts interpret the statutes and regulations. The Fed controls bank reserves and enforces federal banking laws in state banks that are members of the Fed. The OCC enforces federal banking laws in all national banks. The FDIC insures accounts in commercial banks and thrift institutions and is the primary federal regulator for all state-chartered banks with insured deposits that are not members of the Fed. The OTS, an agency of the U.S. Treasury, enforces federal banking laws in most federally chartered thrift institutions. Banks are subject to regular safety and soundness examinations, compliance examinations, and other specialized examinations.

In this chapter we have described the basic method by which banks are governed, as well as how laws and regulations are passed, the difference between a law and a regulation, state and federal jurisdiction, and important state and federal laws that regulate a bank's business transactions. In the chapters that follow we will explore the legal and regulatory systems that relate to many different banking activities.

## QUESTIONS FOR REVIEW AND DISCUSSION

1. What part has the evolution of banking played in the regulation of the banking system today?
2. What is the function of the Federal Reserve Board with regard to bank regulation?
3. What is the difference between a statute and a regulation?

4. What is the process by which a bill becomes law in the U.S. Congress?
5. How do the jurisdictions of state regulators and federal regulators differ?

6. What is the function of the FDIC?

## LEARNING ACTIVITIES FOR CHAPTER 1

### Matching

Match the federal agency that is the primary regulator to each of the types of banks listed, which all have deposits insured by the FDIC.

1. Federal Reserve Board
2. Office of the Comptroller of the Currency
3. Federal Deposit Insurance Corporation
4. Office of Thrift Supervision

a. State-chartered banks—not members of the Federal Reserve System
b. State-chartered banks—members of the Federal Reserve System
c. Federal savings and loan institutions
d. National banks

### Multiple Choice

Circle the one best answer to each question.

1. Regulations are:

   a. enacted by state legislatures
   b. enacted by Congress
   c. written by judges
   d. issued by administrative agencies of government executive branches

2. Banks chartered by the OCC are called:

   a. federal banks
   b. national banks
   c. congressional banks
   d. executive banks

3. Statutory laws originate in the:

   a. legislature
   b. judiciary
   c. regulatory agency
   d. executive branch

4. The Federal Reserve System:

   a. comprises 12 districts known as regional banks
   b. oversees the FDIC
   c. issues charters for national banks
   d. enforces all banking regulations

5. A review of the bank's loans to ensure that they will be repaid in a timely manner and of the bank's internal control procedures to ensure that the bank's business practices will prevent fraud and embezzlement is made in the:

   a. safety and soundness examination
   b. regulatory compliance examination
   c. trust examination
   d. information systems examination

6. Federal circuit courts are known as:

   a. district courts
   b. trial courts
   c. courts of appeal
   d. inferior courts

7. The method of seeking judicial review by the U.S. Supreme Court when the Court has the option to reject the case is known as:

   a. petitioning for certiorari
   b. seeking venue
   c. filing an appeal
   d. seeking original jurisdiction

8. Specialized trial courts:

    a. have general jurisdiction
    b. have limited jurisdiction
    c. function as intermediate courts
    d. may have a magistrate or justice of the peace as a judge

## Completion

1. One of the most comprehensive laws designed to restructure and stabilize the banking system came about as a result of the Great Depression. This law is called _____.

2. Congress enacts banking-related laws to protect the banking system itself and to protect _____.

3. Two types of examinations a bank may have are _____ and _____.

4. Courts that review the decisions of lower courts are called _____.

5. The law that governs the federal rule-making process is _____.

6. The federal districts are grouped together by geographical location into _____ _____.

7. State courts usually include _____ courts, _____ courts, and one or more _____ courts.

8. The Truth in Lending Act and the Equal Credit Opportunity Act are examples of _____ _____ legislation.

# 2

# THE UNIFORM COMMERCIAL CODE

## LEARNING OBJECTIVES

After studying this chapter, you should be able to

- trace the history of the Uniform Commercial Code and list the articles of the UCC that pertain to banking
- list the parties to a negotiable instrument and explain the essential elements that make an item negotiable, according to Article 3
- identify the parties in the collection process and explain posting, priorities of payment, return procedures, and the responsibilities of banks to customers as covered in Article 4
- discuss the coverage of Article 4A and define the duties of a bank when it makes a wire transfer of funds
- differentiate between a commercial letter of credit and a standby letter of credit; explain the issuer's responsibilities, wrongful dishonor, and how to stop payment on a letter of credit as defined by Article 5
- define and use the legal and banking terms that appear in bold in the chapter text

## INTRODUCTION

The Uniform Commercial Code (UCC) is arguably the most important law governing commerce in the United States. Most banking transactions are covered in some fashion by the UCC. However, the UCC is not a federal statute; each state must adopt the UCC for it to regulate transactions within that state.

The significance of the UCC to the banking industry is evident by its history. Before the UCC was adopted in the 1950s, diverse state laws governed commercial transactions, including banking. While these laws had been adequate for the nation when most commerce was conducted on a local level, technological changes—like the invention of the telephone in 1876—promoted commerce on a national level. As technology continued to advance, farsighted legal scholars recognized the need for uniform laws to foster the growing amount of interstate commerce.

The National Conference of Commissioners on Uniform State Laws (NCCUSL), a committee established in 1892 for the purpose of drafting uniform state laws, began to consider a uniform law for commercial transactions. The work of the NCCUSL was not limited to business law. It drafted uniform laws in many other areas, among them partnership law, fraudulent conveyance law, arbitration law, family law, health care, criminal law, and real estate law. Commercial transactions were an important area of consideration for the NCCUSL because the uniformity of the system of commerce directly affected a company's ability to conduct business from state to state. Different state laws covering contracts and sales as well as different requirements for documenting secured transactions would eventually slow the nation's economic growth.

The NCCUSL finished its first draft of the UCC in the early 1950s. By 1967 the code had been adopted by all states except Louisiana. Louisiana has since adopted most articles of the UCC. Because the states are free to amend any provision of the UCC when enacting it, some differences occur in the UCC from state to state. The NCCUSL continues to meet to consider changes to the UCC. Many amendments have been made to the UCC since the early 1950s.

The UCC is divided into nine articles (exhibit 2.1). These articles cover all types of business transactions. The articles most important to bankers include

- Article 3—Negotiable Instruments
- Article 4—Bank Deposits and Collections
- Article 4A—Funds Transfers
- Article 5—Letters of Credit
- Article 9—Secured Transactions

This chapter provides an overview of the UCC articles, other than Article 9, that primarily govern banking transactions. Article 9 is covered in detail in chapter 9. All of these topics are covered in greater depth in *Law and Banking: Applications* (Washington, DC: The American Bankers Association, 2000).

## ARTICLE 3—NEGOTIABLE INSTRUMENTS

An essential part of commercial transactions is the method of payment for goods and services. Payment can be made using cash; however, it is more commonly accomplished by the use of a negotiable instrument, such as a check. Negotiable instruments act like money, so they must meet certain legal standards to be freely transferable. The party receiving a negotiable instrument is called a **holder.**

### Types of Negotiable Instruments

Article 3 of the UCC governs negotiable instruments. The most common types of negotiable instruments are drafts and notes. Some certificates of deposit (CDs) are negotiable instruments.

**Drafts** are instruments that contain an order to pay. A draft has three parties: the **drawer,** the **payee,** and the **drawee.** The drawer is the person who signs the instrument, the payee is the person who will be paid, and the drawee is the person who is ordered to pay. Drafts can be payable at a certain fixed time or they can be payable on demand.

A check is a form of a draft. Checks generally are payable on demand and always are drawn on banks. Other types of drafts may be used in commercial transactions, but checks are the most common.

A **note** is a negotiable instrument with a promise to pay rather than an order to pay. A note has only two parties: a **maker,** who makes the promise to pay, and the **payee,** who receives the promise of payment. A note also may be called a *promissory note.* Notes may promise payment on demand or on a certain date. The maker of a demand note promises to repay it at any time, upon the demand of the payee. Notes that contain a future date for payment cannot be presented for payment until that date, which is called the *maturity date.* Promissory notes frequently are used as a way to defer payment for goods or services purchased.

Originally, CDs were negotiable instruments. Today, however, they rarely are issued in negotiable form. CDs usually are written instruments issued by a bank to represent the deposit of the payee. A CD is payable on a specific date and in a specific amount. Many banks now just issue receipts for CDs and the CD itself is a book entry, not an instrument.

## Elements of Negotiability

For an instrument to qualify as a negotiable instrument and receive all of the benefits of UCC Article 3, it must have each of the six elements discussed below. If the instrument does not contain all of these elements, it is not negotiable. The fact that an instrument is not negotiable does not mean that it lacks value. The instrument may be worth a great deal to the person who owns it; however, that person cannot freely transfer it under Article 3 rules.

The six essential elements of negotiability are

- The instrument must be in writing and signed by the maker or drawer.
- The instrument must contain an unconditional promise or order to pay.

- The instrument must be payable for a fixed amount of money.
- The instrument must be payable on demand or at a definite time.
- The instrument must be payable to the order of a specific payee or to *bearer.*
- The instrument must not state any other undertaking or instruction by the maker or drawer.

### Instrument in Writing and Signed by Maker

All negotiable instruments are written. The writing can be on any tangible object, but paper is usually used. In fact, banks generally require that their customers use specified paper for checks that they pay. This requirement allows banks to process checks at high speed using check-processing machines.

The maker or drawer must sign the negotiable instrument. If an instrument is not signed, no person is obligated to pay it. The person signing the negotiable instrument may use any legal name or trade name. Even marks to represent a signature are acceptable, as are stamped signatures and signatures printed with a facsimile machine.

#### Examples
- Mary Albert uses her maiden name, Mary Carson, to sign checks. Mary Carson is a legal name for her and is a valid signature.

- Ellen Brenner cannot write her name because of an illness. Her mark on her check is a valid signature.

### Unconditional Promise or Order to Pay

To be negotiable, an instrument must contain a promise or order to pay that is not subject to any conditions. For example, the promise to pay cannot be conditioned upon the occurrence of a future event or be subject to the terms of another agreement. The promise or order to pay must be specific and clear.

#### Examples
- If John Withers gives a draft for payment to Ellen Sherwood with these words on it, *"Payable only if Ms. Sherwood sells my house within six months from this date,"* the draft is not a negotiable instrument.

- If Melvin Ward signs a promissory note for $1,000 for the purchase of an antique pedal car and writes on the note that the payment is "subject to the purchase agreement," the note is not negotiable because it has been made subject to another agreement. Melvin is still liable for the amount, but the note is not a negotiable instrument.

Although a negotiable instrument cannot include language that makes it subject to certain conditions or other agreements, certain other clauses can be included without making the instrument nonnegotiable. Negotiability is not destroyed because the instrument contains a reference to another writing or agreement or a statement that a draft is given in full satisfaction of a debt owed by the drawer to the payee.

### Payable for Fixed Amount

A negotiable instrument must be payable in a fixed amount of principal. The promise or order to pay must be definite. While the principal amount must be clear from the face of the instrument, the amount of interest may reference information not contained in the instrument. Such a reference does not affect the negotiability of the instrument.

A negotiable instrument must be payable in money. Money is any medium of exchange that is authorized or adopted by a domestic or foreign government. Therefore, money is not limited to currency.

### Payable on Demand or at a Definite Time

A negotiable instrument must be payable either on demand or at a definite time. An instrument is considered to be payable on demand if it

- states that it is payable on demand
- states that it is payable at site
- otherwise indicates that it is payable at the will of the holder
- does not state any time of payment

To be payable at a definite time, an instrument must be payable at the end of a definite period of time *after* the instrument is accepted or drawn. If the time may be readily ascertainable at the time the instrument is created, then the instrument is payable at a definite time and meets this test of negotiability.

### Payable to a Specific Payee or to *Bearer*

A negotiable instrument is payable either to the order of a specific party or to *bearer.* If the instrument is payable to a specific payee, the payee must be named on the instrument. A check payable to *my teacher* is not a negotiable instrument. A check payable to *cash, bearer,* or *holder* is considered to be a bearer instrument.

### No Other Undertaking or Instruction

The negotiable instrument generally must be free of extraneous instructions or other promises. It must state no other undertaking or instruction by the maker. The UCC does allow the following promises to be in an instrument without affecting its negotiability:

- the promise to give, maintain, or protect collateral that secures payment
- an authorization to allow the holder to confess judgment or dispose of collateral
- a waiver of any law intended for the protection of the maker or drawer

## Other Article 3 Requirements

Many of the rules in Article 3 help to resolve the common problems and ambiguities that arise with negotiable instruments. For example, if a check is ambiguous because the words and the numbers conflict, according to Article 3 the words take priority.

Other rules concern the ways missing, additional, ambiguous, or conflicting language can affect either the negotiability of an instrument or the rights and responsibilities of the parties to them.

## Terms Affecting Rights and Responsibilities

While terms added or omitted may affect an instrument's *negotiability,* other terms or ambiguous language can affect the *rights and responsibilities* of the parties to an instrument. Article 3 and state court decisions have provided some answers to these issues.

One common situation involves the issue of multiple payees. Checks often are made payable to more than one person. For example, if two people jointly own property and sell it, the buyer may make the purchase check payable to *Bill Martin and Arlene Rogers.* When there is more than one payee, Article 3 provides guidance on the rights of the payees and the duties of the bank. Some of the more common rules are

- If the payees are joined by the word *and,* the instrument is payable to all of them; all must endorse the check.
- If the payees are separated by the word *or,* the check is payable to either payee; only one person needs to endorse the check.
- If the payees are joined and separated by the words *and/or,* the check is treated as an *or* check.
- If the payees are separated by a virgule (/), in most states the check is treated as an *or* check.

## ARTICLE 4—BANK DEPOSITS AND COLLECTIONS

UCC Article 4 creates a uniform set of rules for banks to follow when sending checks for collection. It also specifies the rights and responsibilities of banks and their depositors regarding checking accounts.

**Collection** is the process a bank uses to obtain payment on checks that are deposited with it. The check or draft that is the subject of the collection process is called an **item.** Most checks that are deposited in a bank will be drawn on other financial institutions. Therefore, the bank must forward these checks, or items, to the drawee banks for collection. Depending on the route a check takes, many banks may be involved in the collection process.

UCC Article 4 identifies banks in the collection process according to their function in forward collection. A bank might serve more than one function, depending on the collection route that a check follows. For example, if a check is drawn on the bank into which it was deposited, the bank is both the depositary bank and the payor bank.

A **depositary bank** is the first bank to receive an item in the collection process. The **payor bank** is the bank on which an item is payable as drawn. **Intermediary banks** are banks, other than the depositary or payor bank, to which an item is transferred during collection. A **presenting bank** is any bank that presents an item to the payor bank for payment. A **collecting bank** is any bank, other than the payor bank, that handles an item for collection.

A typical check collection route might involve a depositary bank and a different payor bank located in the same metropolitan area, with both banks members of a local clearing house (exhibit 2.2). Banks generally use clearing houses or they may use the clearing and settlement services offered by the Federal Reserve regional banks.

### Collection Process

As the first bank to receive an item, the depositary bank prepares the check for the collection process. The depositary bank encodes the check with the dollar amount, copies the check on microfilm, and puts the bank's endorsement on the back. The check is then sorted according to the geographical location of the bank on which it is drawn. The bank sends all of its sorted checks to the local clearing house or to the Federal Reserve.

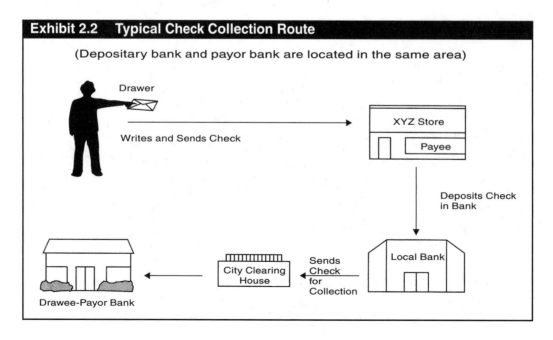

**Exhibit 2.2   Typical Check Collection Route**

(Depositary bank and payor bank are located in the same area)

Drawer
Writes and Sends Check

XYZ Store
Payee

Deposits Check in Bank

Local Bank

Sends Check for Collection

City Clearing House

Drawee-Payor Bank

### Ordinary Care

Under UCC Article 4, all banks must exercise **ordinary care** in handling checks during the collection process. Any bank that fails to exercise ordinary care is subject to damages should another bank or one of the parties to the check suffer an injury because of the bank's actions. The UCC describes ordinary care in relation to several actions taken by banks. One of these actions involves the midnight deadline.

To exercise ordinary care, a collecting bank must take proper action within its midnight deadline—midnight of the banking day following the one on which an item is received. A bank that receives checks for collection on Thursday exercises ordinary care if it forwards or presents them for payment by midnight on Friday.

However, the midnight deadline is not a hard and fast rule. It may be varied by agreements, rules, or regulations; by a bank's establishing earlier cut-off hours for handling items for collection; or by excused delays. Taking proper action within a reasonably longer time may constitute the exercise of ordinary care, but the bank has the burden of establishing timeliness.

The last bank in the collection process is the payor bank. This is the bank on which the check is drawn. The payor bank's duty is to decide by its midnight deadline whether to pay a check or return it unpaid. The bank makes this decision based on many factors, including whether there are enough funds in the account to pay the check. Under Article 4, a payor bank is held accountable for the full amount of any check that it fails to either pay or return by its midnight deadline.

### Posting

The payor bank is responsible for posting the check to the account of the drawer. **Posting** is the process of making debit or credit entries in the customer's account. In most banks, this process no longer requires that a person physically examine the check except at the very beginning when the collecting bank encodes the amount of each check with magnetic ink. Machines read the magnetic ink numbers written on the check, and computers track the account balances. Although a bank may have a policy to physically examine checks over a certain amount, the vast majority of checks go through the collection system without any individual actually looking at the document. If posting a check will overdraw the account, the check is kicked out of the automatic system for return to the person who deposited it.

Article 4 sets no order for the payment of checks. Banks may pay them in any order. However, Article 4 does set up a system for payment priorities.

### Priorities of Payment

Several things can interrupt the normal collection process. For example, the payor bank can

- receive notice that the drawer has filed for bankruptcy
- receive from the drawer an order to stop payment on the check
- receive a court order or other claim against the account for the benefit of the drawer's creditors
- exercise its own right of setoff to use funds in the account to pay a debt owed to it by the customer

Each of these events may create a dispute with the owner of the check over who has first claim, or priority, regarding funds in the account.

Article 4 provides several tests to establish a check owner's priority in relation to others. These tests include the payor bank's certification of the check and actions by the payor bank that demonstrate its final decision to pay the check. Also, a bank must have an opportunity to act before it can be held responsible to carry out instructions it receives. "First come, first served" is the basic test for determining priority in relation to entitlement to funds in the drawer's account.

### Example

State National Bank receives on-us checks for collection at 11:00 each morning. By 4:00 each afternoon, the bank decides whether to pay each check or to return it to the presenting bank. At 3:30 one afternoon, State National receives a letter from a customer requesting that the bank place a stop payment on a check State National received earlier that day for collection. State National does not have sufficient opportunity to act upon this instruction, so it is not responsible to its customer if it pays the item.

## Return Procedures

Article 4 sets forth some procedures for returning checks. A payor bank may take until its midnight deadline to decide whether to pay or return a check that has been presented to it for payment. A dishonored check is returned to the depositary bank and to the depositor who initiated the collection process.

### Returning Banks

A **returning bank** is any bank handling a returned check except the payor bank and the depositary bank. Under Article 4, a returning bank is charged with the duty to exercise ordinary care in returning an item.

### Large-Item Returns

A payor bank must notify the depositary bank when a check in the amount of $2,500 or more is dishonored. The depositary bank must receive this notice by 4:00 p.m. on the second business day following the banking day on which the item was presented for payment. A large-item return notice may be given by any reasonable means, including by mail, telephone, wire, fax, or telex. Once the depositary bank receives the notice, it must notify the depositor of the nonpayment by midnight of the following banking day, unless the bank has a reason for taking longer. If the bank does take longer, the bank assumes the burden of proving that it acted in a reasonable manner and with ordinary care.

A paying bank may take until its midnight deadline to decide whether to pay or **dishonor** (not pay) a check. However, if the paying bank fails to pay or return the check within its midnight deadline, Article 4 imposes strict liability on the bank for the full amount of any check. In other words, a paying bank is accountable for the amount of a check, whether or not it is properly payable, if the bank fails to either pay or return the item within its midnight deadline. Again, in certain circumstances, the bank may act reasonably by taking a longer time period; however, the bank will have the burden of proving the reasonableness of its actions.

## Responsibilities of a Bank to its Customer

Article 4 does not require a bank to overdraw a customer's account if it is presented with a check for which the account has insufficient funds. The bank may pay the check anyway and the customer will owe the funds to the bank. A customer has no duty to pay for a check presented against his or her account if he or she did not sign the check or benefit from the proceeds. Banks may pay postdated checks unless the customer has notified them in advance (before payment is made) of the postdating and provided the bank an opportunity to act. A bank is liable to its customer for actual damages for wrongfully dishonoring any check presented against the customer's account.

## ARTICLE 4A—FUNDS TRANSFERS

UCC Article 4A governs electronic transfers of funds. Before the passage of Article 4A, no single law regulated electronic transfers of funds. Before 1970 virtually all funds transfers were paper transactions, so there was no need for such a law. State contract law, agreements between banks and their customers, and the agreements between banks and the payment networks that facilitated electronic transfers all purported to regulate these funds transfers.

Corporate and business customers particularly liked the speed and efficiency of wire transfers of funds, and these types of transactions became popular as funds management tools. As the number of transactions increased, legal problems began to surface. In 1973 a corporate customer sued a bank, alleging that the customer had lost a large contract because the bank failed to execute a wire transfer order. The lawsuit claimed a large amount in damages. The trial court found against the bank in 1981, but the court's decision was overturned on appeal the next year.

The case put into high relief the dangers in transferring large amounts of funds without an overruling law. Therefore, beginning in 1985, the NCCUSL sought to draft a law to establish the rights and responsibilities of parties to electronic funds transfers. Article 4A also was intended to fairly apportion the liability for mishandled funds transfers.

## Funds Transferred for Business Purposes

Article 4A covers only funds transferred for business purposes. Consumer electronic funds transfers have been covered by the federal Electronic Funds Transfer Act (EFTA) since 1978. Article 4A primarily covers funds that are transferred through automated clearing houses (ACH) or through payment networks, such as Fed-Wire (operated by the Federal Reserve), the Clearing House Interbank Payment System (CHIPS), the Society for Worldwide Interbank Financial Telecommunications (SWIFT), and other networks.

## Parties to a Transfer of Funds

An order to transfer funds is called a **payment order.** The person making a payment order is called the sender or the **originator.** The receiver is called the **beneficiary.** The bank receiving the payment order and sending the funds is called the **originator's bank,** and the bank receiving the funds for payment to a beneficiary is the **beneficiary's bank.** Banks that receive orders from the originator's bank for transmittal of funds to the beneficiary bank are called **intermediary banks.**

## Duties of the Originator's Bank

Originator's banks have a duty to either accept or reject a payment order received from the originator.

### Security Procedures

The originator's bank may establish security procedures for verifying the identity and authority of customers who authorize payment orders the bank receives. Such security procedures usually involve passwords, call-back procedures, audiotaped telephone lines, and other measures to guarantee that only authorized persons can order funds to be transferred from any given account. If a bank sends an erroneous payment order because it did not follow its own security procedures, the bank is liable to the customer for the funds unless it can be shown that the customer failed to exercise ordinary care.

### Cut-off Time

The originator's bank may set a cut-off time by which it must receive payment orders or any cancellations or amendments of previous orders. If the bank receives a payment order after the cut-off time, the receiving bank may treat the payment order as being received at the opening of the next business day. Also, if the bank does not receive an order to cancel or amend by the cut-off time, the bank is not responsible for damages suffered by the originator because the payment was not canceled or amended.

## Duties of the Beneficiary's Bank

A beneficiary's bank is liable to the beneficiary if, after it accepts a payment for the beneficiary, the bank fails to credit the payment to the beneficiary's account in a timely manner. The bank also is liable if it fails to notify the beneficiary of the receipt of the funds by midnight of the day following the day the funds were received. Notice often is given by providing a copy of the entry or deposit into the account.

---

### Critical Terms

*Originator* A person initiating a payment order for a transfer of funds for a business or commercial purpose.

*Beneficiary* The person ultimately receiving the transfer of funds.

*Originator's Bank* The bank executing the payment order for the originator.

*Beneficiary's Bank* The bank receiving the funds for the account of the beneficiary.

---

Article 4A also sets forth guidelines for many technical details, such as how to determine when a payment order is considered to be received and when final settlement occurs.

## ARTICLE 5—LETTERS OF CREDIT

UCC Article 5 governs letters of credit. A letter of credit is a payment device used in many kinds of commercial and financial transactions. The main parties to a letter of credit include the bank customer who contracts with the bank for the letter of credit (the applicant), the bank that issues the letter of credit (the **issuer),** and the company or individual who receives payment under the terms of the letter of credit (the **beneficiary).** There are two types of letters of credit: a **commercial letter of credit** and a **standby letter of credit.**

## Commercial Letters of Credit

Commercial letters of credit involve transactions for the sale of goods (exhibit 2.3). A seller who does not personally know the buyer and who wants some assurance that payment will be received once the goods are shipped may request the buyer to provide a commercial letter of credit. The buyer—who is the bank's customer and the applicant for the letter of credit—arranges with the bank to issue a letter of credit. The bank (issuer) agrees to be responsible to pay for the goods when demanded by the seller and when the terms of the letter of credit have been met. The letter of credit includes a statement of the bank's (issuer's) commitment to pay and the conditions the seller must meet to receive payment. Conditions for the seller normally include documents establishing that the goods were received and inspected and that insurance requirements have been met. The seller also submits a draft for payment made out to the bank or to the buyer's account.

## Standby Letters of Credit

Standby letters of credit simply guarantee a customer's performance of an obligation to a beneficiary. This kind of letter of credit does not involve the purchase or sale of goods. A standby letter of credit would be used

- in real estate development transactions where a contractor must ensure the completion of a construction project to an owner

**Exhibit 2.3    Commercial Letter of Credit**

*ARMORY NATIONAL BANK*
228 De X Boulevard
Armory, LA 70030
(504) 609-2424

CABLE:     ARMNB NEWORLEANS
S.W.I.F.T.:   ANBK USA 48

Irrevocable Credit

DATE:        22 July 2000

MAIL TO:    Centrale des Pas et de Mer Perricolo
38 Rue de Tocqueville
62827 Paris, FRANCE

All drafts must be marked:
Armory National Ref. No.:    5454286

Dear Sir or Madam:

At the request of Chantilly Quest, Inc.,  we hereby open in your favor our Irrevocable Credit, numbered as indicated above, for a sum not exceeding a total of U.S. $300,000 available by your drafts [at SIGHT] on us subject to the following:

Expiration date:      31 December 2004
Trans shipment:      [Not allowed]
Partial shipment:     [Not allowed]
Ship from:             Cherbourg, France
Ship to:                Chantilly Quest, Inc.
                            New Orleans, Louisiana

and accompanied by the following documents:

1) Ocean bills of lading
2) Insurance certificates
3) Customs invoice combined with certificate of origin

When presenting your drafts and documents or when communicating with us please make reference to our reference number shown above.

We hereby agree to honor each draft drawn under and in compliance with the terms of this credit, if duly presented (together with the documents specified) at this office on or before the expiration date.

The credit is subject to the Uniform Customs and Practice for Documentary Credits, 1993 revision, ICC Publication No. 500.

Yours Very Truly,



Gustave J. Chenevert
Vice President

- as security against the nonpayment of a loan
- to ensure payment of a judgment by the losing party in a lawsuit
- to substitute for actual property seized by a court in a lawsuit

With a standby letter of credit the issuing bank pays only if the customer defaults. Payment is made when the beneficiary sends a draft for the amount due (the amount of the credit or the default amount, whichever is less). The bank (issuer) must then collect from the customer (applicant). The bank treats standby letters of credit as if they are loans to the customer. As it would for a loan, the bank takes steps to verify that the customer is creditworthy before issuing a standby letter of credit.

### Issuer's Responsibilities

The issuer must examine the documents received from the beneficiary to ensure that they comply with the letter of credit terms. This review takes longer than the review of an ordinary draft. Therefore, UCC Article 5 allows the issuer a reasonable time—up to seven days maximum upon receipt of the draft—to make a payment decision. The midnight deadline that applies to ordinary drafts does not apply to letters of credit.

If the documents submitted by the beneficiary with the draft for payment do not comply with the letter of credit terms, the issuer must dishonor the draft. In the case of a commercial letter of credit, the issuer notifies the seller (beneficiary) that the documents contain discrepancies and that payment will not be made. Under Article 5 of the UCC, the issuer has no authority to make payment if the documents do not strictly comply with the letter of credit.

### Wrongful Dishonor

If the beneficiary has complied with the letter of credit terms on face value, the issuer is liable to the beneficiary. If the payment is not made, the issuer has **wrongfully dishonored** the letter of credit and may recover damages from the issuer. Article 5 specifies that the issuer is liable for the amount of the draft along with any incidental damages plus interest. If the issuer's obligation under the letter of credit was not for the payment of money but for the performance of some other obligation, the beneficiary may obtain either the specific performance from the issuer or the value of the specific performance.

### Stopping Payment on a Letter of Credit

If the beneficiary properly presents a draft on a letter of credit, the issuing bank must pay it. This is true even if the bank's customer does not want the bank to pay because of some dispute with the beneficiary. The customer's only option is to file a suit in court and ask the court to stop the bank from making payments. Courts usually will not stop a payment except in circumstances involving fraud or forgery. A dispute about the terms of the contract of sale is insufficient to stop the payment of a letter of credit.

In a very limited circumstance, the bank can, without first resorting to the courts, refuse to pay a letter of credit based upon fraud or forgery. First, the documents presented with the letter of credit must appear to comply with the terms and conditions of the letter of credit. If the beneficiary's signature is forged on a document, however, or if one or more of the required documents is fraudulent, the issuing bank can refuse to pay the letter of credit—unless the payment is demanded by a person, acting in good faith with no knowledge of the forgery or fraud, who has given value for some part of the transaction.

## CONCLUSION

The Uniform Commercial Code (UCC) governs most bank transactions. Article 3 determines the negotiability of an instrument as well as the rights and responsibilities of the parties involved. Article 4 regulates the rights and responsibilities of banks and their customers when depositing and collecting checks. Article 4A governs the duties and liabilities of banks and customers when electronically transferring funds for business or commercial purposes. Article 4 governs transactions involving letters of credit. Commercial letters of credit generally are executed in connection with a sales transaction, whereas standby letters of credit simply guarantee a customer's performance of an obligation to a beneficiary

## QUESTIONS FOR REVIEW AND DISCUSSION

1. What are some of the reasons why the UCC was enacted?
2. What are the six elements of negotiability?
3. Why is it beneficial for an instrument to be a negotiable instrument?
4. What are some of the responsibilities of a returning bank in the check collection process?
5. What are the typical responsibilities of an originator's bank when it wires funds for a customer?
6. What are the duties of a beneficiary's bank when it receives a wire transfer of funds and accepts the payment order?
7. What is the difference between a standby letter of credit and a commercial letter of credit?

## LEARNING ACTIVITIES FOR CHAPTER 2

### Multiple Choice

Choose the best answer for each question.

1. Which of the following banking-related transactions is not covered by the UCC?

   a. the check collection process
   b. wire transfers of funds
   c. real estate transactions
   d. letters of credit

2. What is the benefit of using a negotiable instrument?

   a. It is on one piece of paper.
   b. It is signed by only one person.
   c. It is payable to only one person.
   d. It is freely transferable.

3. A negotiable instrument with a *promise* to pay (rather than an *order* to pay) is a:

   a. note
   b. draft
   c. check
   d. bearer instrument

4. The addition of a *subject to* clause in an instrument makes the instrument:

   a. negotiable
   b. nonnegotiable
   c. worthless
   d. more valuable

5. Under Article 3, money includes:

   a. precious metal
   b. commodities
   c. currency
   d. any medium of exchange authorized by a government

6. A negotiable instrument may be payable:

   a. to order
   b. to *bearer*
   c. to a specific payee
   d. all of the above

7. A check payable to *John or Mary* may be endorsed by:

 a. John
 b. Mary
 c. John and Mary
 d. all of the above

8. The first bank to receive an item in the collection process is the:

 a. depositary bank
 b. intermediary bank
 c. returning bank
 d. payor bank

9. Banks in the collection process generally must adhere to the midnight deadline. This deadline is:

 a. midnight of the banking day the check is received
 b. midnight of the day after the banking day the check is received
 c. midnight of the last day of the month in which the check is received
 d. midnight of the day after the calendar day the check is received

10. Large-item return notices must be sent for items in the amount of:

 a. $1,000 or more
 b. $1,500 or more
 c. $2,000 or more
 d. $2,500 or more

## Completion

Fill in the blanks with the word or words that best complete the sentences.

1. The receiver of a negotiable instrument is called a _____.

2. A note is a negotiable instrument with a _____ to pay.

3. A check is a type of _____.

4. A negotiable instrument must contain an _____ promise to pay.

5. A negotiable instrument must be payable in _____.

6. If a draft is *payable at sight,* it is payable _____ _____.

7. Banks in the collection process must exercise _____ _____.

8. A bank that executes an erroneous electronic payment order will be liable if it does not follow its own _____ _____.

9. A letter of credit used in a sales transaction is called a _____ letter of credit.

10. A letter of credit that is a performance guarantee is a _____ letter of credit.

## True/False

Indicate whether each of the following statements is true or false.

T F 1. The fact that an instrument is payable on demand does not affect its status as a negotiable instrument.

T F 2. The signature of the maker of a negotiable instrument can be any legal name, trade name, or assumed name.

T F 3. A negotiable instrument may be conditioned upon the occurrence of a future event.

T F 4. A negotiable instrument may be payable in British Pounds Sterling.

T F 5. The first bank to receive an item in the collection process is the depositary bank.

T F 6. A bank exercises ordinary care if it forwards a properly payable check for collection within three business days of the day the item was received.

T F 7. Most checks are not physically examined during the posting process except to encode the amount of each check.

T F 8. A bank may establish its own security procedures for wire transfers as long as they are commercially reasonable.

T F 9. UCC Article 4A covers all transfers of funds for any purpose.

T F 10. A bank does not have to honor a letter of credit if its customer asks it not to do so.

# 3

# TORTS AND CRIMES

## LEARNING OBJECTIVES

After studying this chapter, you should be able to

- explain the difference between torts and crimes
- describe the principal torts that apply to banking, including negligence, fraud, and defamation
- discuss the crimes to which banks are most vulnerable, including larceny, embezzlement, bribery, and money laundering
- describe situations in which banks have a legal responsibility to file suspicious activity reports
- define and use the legal and banking terms that appear in bold in the chapter text

# INTRODUCTION

Each citizen of the United States has rights and duties under the law. Individuals have a duty to respect the rights of others. When a person's rights are violated, the violation may be considered a crime or a tort.

Crimes are violations of criminal laws enacted by a governmental body. Criminal laws enacted by the U.S. Congress apply in all 50 states plus the District of Columbia—these are federal laws. State and local governments also may enact criminal laws that apply within their jurisdictions. An individual who violates a criminal law commits a **crime.**

According to the law, a crime is not committed against another individual, but rather against the entire city, state, or country. Breaking the law injures society as a whole. Therefore, criminal trials are conducted by a prosecutor who is employed by the government to represent the entire community. This is why criminal trials are brought in the name of the people as a whole, such as *The United States v. Bob Smith* or *The City of Dallas v. Jane Jones.*

Governments are not free to enact criminal statutes at will. All federal and state laws are subject to the U.S. Constitution and the rights it offers all citizens. A local government, for example, is not free to enact a law that prohibits constitutionally protected speech.

All U.S. citizens also have certain rights under civil laws. These rights include the right to use and enjoy one's property, the right to a good reputation, the right to relationships, and the right to be secure in one's person and not be put at risk by someone's careless or reckless behavior. A **tort** is the intentional or negligent interference with the rights of another person. Torts are subject to the civil laws of a jurisdiction rather than to the criminal laws.

Unlike a crime, which is committed against society as a whole, a tort is committed against an individual. Examples of torts include assault, battery, slander, libel, trespass, wrongful death, false imprisonment, and the intentional infliction of emotional distress.

Lawsuits involving torts are brought by the person or entity who has been wronged, or *injured.* Such legal actions are considered *civil* cases, meaning that they involve civil law rather than criminal law. The person who files a civil lawsuit is called the **plaintiff.** A person who is found liable of a tort is called a **tortfeasor.**

Certain actions that constitute torts might also fit the definition of a crime. It is not unusual to see both an individual and "the people" complaining against the same defendant for the same act.

### Example

A state's criminal law defines larceny as "the taking and carrying away of property from the possession of another without consent and with intention to steal." The state's tort laws define a tort called *conversion* as "an act that seriously interferes with another's right to possess property, with intention to do the act that brings about the interference."

A bookkeeper at a bank wrongfully transfers bank funds into his own account over a period of several months. The bank discovers this action during an audit and reports the wrongdoing to the police. The police charge the bookkeeper with larceny (a *crime*). In a separate, civil action, the bank sues the bookkeeper for conversion (a *tort*).

The criminal trial and the civil trial will always be separate proceedings. The outcome of one trial does not necessarily have a bearing on the outcome of the other. For example, if the criminal trial comes first, a finding of not guilty does not necessarily mean that the civil trial will result in a finding that no tort was committed. And vice versa. This fact highlights two other differences between crimes and torts—the elements of each that must be proved, and the standards of proof that must be met to prove each element.

In a criminal case, the government must prove *beyond a reasonable doubt* that the defendant committed each element of the crime as defined in the law. In a tort suit, the plaintiff must prove only that it is *more likely than not* that the defendant committed the tort. In other words, the plaintiff's evidence need only outweigh the defendant's evidence by some degree; it need not prove liability beyond a reasonable doubt.

### Example

In the criminal trial after the incident at the bank, the government proves five elements of the larceny charge. The defendant 1) took and 2) carried away 3) property 4) from possession of the bank 5) without consent. When it comes to the sixth element of the crime—with intention to steal—the defendant claims that stealing was not his intent. He testifies that the bank owed him the money because he worked many hours of overtime for which the bank had not paid him. The $500 is payment for the overtime that he claims to have worked and for which he claims he did not receive proper compensation. This defense—that he believes the money is rightfully his—might make the government unable to prove beyond a reasonable doubt that his *intention* was theft. If all six elements of this crime cannot be proved, the defendant will be found not guilty.

The sole element of intent for the tort of conversion is to *do the act* that caused interference with the bank's possession. The defendant's excuse that his intent was not to steal would be of no help to him in a tort action. He intended to take the money and did so, which seriously interfered with the bank's right to possess it. Most likely, the tort case would result in a finding for the bank and it could get the $500 back from the defendant.

Another difference between torts and crimes is what happens to defendants who are found liable (for tort) or guilty (of crime). In tort suits, plaintiffs seek compensation from the defendant for the interference or wrong that was committed. Usually the compensation is money (called **damages),** but it might also be return of the property that was taken or some other act required of the defendant.

In criminal actions, the object is to punish the defendant for the injury against society. The typical punishments for crimes are loss of liberty (imprisonment) and/or criminal fines paid to the government. A **felony** is a more serious crime that is punishable by imprisonment for one or more years. Lesser crimes are called **misdemeanors** and are punishable by up to one year in jail.

---

### Critical Terms

*Crime* An offense against society at large made punishable under a criminal statute. The maximum punishment for committing a crime is always stated in the law. Crimes are considered public wrongs.

*Tort* A noncriminal interference with the rights of an individual member of society. Torts are considered private wrongs.

*Tortfeasor* A person who is found liable for a tort in a civil proceeding.

---

## TORTS

Although many different torts could conceivably involve a bank, those of particular concern to bankers include negligence, fraud (or deceit), and defamation.

### Negligence

The tort of **negligence** is based on a concept called the *duty of care*, which everyone in society owes to one another. Unlike conversion and some other torts, negligence need not involve wrongful intent. Negligence is defined simply as carelessness in conducting one's affairs that results in injury to someone else. The duty of care is defined as the degree of care that a reasonable person would use under similar circumstances. Acts done without that amount of care and that cause injury to others are legally negligent. Persons who act negligently can be sued and required to pay for the damages they cause.

The duty of care sets standards of conduct for all aspects of society, including banking operations. Like any other member of society, a bank is accountable to anyone who suffers injury as a result of its negligence.

### Example

A bank routinely makes real estate loans and requires its customers to make payments into an escrow account for taxes and insurance. Winston Properties, Inc. has a loan at the bank secured by a small motel it owns. The borrower makes payments monthly for hazard and flood insurance into the bank's escrow account. The bank receives insurance premium payment notices and pays them before the end of the grace period.

On August 1 the bank receives a notice that the Winston Properties motel flood insurance premium is due by September 1. The premium for the next year has increased by 19 percent. The loan assistant in charge of making the insurance payments begins reviewing the property characteristics to verify the premium increase. The payment for the policy premium is not made until September 10. Although the loan assistant did not know it, the flood insurance policy has no grace period. The insurance expires on September 1 when the payment is not made. On September 8 a storm hits the area in which the motel is located. The motel floods and sustains substantial damages. Is the bank liable for negligence in failing to pay the policy on or before the due date?

In some cases the actions of the plaintiff can be important in establishing the damages for a defendant's negligent behavior. If it can be shown that the plaintiff's actions substantially contributed to his or her own injuries, the defendant usually will not be liable for damages in a negligence claim. If the plaintiff's actions were only slightly involved in causing the injury, the damage claim may be lessened.

### Case for Discussion
*The Errant Fire Alarm*

State National Bank had a fire alarm system that was constantly monitored by Acme Safety Systems. The bank paid Acme an annual fee to monitor its fire and burglar alarm systems on a continual basis because the city ordinance required companies with buildings over five stories to have such a constantly monitored system. The State National Bank building was seven stories tall.

On October 1, State National Bank asked to have the system taken off-line for a period of 24 hours for testing. On October 2, the bank asked Acme to bring the system back on-line. Acme reinstated the system's on-line capacity within two hours of the bank's request. However, on October 3, an Acme systems engineer who knew that the bank was testing its system noticed that the system was back on-line and believed this to be a mistake.

The engineer called the bank and spoke to the assistant facilities manager, who was new to the job. The assistant manager told the Acme engineer that he did not know if the system should be on-line, but that he would check into the situation and call back. The facilities manager never called the engineer back.

The engineer, believing that the bank was still testing, took the system off-line. Within the next hour, a fire started on the second floor of the building. When bank employees noticed the fire, they manually activated the building's fire alarm system. If the Acme system had been on-line at the time of the fire, it would have been contained easily and would have done little damage. Because the system was taken off-line, however, the fire caused a great deal of damage to the building's second floor by the time it was extinguished.

**Questions for Discussion**

1. Does the bank have a negligence claim against Acme?
2. Does Acme have an effective defense?

## Fraud

A tort frequently committed in business is **fraud** (also called *deceit* and *misrepresentation*). Fraud has these five essential elements:

- a false statement of fact made by one person to another
- knowledge by the maker of the statement that it is false
- making the statement with the intention that the other person will believe and act upon it
- justifiable reliance by the other person on the truth of the statement
- damage to the other person resulting from his or her relying and acting on the false statement

### Example

In his application to the bank for a $50,000 loan, a woman lists several assets that she does not own. The bank would not make the loan if the woman's true financial status were known. If the bank later discovers that the woman does not actually own the assets, and suffers injury (for example, the loan is not repaid), it could bring a civil suit against the woman for fraud.

As with many torts, this conduct might also constitute a crime. Providing a false loan application to a bank is a federal offense that can result in a fine of up to $5,000, a prison sentence of up to two years, or both.

---

**Critical Terms**

*Slander* A false oral statement that damages a person's reputation. Such a statement is slanderous.

*Libel* A false written statement that damages a person's reputation.

---

## Defamation

**Defamation** is an untrue statement that causes injury to someone's reputation. **Slander** is a spoken defamatory statement, while **libel** is written defamation. Libelous and slanderous statements are defined as those that tend to expose a person to hatred, contempt, or ridicule, or that injure the person in his or her position or business. For example, it is defamatory to spread a false rumor that a person or business is on the brink of bankruptcy, as this would tend to injure the person's reputation and the business.

---

**Case for Discussion**
*The Luncheon Pitch*

Brad Jordan, a young, aggressive, commercial loan officer for First Friendly National Bank, began a year ago to approach Tony Cuisine, a successful restaurateur who was also a longtime customer of rival Big City Federal Bank. Jordan had succeeded in attracting some small loan activity from Cuisine, mostly personal loans unrelated to the business. Jordan began pressing Cuisine to seek larger loans from First Friendly.

During a meeting over lunch, Jordan made his pitch. Cuisine was complaining about Big City Federal and also confided that his restaurant business,

---

although still profitable, was in financial trouble. Seeing an apportunity to sell First Friendly's congenial image, Jordan told Cuisine that he had talked with a dozen businessmen in the past month who also complained about the attitude of Big City Federal's loan officers. Jordan also pointed out that First Friendly had an experienced staff and a solid credit department and worked in partnership with customers to assist in business planning. "If you become a First Friendly customer," he told Cuisine, "you will not have to worry about Big City's bad attitude anymore."

Cuisine said he would think it over. The next day, after talking briefly with Jordan on the telephone, Cuisine made arrangements to pay off his loans at Big City and transfer all his loans and accounts to First Friendly.

Jordan was called out of town on an important problem loan and was gone for two days. When Jordan returned to First Friendly, a telephone message waited for him. It was from Rockwell Moder, corporate counsel, who wanted to talk to him about a call from Big City Federal's attorney concerning slanderous statements.

Does Jordan have reason to be concerned?

### Questions for Discussion
1. What is a *slanderous statement?*
2. What did Jordan do that might provide the basis for a lawsuit by Big City Federal?

A statement is not defamatory unless it is published. Publication does not mean that the statement must be printed. It simply means that the statement has been communicated in some way to a third party—that is, to someone other than the person who is the subject of the statement. For example, saying "I heard you were bankrupt" directly to someone is not pub-

lication. But saying to Loretta, "I heard that George is bankrupt" *is* a publication. A person who simply repeats a defamatory statement also is liable for the statement, even if he or she does not believe it. By repeating the statement, the person is considered to have re-published it. In addition, the original defamer is liable for re-publication if he or she knew or should have known that the statement would be repeated.

### Example
Helen and Pat are tellers at the Mockingbird Avenue branch of Big City Bank. They are familiar with all of the bank's regular customers. George Edwards, a depositor of Big City Bank, frequently conducts his banking business at the Mockingbird Avenue branch. George operates an import-export business and has difficulty with cash flow from time to time, although his business is successful overall. George had two overdrafts last month and one last Monday.

George's friend Milton Ward also banks at Big City Bank. Last Tuesday, when Milton was making a deposit at Helen's teller station, he overheard Helen and Pat discussing George's large overdraft from the previous night. Helen said, "I can't believe that he is still in business with all the overdrafts he has."

Milton did not indicate to Helen and Pat that he knew George personally. However, he does tell George that the bank was discussing George's overdrafts while he was in the teller line. George instructs his attorney to call the bank and threaten to sue them for defamation by slander.

While the statement made by Helen was published in that it was communicated to a third party, in order for George to obtain damages it would need to be shown that George was somehow injured by the statement. In most cases a statement cannot be considered defamatory if it is true. Also, if the person about whom the statement is made consents to the publication of the statement, no defamation exists.

The publication of some defamatory statements, even if they are untrue, cannot be grounds for a lawsuit. Because a democratic form of government requires freedom of speech and public debate, and because speech concerning important public issues may be stifled because of the fear of liability, the Supreme Court has ruled that statements made about public officials and public figures may be *privileged* and may not invoke liability in a tort suit. Under the Court's ruling, public officials and public figures cannot sue for defamation unless the untrue statement about them is published with *actual malice*. Actual malice means that the statement was published with knowledge or reckless disregard of its falsity.

## CRIMES

The crimes that bankers may encounter include larceny, embezzlement, bribery, and money laundering.

### Larceny

**Larceny** is the crime of taking and carrying away personal property from the possession of another without consent and with intent to steal it. If the property taken has a sufficiently high value, the crime will be defined as *grand larceny*—a felony. If the property is of lesser value, the crime is *petty larceny*—a misdemeanor. While bank robbery is a good example of larceny, larceny need not involve the taking of money. Stealing a wastebasket from the lobby or plantings from the walkway also would constitute larceny.

### Embezzlement

**Embezzlement** is the fraudulent use or keeping of money or other property that has been entrusted to one's care. With banks, this crime is also referred to as *misappropriation of funds.*

**Example**

A bank courier takes for his own use $5,000 that he was transporting for the bank. The courier is guilty of embezzlement.

Embezzlement can be proved by showing that the accused 1) had a fiduciary relationship with the bank, such as officer, director, employee, or agent; 2) deliberately misapplied the bank's money or money that was in the bank's custody; and 3) acted with intent to defraud the bank.

**Example**

A loan officer prepares loan applications in false names, approves them, and funds the loan proceeds into an account that she controls. The loan officer uses the funds for her own purposes and resigns from the bank. The bank, through an audit, discovers that the loans were made to fictitious persons and that the loan officer has, in fact, embezzled them from the bank.

The prevention of embezzlement is one reason why federal regulatory agencies generally require bank employees to take two consecutive weeks of vacation each year. Because most ongoing embezzlement schemes require regular activity to conceal them, it is difficult to maintain such a scheme when the perpetrator is out of the bank for two consecutive weeks.

### Bribery

The **Bank Bribery Act** is a federal law that makes it a felony for a bank employee to receive gifts, money, or favors for any bank-related decision or activity.

**Example**

A business customer applies for a $500,000 loan at a bank and two days later pays for the bank president's trip to a beach resort for the weekend. Both the customer and the bank president could be found guilty of violating the Bank Bribery Act.

Federal regulatory agencies have issued guidelines to assist bank officers, directors, employees, and attorneys in complying with this act. These guidelines encourage banks to adopt codes of conduct and written policies that explain what actions the law prohibits. Under these guidelines, banks usually forbid employees from either asking for or accepting anything of value in connection with the business of the bank. Acceptance of marketing or promotional items or items of nominal value do not violate the statute. In addition, bankers may continue to accept items of value from customers with whom they have other social or family ties. Allowing a customer to pay for items that the bank would have paid for (such as lunch or dinner) also is acceptable. Gifts of reasonable value given on commonly recognized events such as for weddings or holidays does not violate the law. However, federal regulators have stated that expensive items that have no demonstrable business value are forbidden. Banks also should require employees who receive or are offered something of value by a customer to disclose the matter to a bank official.

### Procedures

The regulatory agencies have urged banks to adopt procedures to ensure compliance with the Bank Bribery Act. These procedures include providing copies of the code of conduct to all employees and requiring them to read it and agree to comply with it. Banks also should maintain written reports of disclosures made by employees in connection with the code of conduct or written policies.

Federal regulatory agencies also have encouraged all banks to adopt acceptable dollar-values for any benefits that employees are permitted to receive from customers or other parties seeking to do business with the bank. They recommend that banks review employee disclosures to determine whether the items offered or accepted pose any threat to the integrity of the bank. The OCC, the FDIC, and the Fed all caution that an offer of anything with a value above the limits set by the bank's policies, even if not accepted, violates the law if the offer relates to bank business and is made with dishonest intent.

## Money Laundering

In 1970 Congress passed the Currency and Foreign Transaction Reporting Act, commonly known as the **Bank Secrecy Act.** This act has since been amended to strengthen its use in exposing criminal activity. One of its purposes is to combat **money laundering.** This crime involves transferring cash acquired in illegal operations from one bank account to another to conceal the true source of the cash.

### Example

A man takes his proceeds from one day's cocaine sales, $25,000 in cash, to a bank and purchases two $12,500 money orders. He then deposits the money orders in accounts he has at two other banks.

To facilitate detection of these activities, the law requires banks to file a **currency transaction report (CTR)**—also called Form 4789—with the Internal Revenue Service whenever cash transactions with a customer involve more than $10,000 in one day (see exhibit 3.1). For example, if a customer deposits $9,000 at the bank's main office, $4,000 at a branch office, and $7,000 at another branch office on the same day, the bank is required to file a CTR. Some customers, such as other banks, government agencies, businesses that are listed on a major U.S. stock exchange, and retail businesses owned by U.S. residents that have been customers of the bank for at least

**Exhibit 3.1 Form 4789**

Form **4789**
(Rev. June 1998)
Department of the Treasury
Internal Revenue Service

## Currency Transaction Report

▶ Use this 1998 revision effective June 1, 1998.
▶ For Paperwork Reduction Act Notice, see page 3.   ▶ Please type or print.
*(Complete all parts that apply—See instructions)*

OMB No. 1506-0004

**1**   Check all box(es) that apply:

**a** ☐ Amends prior report   **b** ☐ Multiple persons   **c** ☐ Multiple transactions

### Part I   Person(s) Involved in Transaction(s)

### Section A—Person(s) on Whose Behalf Transaction(s) Is Conducted

| 2   Individual's last name or Organization's name | 3   First name | 4   M.I. |
|---|---|---|

| 5   Doing business as (DBA) | 6   SSN or EIN |
|---|---|

| 7   Address (number, street, and apt. or suite no.) | 8   Date of birth   M M D D Y Y Y Y |
|---|---|

| 9   City | 10   State | 11   ZIP code | 12   Country (if not U.S.) | 13   Occupation, profession, or business |
|---|---|---|---|---|

**14**   If an individual, describe method used to verify identity:

**a** ☐ Driver's license/State I.D.   **b** ☐ Passport   **c** ☐ Alien registration   **d** ☐ Other _____

**e** Issued by:        **f** Number:

### Section B—Individual(s) Conducting Transaction(s) (if other than above).
If Section B is left blank or incomplete, check the box(es) below to indicate the reason(s):

**a** ☐ Armored Car Service   **b** ☐ Mail Deposit or Shipment   **c** ☐ Night Deposit or Automated Teller Machine (ATM)

**d** ☐ Multiple Transactions   **e** ☐ Conducted On Own Behalf

| 15   Individual's last name | 16   First name | 17   M.I. |
|---|---|---|

| 18   Address (number, street, and apt. or suite no.) | 19   SSN |
|---|---|

| 20   City | 21   State | 22   ZIP code | 23   Country (if not U.S.) | 24   Date of birth   M M D D Y Y Y Y |
|---|---|---|---|---|

**25**   If an individual, describe method used to verify identity:

**a** ☐ Driver's license/State I.D.   **b** ☐ Passport   **c** ☐ Alien registration   **d** ☐ Other _____

**e** Issued by:        **f** Number:

### Part II   Amount and Type of Transaction(s). Check all boxes that apply.

**26**   Cash In $ _____ .00    **27**   Cash Out $ _____ .00    **28**   Date of Transaction   M M D D Y Y Y Y

**29** ☐ Foreign Currency _____ (Country)   **30** ☐ Wire Transfer(s)   **31** ☐ Negotiable Instrument(s) Purchased

**32** ☐ Negotiable Instrument(s) Cashed   **33** ☐ Currency Exchange(s)   **34** ☐ Deposit(s)/Withdrawal(s)

**35** ☐ Account Number(s) Affected (if any):   **36** ☐ Other (specify)

### Part III   Financial Institution Where Transaction(s) Takes Place

| 37   Name of financial institution | Enter Federal Regulator or BSA Examiner code number from the instructions here. ▶   [        ] |
|---|---|

| 38   Address (number, street, and apt. or suite no.) | 39   SSN or EIN |
|---|---|

| 40   City | 41   State | 42   ZIP code | 43   MICR No. |
|---|---|---|---|

**Sign Here** ▶

| 44   Title of approving official | 45   Signature of approving official | 46   Date of signature   M M D D Y Y Y Y |
|---|---|---|
| 47   Type or print preparer's name | 48   Type or print name of person to contact | 49   Telephone number  (    ) |

Cat. No. 42004W                    Form **4789** (Rev. 6-98)

Note: This exhibit reproduces only page 1 of Form 4789. The complete form, including instructions, can be found on the Financial Crimes Enforcement Network (FinCEN) web site at http://www.ustreas.gov.fincen.

12 months may be exempt from CTR filings if the bank files a special form designating the customer as an exempt person (see exhibit 3.2). Under the Bank Secrecy Act, exempt person status may not be given to businesses engaged in

- serving as an agent of a financial institution of any type
- purchasing or selling motor vehicles of any kind, including vessels, aircraft, farm equipment or mobile homes
- practicing law, accountancy, or medicine
- auctioning of goods
- chartering or operation of ships, buses, or aircraft
- gaming of any kind (other than licensed pari-mutuel betting at race tracks)
- providing investment advisory services or investment banking services
- providing real estate brokerage or pawn brokerage services
- providing title insurance
- arranging for real estate closings
- participating in trade union activities

In addition to CTRs, banks are required to file reports on international transactions involving monetary instruments in amounts over $10,000 (or its equivalent in foreign currency). The regulations also direct that banks keep records on certain loans, transfers of funds, certificates of deposit, deposit accounts, checks, drafts, and other transactions in excess of $10,000. Banks also are required to keep records on cashier's checks, traveler's checks, and money orders that are purchased with more than $3,000 in currency.

Banks are required to appoint individuals to be responsible for coordinating and monitoring daily compliance with the Bank Secrecy Act. Violations of the Bank Secrecy Act have serious consequences for banks, their directors, and officers. Criminal and civil penalties can be imposed for failing to file or properly complete CTRs and for circumventing reporting requirements, even if the failure was unintentional.

## SUSPICIOUS ACTIVITY REPORTING

Banks also have a legal duty to report all known or suspected criminal activity. The federal bank regulatory agencies have adopted procedures that require a bank to report known or suspected crimes that involve the bank. These reports are called *suspicious activity reports* and are made using a specific Suspicious Activity Report (SAR) form (exhibit 3.3). If the suspect is a bank employee, officer, director, or shareholder, a SAR must be filed regardless of the dollar amount of loss or suspected loss. When the bank suspects that a crime or possible crime has been committed involving $5,000 or more and has a basis for identifying a suspect, a SAR must be filed. When there is no basis for identifying a suspect, the loss or suspected loss must be $25,000 or more to trigger the filing requirements. If the criminal activity involves the Bank Secrecy Act, the bank must file a report if the amount involved is $5,000 or more. Robberies and burglaries that are reported to the appropriate law enforcement agencies do not require the filing of a SAR. The law provides a safe harbor to banks that file SARs against claims of libel or slander. If the bank reports in good faith, it is not subject to such claims. The failure to file a SAR can subject a bank's officers and directors to civil money penalties.

SARs must be submitted to the Financial Crimes Enforcement Network of the Treasury Department (FinCEN) within 30 days of the bank's initial detection of facts that give rise to the suspicion. Referrals are not required concerning robberies and burglaries because they are subject to other regulations. Banks must keep copies of all SARs for five years from the date of filing.

## Exhibit 3.2    Designation of Exempt Person

**TD F 90-22.53**
Treasury form

(January 1999)

# Designation of Exempt Person

**Please type or print**

FinCEN

OMB No. 1506-0012

**1** Check appropriate box (see instructions):

**a** ☐ Initial Designation      **b** ☐ Biennial Renewal

**2** Check appropriate box

**a** ☐ Exemption Amended      **b** ☐ Exemption Revoked

### Part I    Exempt Person

**3** Business Name or Name of Sole Proprietor

**4** Doing Business As (DBA)

**5** Address (Number, Street, and Apt. or Suite No.)

**6** City

**7** State

**8** Zip/Postal Code

**9** Taxpayer Identification Number

### Part II    Basis for Exemption

**10** Exemption Basis

**a** ☐ Bank      **b** ☐ Government Agency / Governmental Authority      **c** ☐ Listed company      **d** ☐ Listed Company Subsidiary

**e** ☐ Eligible Non-listed business      **f** ☐ Payroll Customer

**11** Effective date of the exemption
M  M    D  D    Y  Y  Y  Y

**12** Has there been a change in control of the exempt person? For 10(e) and (f) only.
**a** ☐ Yes      **b** ☐ No

### Part III    Bank Granting or Revoking Exemption

**13** Name of Bank

**14** Primary Federal Regulator  (check **only one**)

**a** ☐ OCC   **b** ☐ FDIC   **c** ☐ FRS   **d** ☐ OTS   **e** ☐ NCUA

**15** Address (Number, Street, and Apt. or Suite No.)

**16** City

**17** State

**18** Zip/Postal Code

**19** Taxpayer Identification Number

**Sign Here**

**20** Title of approving official

**21** Signature of approving official

**22** Date of Signature
M  M    D  D    Y  Y  Y  Y

**23** Last name of person to contact

**24** First name of person to contact

**25** Telephone number
(          )          –

**26 For Biennial Updates ONLY (see item 1(b))**

I certify on behalf of the above listed bank that its system of monitoring the transactions in currency of an exempt person for suspicious activity has been applied as necessary, and at least annually, to the account of this exempt person.

**Sign Here**      Signature of Approving Official _____

This form must be used by a bank or other depository institution to designate an eligible customer as an exempt person from currency transaction reporting rules of the Department of the Treasury (31 CFR 103.22). File this form with:

### U.S. Department of the Treasury, P.O. Box 33112, Detroit, MI 48232-0112.

**Paperwork Reduction Act Notice:** The purpose of this form is to provide an effective means for banks and depository institutions to exempt eligible customers from currency transaction reporting. This report is required by law, pursuant to 31 CFR 103.22. Federal law enforcement and regulatory agencies, including the U.S. Department the Treasury and other authorized authorities may use and share this information. You are not required to provide the requested information unless a form displays a valid OMB control number. Public reporting and recordkeeping burden for this form is estimated to average 70 minutes per response, and includes time to gather and maintain information the required report, review the instructions, and complete the information collection. The record retention period is five years. Send comments regarding this burden estimate, including suggestions for reducing the burden, to the Financial Crimes Enforcement Network, Attn: Paperwork Reduction Act; Suite 200; 2070 Chain Bridge Road, Vienna VA 22182-2536

Cat. No. 26697V

Note:  This exhibit reproduces only page 1 of Form TD F 90-22.53, Designation of Exempt Person. The complete form, including instructions, can be found on the Financial Crimes Enforcement Network (FinCEN) web site at http://www.ustreas.gov.fincen.

## Exhibit 3.3    Suspicious Activity Report

### Suspicious Activity Report

**ALWAYS COMPLETE ENTIRE REPORT**

| | | |
|---|---|---|
| FRB: | FR 2230 | OMB No. 7100-0212 |
| FDIC: | 6710/06 | OMB No. 3064-0077 |
| OCC: | 8010-9,8010-1 | OMB No. 1557-0180 |
| OTS: | 1601 | OMB No. 1550-0003 |
| NCUA: | 2362 | OMB No. 3133-0094 |
| TREASURY: | TD F 90-22.47 | OMB No. 1506-0001 |

Expires September 30, 1998

1 Check appropriate box:
a ☐ Initial Report    b ☐ Corrected Report    c ☐ Supplemental Report

### Part I    Reporting Financial Institution Information

2 Name of Financial Institution

3 Primary Federal Regulator
a ☐ Federal Reserve   d ☐ OCC
b ☐ FDIC            e ☐ OTS
c ☐ NCUA

4 Address of Financial Institution

5 City    6 State    7 Zip Code    8 EIN or TIN

9 Address of Branch Office(s) where activity occurred

10 Asset size of financial institution
$                    .00

11 City    12 State    13 Zip Code

14 If institution closed, date closed
___/___/___
MM   DD   YYYY

15 Account number(s) affected, if any
a _____
b _____

16 Have any of the institution's accounts related to this matter been closed?
☐ Yes    ☐ No    If yes, identify _____

### Part II    Suspect Information

17 Last Name or Name of Entity    18 First Name    19 Middle Initial

20 Address    21 SSN, EIN or TIN (as applicable)

22 City    23 State    24 Zip Code    25 Country    26 Date of Birth
___/___/___
MM   DD   YYYY

27 Phone Number - Residence (include area code)    (    )

28 Phone Number - Work (include area code)    (    )

29 Occupation

30 Forms of Identification for Suspect:
a ☐ Driver's License/    b ☐ Passport    c ☐ Alien Registration    d ☐ Other _____

e ☐ Number _____    f ☐ Issuing Authority _____

31 Relationship to Financial Institution:
a ☐ Accountant    d ☐ Attorney    g ☐ Customer    j ☐ Officer
b ☐ Agent         e ☐ Borrower    h ☐ Director    k ☐ Shareholder
c ☐ Appraiser     f ☐ Broker      i ☐ Employee    l ☐ Other _____

32 Is insider suspect still affiliated with the financial institution?
a ☐ Yes
b ☐ No    If no, specify { c ☐ Suspended    e ☐ Resigned
                            d ☐ Terminated

33 Date of Suspension, Termination, Resignation
___/___/___
MM   DD   YYYY

34 Admission/Confession
a ☐ Yes    b ☐ No

Note: This exhibit reproduces only page 1 of the Suspicious Activity Report. The complete form, including instructions, can be found on the Financial Crimes Enforcement Network (FinCEN) web site at http://www.ustreas.gov.fincen.

## CONCLUSION

A crime is an offense against society made punishable under a criminal statute. A tort, which may be defined in the common law or by statute, is a breach of a legally defined duty of care that members of society owe to one another. With one act, a person, organization, or institution can commit both a tort and a crime. The government represents society in prosecuting persons or businesses accused of crimes. Victims of torts bring suit for compensation for their injuries in their own names, without government involvement.

Because of the critical role banks play in the nation's economy, protection of bank assets from wrongdoing is an important goal of criminal law. Wrongful conduct, such as failing to provide accurate information that might be only a tort in another business setting, often is also a criminal offense if it involves a bank. To avoid committing crimes in even seemingly innocent activities, bank directors, officers, employees, and agents must take great care to comply with banking laws and regulations.

## QUESTIONS FOR REVIEW AND DISCUSSION

1. Who is harmed by a crime? By a tort?
2. What is the general duty of care in a negligence action?
3. Why is publication an essential element of a defamation action?
4. What is a CTR?
5. What must a bank do when it detects facts that lead it to believe a financial crime has been committed?

## LEARNING ACTIVITIES FOR CHAPTER 3

### Multiple Choice

Choose the best answer for each question.

1. When an individual stands accused of a tort, liability must be established:

    a. as more likely than not
    b. beyond a reasonable doubt
    c. without a doubt
    d. to the satisfaction of the judge

2. Which of the following is *not* a tort?

    a. false imprisonment
    b. conversion
    c. defamation
    d. robbery

3. Misappropriation of funds is a form of:

    a. negligence
    b. embezzlement
    c. fraud
    d. larceny

4. To convict an individual of larceny, a prosecutor must establish that:

    a. the individual was employed by the person from whom the property was taken
    b. amounts in excess of $5,000 are involved
    c. amounts of less than $5,000 are involved
    d. the individual intended to steal the property

5. Johnson is a longtime customer of the bank. Every year Johnson takes a group of business associates on a week-long hunting trip to Mexico. Johnson pays all expenses for the trip. Johnson invites Smith, his loan officer at the bank, to go. Can Smith go on this trip?

    a. Yes, if Smith discloses it to the bank.
    b. Yes, if bank policy permits it.
    c. No, unless Smith or the bank reimburses Johnson for Smith's portion of the expenses.
    d. No, unless Johnson signs a statement that he does not intend to unduly influence Smith or the bank by offering the trip.

6. To demonstrate compliance with the Bank Bribery Act, banks should have:

   a. codes of conduct
   b. lie detector tests administered regularly on a random basis
   c. two-way mirrors in loan interview rooms
   d. regular staff meetings

7. The Bank Secrecy Act is aimed at combating:

   a. bribery
   b. negligence
   c. money laundering
   d. embezzlement

8. Falsely stating that someone has filed for bankruptcy can be a tort of:

   a. negligence
   b. defamation
   c. deceit
   d. misrepresentation

9. For which customer may the bank file an exempt person designation to exempt it from the requirement to file CTRs on a regular basis when deposits of over $10,000 in currency are made?

   a. a local restaurant
   b. a local car dealership
   c. a local real estate brokerage
   d. a local CPA firm

10. Bob Smith, a loan officer, tells his customer, Rhonda Barton, that he has heard that the town's most prominent lawyer is being investigated for money laundering crimes. If this statement is not true, what action could the lawyer bring against Mr. Smith?

    a. negligence
    b. slander
    c. libel
    d. fraud

## True/False

Indicate whether each of the following statements is true or false.

T  F  1.  All torts are crimes.

T  F  2.  All crimes are torts.

T  F  3.  All torts involve either intentional or negligent wrongdoing.

T  F  4.  Statements made about public officials and public figures, even when false may not constitute defamation.

T  F  5.  One who repeats slander is not liable for defamation.

T  F  6.  Any time an individual gives a bank officer a present, the Bank Bribery Act is violated.

T  F  7.  Money laundering has to do with keeping the supply of circulating bills and coins in good condition.

T  F  8.  Unlike bank officers, other bank employees do not have to report gifts or offers of gifts from bank customers.

T  F  9.  Embezzlement differs from larceny in that the amount of money stolen is greater.

T  F  10.  The acceptance by a bank officer of a gift of baseball World's Series tickets from a loan customer would likely be a violation of the Bank Bribery Act.

# 4

# LEGAL ENTITIES: INDIVIDUALS, SOLE PROPRIETORSHIPS, AND PARTNERSHIPS

## LEARNING OBJECTIVES

After studying this chapter, you should be able to

- define the term *legal entity* and identify sole proprietorships and partnerships as some of the types of legal entities that are customers of banks
- explain why banks must be sure that individual customers have the legal capacity to assume obligations
- describe a sole proprietorship and suggest how banks should set up accounts with sole proprietors doing business under an assumed name
- describe how agency relationships are created and terminated and explain the authority and liabilities of the parties in an agency relationship
- distinguish between the formation and authorities of general partnerships and limited partnerships
- define and use the legal and banking terms that appear in bold in the chapter text

# INTRODUCTION

Banks have several different types of customers. Most customers are individual people who conduct personal transactions. However, many bank customers are not natural persons but legal entities, or *artificial persons*. A legal entity might be a business organization such as a partnership or corporation, or it might be an estate or a trust, consisting only of property managed by someone other than its owner.

A person also may transact business at the bank not on his or her own behalf but as an employee or representative of another entity. When an individual transacts banking business as an employee or representative of another entity, the bank needs to know if the person has the proper authority to do so. For example, if a company is seeking a loan it is especially important that the bank know if the individual executing the loan documents has the authority to act on behalf of the company. If the signer does not have the proper authority, the bank may not be able to collect the loan from the company or foreclose on any collateral owned by the company.

The bank must always know who has final responsibility in a banking transaction with an individual who is acting on behalf of another person or business entity. At least two reasons prompt this rule. First, if the bank does not deal with a person who has the authority to obligate the customer, the bank is subject to losses through fraud. Second, the increasing regulatory emphasis on knowing your customers means the bank is responsible for ensuring that businesses that open accounts are legitimate and are not using the bank's services for illegal purposes, such as money laundering.

This chapter discusses business entities that are organized as sole proprietorships and partnerships. Exhibit 4.1 shows an overview of the characteristics of bank customers who do business as individuals, sole proprietorships, and partnerships. The next chapter will discuss corporations and trusts.

# INDIVIDUALS

Most of the bank's customers are individuals. These customers represent themselves when they enter into a banking transaction.

| Exhibit 4.1 | Legal Entities—Sole Proprietorships and Partnerships | | |
|---|---|---|---|
| *Type of Entity* | *Owner* | *Authority* | *Liability* |
| Individual | Natural person | Owner has authority to conduct all business. | Owner is fully liable for all transactions. |
| Sole proprietorship | Natural person | Owner has authority to conduct all business. | Owner is fully liable for all transactions. |
| General partnership | Natural persons, corporations, or partnerships | All partners have authority to conduct partnership business. | Partners are each fully liable for partnership transactions. |
| Limited partnership | Natural persons, corporations, or partnerships | General partners have authority to conduct partnership business. | General partners have full liability for partnership transactions; limited partners have little or no liability other than their investment in the partnership. |

They conduct business in their own name and on their own account. When dealing with individual customers, a bank must assure itself that the customer has the ability, under the law, to assume obligations. If the bank deals with a customer who lacks **legal capacity**—someone who is a juvenile or mentally incompetent at the time of the transaction, for example—the customer may not be held responsible for the transactions he or she conducts. If the bank enters into transactions with such a person by opening deposit accounts or making loans, the bank may not be able to hold the person responsible for any losses incurred by the bank.

---

### Critical Terms

*Legal Obligation* A duty or responsibility legally placed upon a person. A person who rents an apartment promises to pay the rent at the beginning of each month. Another person who uses a credit card to make a purchase promises to pay the amount due with interest each month until the bill is paid. These are examples of legal obligations. If the people in these two examples fail to pay as they promised, they are legally liable for the obligations.

*Legal Capacity* The mental ability (as defined by law) to enter into contracts. If a person can be required by law to repay a loan or other debt as promised, that person has the legal capacity to obtain credit. Juveniles (in most states, persons under age 18) and adults who have been declared by a court of law to be mentally incompetent, generally cannot be required to honor contracts into which they have entered. Therefore these individuals, as a rule, do not have the legal capacity to obtain credit.

---

## SOLE PROPRIETORSHIPS

A **sole proprietorship** is a business that is owned by an individual. It is not incorporated. It is the simplest form of business organization. A shoe store that is owned by one person is a sole proprietorship, as is an insurance agency that is owned by an individual insurance agent. The hiring of employees to work in a business does not affect its status as a sole proprietorship as long as only one person owns the business.

## Assumed Names

While many sole proprietors do business under the name of the individual owner, it is also common to find owners operating the business under an assumed name. The assumed name is what the owner is doing business as (usually abbreviated dba). Many states require individuals who use an assumed name to file an assumed-name certificate with a local or state office. This certificate becomes a part of the public record for the purpose of disclosing the real name of the owner of the business.

When a bank sets up an account with a sole proprietorship, it is wise to require that the account be opened in the legal name of the owner. If the business has an assumed name, the assumed name also can be recorded on the account (for example, Samuel Brown dba Acme Cleaners). If the account is to be opened in the assumed name and not the owner's name, the bank should ask for a copy of the assumed-name certificate before any bank business is transacted.

A bank dealing with a sole proprietorship may transact business in the same way it does with an individual. As far as the bank is concerned, the sole proprietorship and its owner are the same person. A sole proprietorship generally has no one responsible for its financial transactions except the owner, who is personally obligated to pay the business's debts.

### Example
Katherine Henderson opens an account under the name *Katherine Henderson dba Kitty's Collectibles.* The bank obtains a copy of the assumed-name certificate filed by Ms. Henderson showing her assumed name, Kitty's

Collectibles. The bank is dealing with Katherine Henderson, personally. If it makes a loan to her, the assumed name can be listed on the documents too, but because Ms. Henderson is the borrower in her individual capacity, all the documents should reflect that fact. The bank could allow her to sign the loan documents as Katherine Henderson or as Katherine Henderson dba Kitty's Collectibles.

## AGENTS

In addition to dealing with individuals transacting their personal or business matters, banks sometimes deal with individuals who are transacting business for someone else. An individual who does this is called an **agent.** An agent has the authority to act for another. Agents represent the **principal** in business and commercial matters. Agents can represent individuals, partnerships, or corporations.

### Creation of Agency Relationships

Agency relationships are common. In the business world, a company's employees act as agents when they conduct business on behalf of the company. For example, bank employees are agents of the bank when they open accounts and grant loans to the bank's customers. Generally, whenever one person acts for another in a representative capacity, an agency relationship exists.

#### Example
A man comes into the bank and asks to speak with a loan officer concerning a business loan for his company. Meanwhile, a woman with the key to her employer's safe deposit box has come to pick up the employer's passport from the box. In the teller line is a young man whose job with a nearby restaurant requires him to bring daily receipts to the bank for deposit in the restaurant's

account. The woman behind him in the line has her employer's corporate check in hand, made out to *Petty Cash,* for which she will be given $250 to bring back to her employer. Just coming through the door is a woman who represents a local printing firm. She wants to see the bank's purchasing officer about having the firm supply stationery and printed forms to the bank. Everyone mentioned in this scenario—including the loan officer, the purchasing officer, and the teller—is an agent. What they have in common is that none of them is in the bank to transact personal business; all are engaged in the business of others.

Individuals also can appoint agents to act on their behalf. Although the law does not always require a written agency agreement, a bank should not rely on an oral (spoken) appointment. If the transaction is later called into question or is challenged in court, the bank will need written documentation to prove that the agent was acting under authority from the principal. In many cases, state laws require that certain agency agreements be in writing to be valid. For example, often the agreement between a homeowner and real estate agent must be written.

**Powers of attorney** also must be in writing. A power of attorney is a type of agency agreement. It appoints an agent to perform specific acts on behalf of an individual. In a power of attorney relationship the agent is called an **attorney-in-fact.** The authority of the attorney-in-fact may be limited to one particular transaction or it may be very broad. For example, a person being transferred overseas might create a power of attorney to give a friend or relative the authority to close bank accounts, sell the car, and find a renter for the house. Powers of attorney may also be very general, giving broad authority to withdraw from accounts, enter into contracts, sell property, and endorse checks in the name of the individual. A bank should always obtain the original power of attorney and maintain a copy of it for its records before permitting an agent to act on behalf of the bank's customer. If applicable law requires a power of attorney to be filed in the public records, the bank should obtain proof that the power of attorney has been properly recorded.

---

### Critical Terms

*Agent* A person or other legal entity who has authority to transact business or otherwise act on behalf of another.

*Express Authority* Permission specifically given either orally or in writing for an agent to do something.

*Implied Authority* Authority that is necessary for an agent to accomplish the tasks for which he or she has been given express authority. This type of permission is not actually stated. In many states the authority to negotiate usually constitutes implied authority.

---

The principal may sometimes revoke an agency agreement or power of attorney. Revocations may not always be evident on the face of the document itself. Therefore, the bank should take all reasonable precautions to ensure that the agreement is valid before allowing the transaction to occur.

## Agents' Authority to Act for Principals

An agent's authority is defined by and limited to that granted by the principal. Generally the highest level of authority is the authority to make contracts with others in the name of the principal. Making a contract on behalf of a principal affects the principal's relationships with third parties because the contract can be enforced against the principal. For example, if the contract is for a loan, it is the principal who must repay it; if the contract is to pro- vide a product, the principal has a **legal obligation** to provide it; if the contract is for the sale of something belonging to the principal, it becomes the principal's legal duty to accept the price agreed to and deliver the item to the buyer.

Agents may be given the authority to withdraw money from the principal's bank account, sign the principal's checks with their own names, and endorse in their own names checks made out to the principal. These actions must always be for the principal's benefit and undertaken only while transacting the principal's business.

### Example
The purchasing officer at the bank and the woman representing the printing firm make a contract in which the firm agrees to supply certain forms to the bank, and the bank agrees to pay for them upon delivery. The woman signs her name to the contract, and the purchasing officer signs with his name and title. Each of these agents has affected the legal relations of their principals, the printing firm and the bank. The principals now are legally obligated to do what the contract requires. The printing firm must deliver the forms and the bank must pay the agreed-upon price for them.

Not all agents are given a level of authority that allows them to affect the principal's legal relationships. Most agents are employees whose actions for the principal involve little or no independent judgment or discretion. These agents must act under the direction and supervision of a superior, doing what they are told to do and acting within the limits of their defined jobs. If they deal with customers or other parties in the course of the job, their authority is limited to particular, supervised transactions. Anything beyond those limits must be referred to the supervisor. Limitations on authority should be disclosed to third persons.

### Example

Elizabeth is a new customer opening an account with the bank. She is talking to Richard, the new accounts representative, while the account is being processed. Elizabeth asks Richard what are the underwriting criteria for a home loan at the bank. Because Richard does not work in the loan department and is not trained to assist loan customers, the question falls outside the scope of his job. He directs Elizabeth to a lending department representative.

### Types of Authority

Two kinds of authority exist in agency relationships—actual authority and apparent authority. A principal will not be responsible for the actions of an agent unless the agent has one of these two types of authority. If an agent has the authority to take the action, the principal will be responsible for it. If not, the principal will not be responsible. **Actual authority** can be either express or implied. **Express authority** is based on definite oral or written representations specifically given by the principal to the agent to perform the act in question. **Implied authority** is not specifically given by the principal, but involves those actions an agent must take to do what the agent is expressly authorized to do. Thus, implied authority, even though not given specifically, can be assumed to be a necessary part of the express authority granted. Authority to negotiate an agreement usually constitutes authority to sign the agreement unless the principal has specified otherwise.

### Examples

- Robin Lockwood hires John Bessman as her agent to manage several rental properties she owns. She gives him express authority to lease the properties and maintain them on an ongoing basis. Because he has *express* authority to maintain the properties, he has the *implied* authority to hire cleaning companies and repairmen to keep the properties in good operating condition.

- Millard Johnson is a dentist who maintains his personal and business accounts at the bank. His office manager, Rita Atwood, writes most of the checks to pay the bills for the business and Dr. Johnson signs them. Dr. Johnson receives all the bank statements for all the accounts at his home and brings them to the office for Ms. Atwood's use. Ms. Atwood makes the bank deposits in person, orders checks, and generally performs all of the banking on the business account. Although the bank deals almost exclusively with Ms. Atwood, Dr. Johnson is the only authorized signer on the account. One day Ms. Atwood asks the bank to change the address for the statements to the office address rather than Dr. Johnson's home. The bank complies with her request. Ms. Atwood intercepts the statement at the office the next month to hide the fact that she is embezzling from Dr. Johnson's business account. By the time Dr. Johnson realizes that he does not have the statement, Ms. Atwood has resigned and left the city.

It might seem that because Ms. Atwood had express authority to handle routine banking matters, she had the implied authority to have control of the account statement; however, implied authority still must be *actual* authority. Her actions did not imply that she had the authority to change the statement address. She was not a signer on the account. Therefore, the bank could be liable for the funds taken from Dr. Johnson's account after Ms. Atwood changed the statement address.

**Apparent authority,** unlike actual authority, is neither expressly given nor implied from the nature of authorized actions. The principal creates apparent authority, either intentionally or accidentally, by conduct or communication that leads a third party to believe that the agent has authority. If the principal allows the agent to look like he or she has authority and a third party reasonably believes that the agent has such authority, the principal will be bound by the actions of the agent. This occurs even if there was no intention to create the appearance of authority.

### Example

A woman who consistently allows her boyfriend to endorse her paychecks for deposit into their joint account could create an appearance that the boyfriend has the authority to endorse and cash her paycheck. The bank that cashes the check in reliance on the boyfriend's apparent authority may not be held accountable (liable) to the woman should the boyfriend keep or spend the money against her wishes.

### Liability

**Liability** refers to a person's legal obligation. Examples of liabilities are the requirement to repay a loan or to make restitution for some loss or damage resulting from a transaction. The central foundation of agency law is that principals are liable for all debts, losses, or damage that may result from authorized acts of their agents. Transactions and commitments made by an agent are considered by law to have been made by the principal. Four types of liabilities are created by agency relationships:

- liability of principals to third parties
- liability of agents to third parties
- liability of principals to agents
- liability of agents to principals

An agent's authorized acts are **binding** on the principal. This means that the principal becomes legally responsible to the other party to the transaction. A principal is not **bound** by the acts of its agent unless those acts are performed with actual or apparent authority. If the agent engages in a transaction without authority, the principal has no obligation to accept it as legally binding. However, the principal may choose to ratify an unauthorized transaction. **Ratification** means that the principal approves the agent's unauthorized act and consents to assume the obligation. The principal may expressly ratify an agent's action or the principle may ratify it by implication (for example, by keeping or taking benefits from the action). After ratification of either type, the principal becomes legally bound by the transaction.

### Example

A man seeking a business loan for his company requests $50,000. The loan officer's lending limit is $40,000. Nevertheless, she approves the loan as requested. After reviewing the application, the bank's president allows the approval to proceed and the loan is funded. The bank has effectively ratified the transaction in this case. If the bank president did not allow the loan to be funded but simply warned the loan officer to stay within her lending limit, the unauthorized loan decision would not have been ratified.

Not only is the principal bound by agent transactions, but he or she also is presumed to know, and be bound by, all relevant facts of which the agent gains knowledge in the course of the transaction. This is called attributing or *imputing* the agent's knowledge to the principal. The reasoning behind the concept of imputed knowledge is that, under the law, the principal and the agent are considered to be one person. Facts known by the agent are said to be known by the principal. The principal cannot later claim personal ignorance of certain facts as a way to avoid an obligation.

### Example

The woman with the petty cash check deals with a teller who is personally familiar with the corporate employer. The teller knows that only two people are authorized to sign corporate checks—the president and the treasurer. Despite this knowledge, the teller is persuaded by the woman to cash the check because "no one's there" at the office and last week's petty cash is gone. The teller's knowledge that the woman's signature was unauthorized is considered to be the bank's knowledge. If it comes to a legal dispute, with the company insisting that the bank refund the money to its account because the woman left town with it, the bank will be obligated to make the refund. The bank has cashed a check "knowing" that the woman's signature was unauthorized.

The actions of agents also may expose their principals to *tort liability*. A tort is the intentional or negligent interference with the rights of another person. Usually a tort is committed when a person has an accident or makes a mistake that causes loss or damage to an innocent party. The accident or mistake may result from negligence or fault on the part of the person who commits the tort. If an agent commits a tort while acting within his or her authority and on behalf of the principal, both the principal and the agent can be held liable for the damages caused by the agent's tort. Again, in the eyes of the law the principal and agent are considered to be one person. The agent acting on the principal's behalf and in the course of the principal's business is, in effect, the principal. Therefore the agent's tort is considered to be the principal's tort—at least for purposes of paying for the damage.

### Liability of Agents to Third Parties

If the agent who is acting with authority on behalf of a principal discloses his or her representative capacity and the principal's name, the agent has no liability to the other party. The transaction is considered to be between the principal and the third party, and the agent incurs no rights or responsibilities regarding the third party.

By engaging in a transaction on behalf of a principal, an agent is considered by law to be giving a guarantee that the transaction is authorized. If the transaction is *unauthorized,* then the agent has violated the guarantee and must pay for any losses to the third party. For example, a company's sales agent who contracts with a customer to sell the company's product at a lower price than authorized becomes liable for the difference in price if the company refuses to perform the contract at the lower price. Of course, if the company ratifies the contract by consenting to the unauthorized price, the agent is no longer liable.

At the principal's direction an agent may conceal that he or she is acting for a principal. The agent has authority to make the deal on behalf of the principal, but the third party is not told of the principal's existence. To protect the third party's rights in such cases, the law requires the agent to accept legal responsibility in transactions made on behalf of an undisclosed principal. After discovery of the principal's existence, the third party can require the principal to be responsible instead. In most states, the third party must choose which of the two—agent or principal—to deal with, and once the election is made, the other one is discharged from any responsibility in the transaction.

### Liability of Principals to Agents

The agent has two rights against the principal:

- a right to compensation
- a right to reimbursement for money paid or for losses suffered in the course of employment

If the principal has agreed to pay the agent a salary or commission, the agent has a legally enforceable *right to compensation* (right to be paid). Occasionally, an agent will agree to work for no compensation, which removes any right to demand wages later.

All authorized expenses the agent incurs while working for the principal are reimbursable. The agent also is entitled to protection against any financial losses that may result from carrying out his or her actual authority. As discussed earlier, an agent may be personally responsible in transactions in which the principal is not disclosed. If the principal has required the nondisclosure, the agent is entitled to reimbursement for any financial loss or liability on his or her part that may result from the agent's proper exercise of authority granted by the undisclosed principal.

### Liability of Agents to Principals

A **fiduciary** relationship—that is, a relationship founded on confidence and trust—exists between agent and principal, which gives rise to certain obligations. An agent is obligated to act in good faith and with loyalty in all dealings undertaken on the principal's behalf. The law also requires the agent to act with a certain degree of care and attention. Failure to meet any of these duties exposes the agent to liability for losses to the principal.

One of the most common violations of an agent's duty of loyalty or fidelity occurs when one person undertakes to act as agent for two parties to the same transaction. An agent in this case would be liable to both principals for any losses caused to them.

The principal has a right to require that the agent give reasonably skillful service. The amount of skill that the principal can fairly demand depends upon the particular agency relationship. For example, a bank hiring a vice president with a graduate degree and 10 years of banking experience has a right to expect greater skill than when

hiring a teller who has just graduated from high school. The amount of compensation paid frequently determines the amount of skill the employer is entitled to expect. The agent who fails to act with the required skill, causing financial loss to the principal, may well be liable for the loss.

The principal also has a right to have the agent obey instructions and act within the defined limits of authority. The agent is liable for any losses to the principal that result from any transactions falling outside the agent's actual authority.

## Termination of Agency

If the principal and agent have agreed that the agency will end at a certain time, the agency relationship terminates at that designated time. However, third parties who have previously dealt with the agent may be unaware of the termination, and failure to inform others can give the agent apparent authority to continue to act. Thus, the principal may be bound by contracts made by the agent until third parties are notified of the agency termination.

Even though a principal and agent may have agreed to a particular period of employment, the principal may dismiss the agent or the agent may quit before the agreed-upon time. However, the party terminating the relationship in this way may have to pay the other for breaking their agreement. If the agency has no specific time period, it is deemed to be terminable *at will,* and either the principal or agent may terminate it at any time without liability.

Finally, an agency agreement may terminate by operation of law upon the occurrence of certain events that make it impossible to continue the relationship. The destruction of the subject matter of the agency and the death of either the principal or agent are such terminating events.

### Example
A bank located next to a large commercial building retains an agent to negotiate

with the building's manager about having a door installed to lead from the lobby of the building into the bank. Three days later the owner of the building announces that, under a recent agreement with a local businessman, the area in the lobby next to the bank will be converted into a newsstand and card shop. Because this effectively destroys the subject matter of the agency, the agent's employment with the bank is terminated.

## PARTNERSHIPS

There are two types of partnerships—general partnerships and limited partnerships. Banks deal with customers who are organized as general partners and as limited partners. The formation and authority of these types of partnerships are quite different. Bank employees need to know the differences.

A **partnership** is an unincorporated business owned by two or more persons who carry on the business for profit. A partnership is considered to be a legal entity separate and apart from the partners who own it. The partners contribute money, labor, property, and skills to the business, and share the profits and losses. As a business entity, a partnership is much like a sole proprietorship, except for the fact that more than one person owns the business. This fact makes the issue of responsibility for the debts and obligations of the business a bit more complicated.

### General Partnerships

General partnerships can be formal or informal. The ownership of partnership property resides with the partnership itself. Profits and losses are either divided equally among partners or shared according to the specifications of a partnership agreement.

### Formation

A general partnership can be created with or without a formal, written agreement. Any two or more individuals who join together with a common purpose to contribute their labor, money, and skills to operate a business and share in its profits and losses have formed a partnership. Lack of a written agreement to be partners makes the business informal, but it is still a partnership subject to rules of law.

Although partnerships can be established without a formal written agreement, it is best to make the rules of operation definite, beginning with a document that sets forth the agreement of the parties. This document, called the *partnership agreement* or *articles of partnership,* usually contains provisions for matters such as

- the partnership's name and place of business
- the nature of the partnership business
- the dates when the relationship is to begin and end
- the amount of capital contributed by each partner
- when and in what form capital will be contributed
- each partner's share in the partnership

The partnership agreement can address any matter concerning the relationship that the partners wish to include, such as management responsibilities and the authority of partners to transact business in the partnership's name. Matters not addressed in a partnership agreement are governed by the Uniform Partnership Act, as are informal partnerships. This law governs the individual partners' rights and responsibilities to each other and regulates the obligations of the individual partners to partnership creditors.

## Partnership Property

Partnership property consists of contributions from the partners. Individual partners usually contribute money to start up the business or to maintain it when income is low. Partners also may contribute other types of property, such as stocks, bonds, real estate, equipment, or other assets. The partnership itself becomes the owner of the property contributed and, unless otherwise agreed, no partner has a greater right than any other partner to use it.

### Case for Discussion
*South of the Border*

For many years John Smith and Charles Jones have operated a fresh produce business at a busy intersection in Dale City, California. Although Smith and Jones have never signed articles of partnership or a formal partnership agreement, they have been in business at the same location for almost 20 years.

When the business needed working capital they obtained loans from Pacific Horizon Bank. Sometimes Smith would sign the promissory note and on other occasions Jones would sign. The word *partner* always was noted next to the name of the person signing the note.

Two years ago Jones decided to move to Mexico to start a wholesale flower business. Before leaving for Mexico he obtained a loan from Pacific Horizon for $25,000. Several months passed and no payments were made on the loan. Unable to locate Jones, the bank decided to sue his business partner, John Smith. Smith's attorney notified the bank that no formal partnership agreement existed between his client and Jones.

Not long before he left for Mexico, Jones purchased a new pickup truck from a dealer in another part of the state. Although he did not identify the business, he indicated to the dealer that the truck would be used in his business. He made a small downpayment and signed an agreement to pay the balance within 30 days. When the dealer failed to receive the promised balance and was unable to contact Jones, he proceeded to sue John Smith. Again, Smith's attorney claimed that his client was not liable because no formal partnership agreement existed between Smith and Jones.

In the first case the court ruled in favor of Pacific Horizon Bank. The longstanding arrangement between Smith and Jones created an informal partnership as defined by the Uniform Partnership Act. Both partners clearly had authority to borrow money for the business and the fact that both had obtained loans in the past was well documented. Pacific Horizon made the loan based on the outward representation that Smith and Jones were business partners. Smith was required to repay the loan.

In the second case Smith was not held liable for the balance owed on the pickup truck. The court ruled that the dealer relied on no representation that Smith and Jones were partners. The dealer admitted that he had never heard of the business nor had he ever met John Smith.

#### Questions for Discussion

1. Why did the small-business credit department at Pacific Horizon assume that Smith and Jones were business partners?
2. What documents should the bank's loan officer have requested before approving Jones's loan application?
3. Under what change in circumstances might Smith be liable for the balance on Jones's debt to the truck dealer?

The partners have equal rights to use partnership property to carry on the business of the partnership, but they cannot use it for personal purposes. This type of arrangement has the following basic elements:

- All partners have an equal right to use partnership property for partnership purposes.
- A partner cannot transfer any interest in partnership property as security in connection with personal loans or other business.
- Partnership property is not subject to court order in connection with a partner's individual debts but is subject to court order for partnership debts.
- When a partner dies the partnership property passes to the surviving partners. No interest passes to the deceased partner's heirs, unless the deceased was the last surviving partner.

The partners can modify any of these elements, but if no modifications are made, the partners are bound by these limitations on their personal interest in the partnership property. The purpose of this type of ownership is to give the partnership the ability to continue use of its assets despite financial difficulties that may be suffered by any one partner.

### Example

A general partnership purchases three cars for the use of its three partners. Even though the partners keep the cars at home and use them from time to time for personal trips, the cars are not among their personal assets. They may not pledge the cars as security for personal loans or transfer their interests in the cars as part of a property division or debt-settlement procedure. The cars are assets of the partnership, not of the partners themselves.

### Division of Profits

Profits are the money remaining after the partnership pays its debts and other liabilities. After profits are used to repay the value of what each partner contributed, any remaining profits are divided equally among the partners. Under a partnership agreement, partners may decide on a different way to share profits. If this is the case, usually the partners divide the total amount of profits according to how much each partner contributed. If two partners contribute 35 percent and 65 percent of the partnership assets, respectively, then they will divide the profits according to that same ratio.

### Partners' Authority

Individual partners in a general partnership may transact business daily on behalf of the partnership, including ordering and selling goods, buying or leasing real estate, borrowing money, or creating deposit accounts. Each partner is considered an agent of the partnership for the purpose of carrying on its business. The partnership is bound by actions each partner undertakes in the name of the partnership if these actions appear to have had the purpose of carrying on the partnership's business in the usual way. As with any agency relationship, a bank dealing with a person claiming to represent a general partnership must determine whether the individual is in fact an agent of the partnership and, if so, with what level of authority.

Because the law holds that each partner is an agent of the partnership, the first determination is whether the individual representing the partnership is, in fact, a partner. An examination of the articles of partnership or partnership agreement will reveal whether the person is a partner. If the bank does not have a copy of the articles or agreement on file, it should ask the person to produce one. If the partnership is informal and has no written agreement, the bank might check with the state or county authorities to determine whether a certificate of partnership is on file. Many states require the filing of such a certificate, which reveals the names and addresses of the partnership's partners, its purpose, and its terms of existence.

When it is determined that the individual is indeed a partner—and thus an agent—of the partnership, a bank must then assure itself of the partner's authority to undertake the particular transaction. Under the law, a partner has authority to undertake transactions that are in the ordinary course of the partnership's business. For example, if the partner is seeking a loan, the loan should be similar in amount and terms to previous loans made to the partnership, or its purpose should relate to the nature of the partnership business as stated in its articles or on a certificate of partnership.

Even if the transaction has every appearance of carrying on the partnership's business in the usual way, the bank should still determine whether the partner possesses or lacks the authority to undertake the particular transaction. For example, a partnership agreement might state that three of the partnership's five partners must sign any loan documents. This would mean that a single partner seeking a loan lacks authority even if the loan is for the purpose of carrying on partnership business in the usual way. If the partnership agreement has been reviewed or is on file at the bank, the bank is considered to know the scope and limitations of the partners' authority. If the bank makes the loan to a single partner despite such imputed knowledge, the partnership will not be legally bound to repay the loan.

### Partners' Personal Liability

An important feature of general partnerships is a partner's **personal liability** for obligations of the partnership. By operating the business as a partnership, the partners have agreed to share both the profits and the losses of the business. This means that they have each agreed to contribute as much as may be required from their own personal funds to pay the partnership's obligations. If a partner validly obligates the partnership to the bank and the partnership is unable to pay, all the partners are liable for the repayment of the debt.

Typically, in a partnership the partners share losses as they do profits, whether equally or according to a certain percentage for each partner. By agreement, however, partners can alter the pattern of sharing when it comes to losses.

Once the amount of loss is determined and the partnership itself cannot pay, the partners are obligated to each contribute a share to make up the entire amount. If a partner is unable to pay his or her share, the burden falls on the other partner(s) to pay off the loss from personal assets.

If a partner has committed a tort, such as negligence or fraud, while engaged in partnership business, the injured party has a right to sue the partnership or any of the partners individually. In this situation, a partner's liability for partnership obligations can be nearly unlimited. Each of the partners is considered liable to pay damages for the tort, and the injured party has the option to sue any or all of the partners for damages payable out of their personal assets.

### Limited Partnerships

To avoid the personal liability that general partnerships require, many business owners prefer to form corporations, which offer protection from personal liability. Sometimes, however, incorporating is not advantageous for tax purposes or for other reasons. In those situations, a business may want to take the form of a limited partnership.

A **limited partnership** enables one or more individuals to invest money in a partnership business without risking personal liability for partnership debts. Such investors are called *limited partners,* which means that their liability for debts of the partnership is limited to the amount they invest. In contrast to general partners, limited partners may not participate in the management of the limited partnership. Limited partnerships are governed in 48 states (all but Vermont and Louisiana) by the Revised Uniform Limited Partnership Act.

### Formation

Unlike a general partnership, a limited partnership cannot be informally created. To qualify as a limited partnership, a certificate of limited partnership must be filed, typically in the office of the state's secretary of state. This certificate must furnish the

- name of the partnership (which must include the words *limited partnership)*
- office address, and the name and address of an agent on whom a summons can be served if the partnership is sued
- name and business address of each general partner
- latest date on which the partnership is to dissolve

Most states also require that the certificate of limited partnership include

- a description of the partnership's business
- the names and addresses of limited partners
- a description of the value of partnership contributions
- the method for changing partners

The certificate of limited partnership is a public record and is considered notice to the world that the partnership is a limited partnership and that the persons so designated are general partners. This allows third parties to know which partners have the authority to bind the partnership.

## Case for Discussion
*Not Ready to Retire*

In 1987 John Collingwood and Marvin Killmer formed a limited partnership. Collingwood and Killmer persuaded five of their friends to invest in the newly formed company as limited partners. The firm operated under the name Collingwood and Killmer, Limited Partnership. In 1994 Collingwood had a heart attack and decided it was time to retire. That year he sold his interest in the company to one of the five limited partners, a fellow named George Hacker.

Collingwood decided to maintain ties with the firm by investing as a limited partner. Because the business had been very successful from the outset and valuable goodwill was attached to the name, no one wanted to change the name—especially not to Hacker and Killmer. So, although George Hacker was correctly identified as a general partner on the certificate of limited partnership, the firm continued to operate as Collingwood and Killmer.

In 1997 the local economy entered a recession and the company suffered major losses. Creditors lined up to pursue claims against the partnership. Several lenders were surprised to learn that John Collingwood was no longer a general partner. He was frequently seen at the office and, since recovering from his heart attack, had participated in making most of the partnership's important business decisions. The lenders decided to file a suit against the partnership, maintaining that credit had been extended to Collingwood and Killmer on the assumption that Collingwood was still a general partner.

The court ruled in favor of the creditors. In view of the fact that John

Collingwood continued to attend executive meetings and was still very much involved in the management of the business, the creditors' assumption that he was still a general partner was understandable. Continued use of the firm's original name also contributed to this perception.

Collingwood was ordered to pay the creditors an amount equivalent to the money he had originally invested in the company when it was founded in 1987. However, the court ruled that only those creditors who had done business with the company before Collingwood's retirement were eligible to receive payment under this arrangement.

**Questions for Discussion**

1. How could the creditors have determined the identity of the general partners?
2. How could Collingwood and Killmer, Limited Partnership, have protected itself from this type of adverse legal action while retaining its well-known name?
3. Why would the court be unlikely to rule in favor of a commercial bank creditor in cases of this nature?

A limited partner is not personally liable for the partnership obligations unless

- the limited partner participates in control of the business
- the limited partner permits his or her name to be used in the partnership's name

If the limited partner participates in control of the business, he or she will be liable only to those who transact business with the partnership and reasonably believe, based on the limited partner's conduct, that he or she is a general partner. If the limited partner permits his or her name to be used in the partnership's name, then liability extends to any creditor who makes loans without knowing that the limited partner is not a general partner.

### Partners' Authority

Only a general partner has the authority to bind a limited partnership. Most limited partnerships operate under specific partnership agreements. The agreement usually designates the partner who has the authority to bind the partnership. Banks should review the partnership agreement before transacting business with a limited partnership.

## CONCLUSION

Banks deal with many types of customers. It is very important to know what kind of customer you are dealing with—an individual, agent, or other legal entity—to protect the bank from fraud and to comply with "Know Your Customer" regulatory guidelines. A sole proprietorship is owned by one person. The bank may deal with a sole proprietorship as though it is dealing with the individual who owns it. An agent acts for another entity, the principal, by actual or apparent authority.

Actual authority can be expressly given by actions or words, or it can be implied. A general partnership may be formed through a written agreement or it may operate informally, without an agreement.

General partners usually have the authority to bind the partnership and usually are personally liable for its obligations. Limited partners do not have the authority to bind the partnership and are not personally liable for the obligations of the partnership.

## QUESTIONS FOR REVIEW AND DISCUSSION

1. Who are the majority of the bank's customers? What is the primary concern of banks when dealing with these customers?

2. How does a bank do business with a sole proprietorship? With a general partnership?
3. What is the difference between actual authority and apparent authority as exercised by an agent? Give an example of each. In the example of actual authority, use facts giving rise to implied authority.
4. What is the difference between a general partnership and a limited partnership?
5. How can an agent expose a principal to liability, both in contract and in tort?
6. When might a principal be liable for an agent's unauthorized acts?

## LEARNING ACTIVITIES FOR CHAPTER 4

### Multiple Choice

Choose the best answer for each question.

1. Daniel Barton is the owner and operator of a business called Big Town Bingo Parlor. Big Town Bingo Parlor is:
   a. a suitable name for such an enterprise
   b. an assumed name
   c. a corporation
   d. a principal enterprise

2. Tom Smith is an agent for Fred Small. Fred Small is a:
   a. sole proprietor
   b. guarantor
   c. principal
   d. partner of Tom Smith

3. Actual authority is:
   a. express authority
   b. implied authority
   c. apparent authority
   d. both *a* and *b*

4. Knowledge that is acquired by an agent is imputed to the principal because:
   a. The relationship between agent and principal is a fiduciary one.
   b. The agent must remain in close communication with the principal.
   c. The agent may be working on behalf of an undisclosed principal.
   d. The principal and the agent are considered legally to be one person.

5. A power of attorney is a:
   a. document that appoints an agent to perform specific acts on behalf of an individual
   b. document signed by a judge
   c. part of a partnership agreement
   d. written or oral agreement whereby an agent is appointed to act on behalf of a principal

### Completion

Fill in the blanks with the word or words that best complete the sentences.

1. One reason banks must be aware of who has final responsibility in a banking transaction is the regulators' emphasis on _____ _____ _____.

2. The simplest form of business organization, a _____ _____, is owned and operated by one person.

3. A _____ is a business owned by two or more persons who carry on the business for profit.

4. _____ is the legal obligation to pay a debt.

5. By the act of _____, a principal approves an agent's unauthorized act and consents to assume the obligation.

6. The relationship between an agent and principal is founded on confidence and trust and is legally known as a _____ relationship.

## Short Answer

Briefly answer each of the following questions.

1. Give an example of an individual bank customer who might not have the legal capacity to transact bank business.

 

2. Could Joe Smith, Frank Jones, and Sally Lehann set up a sole proprietorship? Why or why not?

 

3. What type of document must be filed with local or state authorities if an individual operates a sole proprietorship under a name other than his or her own?

 

4. What is the term for an individual legally acting for another individual?

 

5. What is critical for a bank to determine when dealing with an individual representing another individual or entity?

 

6. If an agent signs a promissory note on behalf of a principal, what is the responsibility of the agent to pay the note?

 

7. What is the document that sets forth the agreement of the parties to a partnership?

 

8. What is a limited partnership?

## True/False

Indicate whether each of the following statements is true or false.

T  F  1.  Partnership liabilities in a general partnership are personal liabilities for each partner.

T  F  2.  A general partnership can only be created by a written agreement.

T  F  3.  An agent may bind a principal to a contract.

T  F  4.  If a limited partner participates in the control of a partnership business, the limited partner can become personally liable for its debts.

# 5

# LEGAL ENTITIES: CORPORATIONS, LIMITED CORPORATIONS, TRUSTS, AND ESTATES

## LEARNING OBJECTIVES

After studying this chapter, you should be able to

- define and describe corporations as legal entities, including how they are organized, issue and transfer stock, and interact with banks
- identify the responsibilities and liabilities of corporate shareholders, directors, and corporate officers
- describe the purpose and structure of limited liability companies and professional corporations and note how banks should interact with these entities
- give examples of government agencies with which banks do business and note important considerations in their relationship with banks
- distinguish between trusts and estates and explain how banks do business with these entities
- explain the difference between a surety and a guarantor.
- define and use the legal and banking terms that appear in bold in the chapter text

## INTRODUCTION

Chapter 4 discussed the documentation a bank needs when it does business with individual customers, sole proprietorships, and partnerships. Banks have other types of customers besides individual persons and partnerships. Large companies usually are formed as corporations. However, small businesses, such as those owned by families, may also be corporations. Other forms of business entities, such as trusts and estates, also use banking services—so bank employees must be aware of the legal requirements that authorize persons to act on behalf of corporations, trusts, and estates.

Throughout this chapter important issues for banks in dealing with corporations and other legal entities will be highlighted. Moreover, most banks are themselves corporations, with specific legal requirements and obligations to their shareholders. Some of these considerations also will be discussed.

## CORPORATIONS

A **corporation** is separate from the people who own it. Legally, it is a person unto itself. A corporation is owned by its shareholders and managed by a board of directors, but the corporation itself is separate from either. Thus, under normal circumstances, a corporation's shareholders, directors, or officers would not be liable for the corporation's debt.

A corporation's assets and liabilities also stand apart. This legal independence makes the corporation an attractive business form. For example, a person with a construction company might be motivated to organize it as a corporation so that if injuries or accidents occur on the job, the corporation's assets are the ones at risk rather than those of the individual owner. Raising capital is easier with a corporation—it issues stock. And transferring ownership also is convenient—one simply sells the stock.

## Organization of a Corporation

State law governs the creation of a corporation. Incorporators are the persons who first invest in the corporation. Often a business promoter who has the initial idea for a company will recruit investors to become the incorporators of the corporation. Incorporators promise to buy a specified number of shares of the corporation to constitute its initial capitalization. The number of incorporators needed depends on the amount of money required to start the company and how much each incorporator is willing to invest. Once a sufficient amount of money (and number of incorporators) has been found, the corporation begins life by filing **articles of incorporation** with the appropriate state agency (exhibit 5.1). Articles of incorporation typically define the

- name of the corporation
- name and address of each incorporator
- broad purposes or objectives of the corporation
- street address of the corporation's principal office, and the name of its agent on whom a summons can be served if the corporation is sued
- length of time the corporation is to last (often called the *maximum duration)*
- number of shares of stock the corporation is authorized to issue
- par value of the stock (amount of money in corporate assets represented by each share of stock)

State officials review the articles for compliance with state law. If the articles meet the legal requirements, the state issues a certificate of incorporation, or charter. The corporation comes into existence only with the proper approval by the state. Without that approval, the corporation is lifeless. If the corporation fails to maintain good standing in the eyes of the state, it technically dies. For example, if the corporation fails to pay its state taxes, it could be considered to be dead.

**Exhibit 5.1    Sample Articles of Incorporation**

*Articles of Incorporation of the ABC Corporation*

*Article One*
Name of the Corporation
The name of the corporation is the ABC Corporation.

*Article Two*
Address of the Corporation and its Registered Agent
The address of the corporation is 2435 Waters Avenue, Anywhere, Any State, USA 00321. The name of its registered agent at such address is John B. Doe, Jr.

*Article Three*
Duration of the Corporation
The period of duration for which the corporation is incorporated is perpetual.

*Article Four*
Shares of Stock
The aggregate number of shares which the corporation shall have the authority to issue is 1,000,000. The shares shall all be of one class and shall have no par value.

*Article Five*
Board of Directors
The number of directors to constitute the initial board of directors of the corporation shall be three. Such initial directors, which shall serve until the first annual meeting of shareholders, or until their successors are elected and qualify are

Tom M. Daniels, 11402 Bedford St., Anytown, Anywhere, USA

Ellen McMichael, 702 Third Ave., Suite 1705, Anytown, Anywhere, USA

Justin Martinez, 1914 Becker Rd., Anytown, Anywhere, USA

*Article Six*
Purpose of Corporation
The Corporation is formed for the transaction of all lawful business for which a corporation may be incorporated under applicable laws, including, but not limited to, the manufacture and sale of farm machinery.

In witness whereof, these articles of incorporation have been signed on this 20th day November, 2000.

_____
Incorporator

_____
Witness

_____
Witness

The corporation's shareholders meet to elect directors and may adopt bylaws to govern the conduct of the corporation's internal affairs. Before the corporation can transact business, the directors must appoint the necessary officers and agents to act on the corporation's behalf.

When dealing with customers claiming to do business as corporations, banks should assure themselves that the corporation is in fact legally incorporated and in good standing with the state. In the past banks have unknowingly opened corporate checking accounts for dishonest individuals who then wrote checks without sufficient funds on deposit. Such criminals rely on the official look of a corporate check to lure payees into accepting checks they might not otherwise take.

### Stock

Stock represents an ownership interest in a corporation. A corporation issues stock to investors in exchange for the money they invest. The investors receive a stock certificate that indicates how many shares of stock they own. The owner of a stock certificate is called a *stockholder* or *shareholder.* Stock can be purchased from individuals who own it or it can be purchased from the corporation itself when it issues new shares.

A corporation that grows large enough may decide to sell its stock to the public. Any time a corporation sells stock to the public, it becomes subject to federal and state securities laws and regulations designed to protect the public from fraud. The primary law that regulates the issuing and selling of stock is the Securities Exchange Act of 1933. This law requires corporations to register a statement with the Securities and Exchange Commission (SEC) truthfully presenting all relevant facts about the corporation. The registration statement allows the public to read all about the corporation and its financial condition. A summary of the registration statement, called a prospectus, describes

the corporation and the stock it wants to sell, and contains other information to help the public make an intelligent decision about purchasing the stock. The prospectus is sent to potential investors so that they can evaluate the stock before purchasing it.

State laws and regulations that govern the issuing and selling of stock and other securities are labeled Blue Sky laws. Like federal securities law, these laws were enacted to ensure that people purchasing stock receive more than "blue sky" for their money. Blue Sky legislation requires corporations and stockbrokers acting on their behalf to file an application for permission to sell the stock. This application must contain detailed information about the financial condition of the company. If stock is sold before permission has been granted by the state, the seller can suffer serious penalties, including cancellation of the sales, fines, and imprisonment.

### Close Corporations

Unlike a publicly traded company, a close corporation finds issuing stock to be a relatively simple transaction. A **close corporation** (also called a closely held corporation) is one whose stock is not generally traded in the securities markets. Often the only shareholders of a close corporation are its directors and officers, although it may have one or two other shareholders who are investors. As long as the transactions are isolated and few in number, a close corporation may sell its stock without being subject to state or federal securities laws and regulations.

Most corporations in the United States are close corporations. While most close corporations are small enterprises, a number of large corporations do exist whose stock is held by only a few shareholders and is not traded in securities markets. For example, until the Ford Motor Company went public in 1955, the only stockholders in the company were members of the Ford family.

## Stock Transfers

Whether a corporation is closely or publicly held, its stock can usually be transferred or sold. Stock transfers have become mainly electronic transactions where the shares are not certificated, but the ownership interest is recorded on the books of the corporation. Documentary transfers involving stock certificates still occur, however, and stock certificates generally contain a form for documenting transfers (exhibit 5.2). The form generally appears on the reverse side of the stock certificate.

The new owner receives the certificate and sends it to the corporation that issued it or to the corporation's **transfer agent** (a person or company responsible for documenting stock transfers). Banks often serve as transfer agents for corporations. As an agent, the bank receives the stock certificate, cancels it, and issues a new certificate in the name of the new owner. The new owner's name is then registered on the corporation's books and the prior owner's name is deleted.

Although registration on the corporation's books is not necessary to transfer ownership of the stock certificate, the new owner is not entitled to be treated as a stockholder by the corporation until this registration occurs. Article 8 of the Uniform Commercial Code (UCC) governs the transfer of investment securities.

## Ownership and Management

While shareholders own the corporation, they cannot act for it. Their power is limited to electing a board of directors and adopting changes to bylaws and the articles of incorporation. The board of directors has general oversight over the corporation, but the appointed officers of the corporation usually undertake the day-to-day management of the corporation.

## Shareholders

A corporation may have few or many shareholders. All shareholders have contributed capital to the corporation, thus purchasing a share in the company. Shareholders have specific rights and powers in relation to the corporation. Shareholders' liability is limited because the corporation is considered to be a separate legal entity.

### Shareholders' Rights and Powers

Shareholders profit from their stock ownership by the appreciation of the value of their stock and by the receipt of dividends. **Dividends** are that portion of a corporation's profits paid to its shareholders. Dividends are not payable except when the corporation has profits or a surplus of capital and its directors decide that this money should be divided among the shareholders. Some corporations never declare dividends but instead invest all the corporation's profits back into the business itself.

Shareholders also have the right to bring lawsuits on behalf of the corporation against officers or directors who abuse their responsibilities. If such a lawsuit is successful, the officers or directors whose abuses have caused losses to the corporation are required to repay the amount of the loss.

---

**Exhibit 5.2    Stock Certificate**

FOR VALUE RECEIVED, I __(Owner of Stock)__ do hereby sell, assign, and transfer unto _(New Owner)_ , _(amount)_ shares of Common Stock represented by the within Certificate, and appoint _____ attorney to transfer the said shares of the books of the within-named Corporation with full power of substitution in the premises.

_____          Dated: _____

---

Shareholders can sue the corporation and its officers or directors for fraud if they believe that incorrect financial information was released to the public (or that correct financial information was withheld) and that such actions caused the stock price to be unfavorable.

### Shareholders' Liability

One of the most attractive aspects of a business operated as a corporation is that shareholders are not personally liable for corporate obligations. Shareholders risk a limited amount of money on the management skills of others, but they are unwilling to risk their entire financial worth in the way that sole proprietors and general partners do.

When they conduct business with close corporations, bankers must be aware that incorporation does not of itself improve creditworthiness. Because the stockholders have no personal liability for corporate debt, a corporation's creditworthiness may even be more suspect than that of a sole proprietorship or partnership. Many banks require the major shareholders of close corporations to cosign or personally guarantee the loans.

**Publicly held corporations** usually have sufficient assets and income to justify loans without personal guarantees by their shareholders. Therefore, most banks treat publicly held corporations as separate entities to a greater degree than they do close corporations.

Although shareholders usually are not held personally liable for a corporation's debts and actions, exceptional situations do arise when a court will put aside the protective veil that the corporate form provides and hold shareholders personally liable. Such liability can arise when a corporation is inadequately funded; when the corporate form is used to evade an obligation or to commit a fraud; or when the corporation's identity as a separate entity has been ignored.

### Example

A taxicab owner decides to incorporate his cab business, naming it General Cab Corp. The owner is the sole incorporator. After filing articles of incorporation with the state, he issues stock to himself in exchange for his contribution to the business. His contribution is the taxicab itself and nothing more. The owner then leases the cab to a driver who pays a monthly fee in cash to the corporation. Because the corporation has no separate bank account, the fee is put each month into the sole incorporator's personal account.

One day, while transporting a passenger, the cab becomes involved in a serious accident for which the driver is entirely responsible. The passenger is injured along with a pedestrian, and another car is badly damaged. In the resulting lawsuit against General Cab Corp., the parties discover that while the corporation has no assets to pay any claims, the sole owner of the corporation is personally wealthy.

The court in this situation "pierces the corporate veil" behind which the owner was hiding. The court rules that the owner is personally liable in this case, because he has placed all corporate proceeds in his personal account. This commingling of assets is one of the factors that courts consider when determining whether to pierce the corporate veil.

### Board of Directors

Corporations are managed by **boards of directors** whose responsibilities include establishing corporate policy, approving major transactions, and appointing and supervising the corporate officers who carry out the day-to-day management responsibilities. Board members have no authority to take individual action regarding the corporation unless the board as a whole specifically authorizes a member to act in a particular matter.

Boards of directors often appoint committees that meet separately to consider time-consuming matters. Bank board committees, for example, might consider issues relating to audits, loans, and investments. Such committees make recommendations to the full board, which remains responsible for final decisions. In some cases the board of directors may delegate specific authority to one or more committees.

### Election of Directors

The corporation's shareholders elect the board of directors. In electing directors, shareholders usually vote their shares either on the basis of one-share/one-vote or by cumulative voting.

In a one-share/one-vote system, a shareholder gets as many votes as the number of shares he or she owns. If the shareholder owns 100 shares, he or she can vote 100 times.

Cumulative voting permits each stockholder to have as many votes as shares of stock owned, multiplied by the number of directors to be elected. The shareholder may cast all of his or her votes for one candidate or divide them among the candidates as he or she chooses. For example, if five directors are to be elected, a shareholder may concentrate all votes on only one or two of the candidates and is not required to split the votes among the five board seats.

National banks are required by federal law to use cumulative voting when electing candidates to the board of directors.

### Duties and Responsibilities of Directors

Directors of corporations, and particularly of banks, have important responsibilities. A board's most important duty is to appoint officers who are qualified to manage the corporation's business. Except in cases of closely held corporations, directors usually do not involve themselves in the day-to-day operation of corporations, but they should be aware of and approve major transactions.

To supervise a corporation properly, directors must spend enough time to become familiar with its business and ongoing financial condition. Larger corporations, including banks, employ both internal and outside auditors to monitor the corporation's financial condition continually for the board of directors.

Directors establish a corporation's policies and objectives, which its officers and employees then follow. Corporate policies relate to such topics as profit planning, budgeting, and personnel practices. Directors also are responsible for a corporation's compliance with the laws and regulations governing the business in which the corporation is engaged.

Directors are considered to be fiduciaries to the corporation and are required to exercise a duty of loyalty to the corporation and its owners, the shareholders. Their relationship to the corporation is based on confidence and trust. Directors must avoid self-serving practices, such as using corporate property for personal gain or benefit, or competing with or failing to be loyal to the corporation, unless such practices are disclosed to the directors and the shareholders and are ratified by the directors and the shareholders.

### Directors' Liability

In managing the corporation's affairs, directors exercise considerable freedom to make decisions. They can be held liable to the corporation if they are negligent or involved in fraud, criminal activity, or a conflict of interest. If the corporation will not pursue a claim against a director, the shareholders may bring a lawsuit (called a *derivative action*) against the director on behalf of the corporation. In such an action, whatever the shareholders recover is for the corporation's benefit.

## Corporate Officers

The board of directors of a corporation appoints **officers** to be responsible for the day-to-day management of the business and to carry out the policies established by the board. Like other corporations, banks are managed primarily by their officers.

The senior officer of a corporation usually is the chairperson of the board of directors. For example, in a bank the board chair and the president usually are the two officers who have the most day-to-day control.

Other officers may include one or more vice-presidents, who manage specific parts of the bank; the chief financial officer, who oversees the bank's accounting and reporting functions; and the auditor, who examines and verifies the bank's internal records and procedures.

The officers generally are the individuals who conduct transactions on behalf of the corporation. A bank needs to obtain proof that an individual who claims to be a corporate officer has indeed been given the authority to conduct the transaction. The documentation the bank needs to verify this authority is a resolution of the board of the directors appointing the officer or officers to conduct the banking business. A corporate resolution should specify what actions each officer is empowered to undertake. The appropriate director (usually the secretary to the board) should sign the resolution.

## PROFESSIONAL CORPORATIONS

Professional corporations are another type of business entity created by state law. Professional corporations allow professionals such as doctors, lawyers, accountants, architects, and engineers to form corporations for the tax benefits that such organization offers. Although most professional corporations have the trappings of a regular corporation, such as articles of

### Case for Discussion
*The Case of the Amended Resolution*

Fletcher Corporation had been a deposit and loan customer of State National Bank for many years. Both Roger Evinton, the chairman of the board, and Will Bowers, the president, were well known to State National employees and both conducted business on behalf of Fletcher Corporation for several years.

The bank had a copy of a resolution of the Fletcher Corporation board of directors giving either Mr. Evinton, as the chairman, or Mr. Bowers, as the president, the right to execute lending documents and pledge collateral up to a value of $50,000. Any transaction with a value greater than $50,000 had to be signed by both the president and the chairman. The resolution was signed by the secretary of the board of directors. The chairman and president also signed the resolution to provide specimen signatures to the bank.

One day Mr. Evinton came to the bank and told Steve Woodruff, the bank president, that Mr. Bowers had resigned from Fletcher and would no longer be able to conduct business for the company. He introduced Mr. Woodruff to Wanda Leverton, the new president of Fletcher, and stated that she would now sign on behalf of the company instead of Mr. Bowers. Mr. Evinton asked to see the bank's corporate resolution authorizing transactions for the company and proceeded to cross out Mr. Bowers's name and replace it with Ms. Leverton's name. Mr. Woodruff had Ms. Leverton sign the resolution signature specimen page and approved the amended resolution.

The next day Mr. Evinton asked for a $75,000 loan to purchase new equipment and the bank prepared the promissory note for his and Ms. Leverton's incorporation, issuance of stock, boards of directors, and so forth, the professionals who own it cannot use the professional corporation to shield them from liability for professional malpractice. As they do when dealing with other types of corporations, banks need to obtain corporate resolutions from professional corporations authorizing one or more individuals to act on the corporations' behalf.

## LIMITED LIABILITY COMPANIES

A relatively new form of business organization in the United States is the **limited liability company (LLC).** Since 1977 many states have passed legislation permitting this form of organization in their jurisdictions. An LLC is a mix between a partnership and a corporation. Its owners can manage it, as in a partnership, yet the owners are shielded from the company's liability, as in a corporation.

Owners of LLCs are called *members.* Members often operate the LLC themselves, or they may delegate that responsibility to managers.

Liability of owners of LLCs is similar to that of shareholders of a corporation, but the tax treatment of the entities is quite different. For federal income and most state tax purposes, corporations are separate legal entities—that is, separate taxpayers. LLCs are classified as partnerships for federal income tax purposes and thus are not subject to income tax. Instead, all income, losses, deductions, and credits are allocated to the members. Thus, LLCs offer their owners the legal protection of the corporate form and the tax treatment of the partnership.

State law dictates the formation of an LLC, as it does with sole proprietorships, partnerships, and corporations. Like a corporation, an LLC is created by filing articles with the state. Often an LLC will have an operating agreement (similar to corporate bylaws) that sets forth how its business will be conducted.

### Governance

Banks that conduct business with an LLC should obtain copies of the operating agreement to determine what individual can act on behalf of the company. The member or manager negotiating with the bank on behalf of an LLC must have the authority to do so. A review of the LLC's articles and operating agreement will assist the bank in making this determination. As with any agent relationship, however, not only must the bank verify that the individual is an agent of the LLC, but also that the contemplated transaction is within the agent's authority.

Many LLC statutes require that the LLC maintain a list of its members and managers. It is important to make sure that the individual the bank is dealing with is on that list.

#### Example

Amy Smith approaches Central Bank for a loan on behalf of Acme LLC. Smith identifies herself as a member of the LLC. Central Bank obtains a copy of the LLC's articles from the state, and a copy of the operating agreement and member and manager list from the LLC. A review of the list does disclose Smith's name; however, both the articles and operating agreement indicate the LLC will act only through a *manager* elected by the members. Smith is not the manager and thus is not authorized to bind the LLC to a contract, including a loan.

### Life of an LLC

Many state statutes provide for the dissolution of an LLC upon the death of a member or the occurrence of other triggering events, such as insanity, bankruptcy, resignation, or expulsion of a member. Because an LLC must be active to be able to conduct business with a bank, it is important to examine the articles of an LLC to determine the term of its existence and any event that can cause its dissolution. A bank may decide to obtain personal guarantees from the principals of an LLC to protect the bank against losses resulting from transactions that occur with the company before the bank has knowledge of its dissolution.

### Assets of an LLC

LLCs own real and personal property, as do corporations or any other legal entity. Assets can be purchased, sold, and used as collateral by an LLC through members or managers who have authority to undertake such transactions.

No member has the authority to use an LLC's assets for his or her own personal purposes, any more than a shareholder of a corporation can use corporate assets or a partner can make personal use of partnership assets. Only upon dissolution may a member obtain an LLC's assets, and then only after creditors have been paid.

#### Example

Tom Jones applies for a loan at First Bank. Jones indicates that he is one of three members of an LLC that owns a widget factory. Jones indicates a willingness to use LLC assets as collateral for the personal loan he is seeking.

Because Jones has no individual interest in any of the LLC's assets, he cannot use its property as collateral for an individual loan. Even if the bank were to accept the property as collateral, it could not foreclose on it should Jones default on the loan.

## GOVERNMENTS AND GOVERNMENT AGENCIES

Banks do business with various government entities, which may be both depositors and borrowers. Governments and government agencies are distinct legal entities, separate from the elected officials and employees who act on their behalf. Examples of government entities include

- state board of education
- state department of transportation
- regional park commission
- metropolitan airport authority
- county government
- county school district
- department of child and family services
- municipal housing authority

When dealing with such entities, a bank must be extremely careful to make certain that the proposed transactions are within the authority not only of the government employees involved (the agents with whom the bank is dealing), but also of the government entity itself as granted by federal, state, or local law. If either of those basic elements is missing, the transaction could easily be declared ineffective and void.

#### Example

The county director of transportation goes to a bank seeking a loan for a new computerized traffic signal system. The director's predecessor had received loans from the bank twice before, both in the $90,000 to $100,000 range. This loan request is for $117,000, which the bank approves. Subsequently, the county fails to make any payments on the loan. Having made repeated demands for payment, the bank decides to sue. After some research into the county's laws, the bank discovers that any transactions involving more than $100,000 must be approved and signed by the county administrator. The director of transportation had no authority to sign for the $117,000 loan, and in doing so has created no legal obligation on the part of the county.

## ESTATES

The term **estate** refers to all the property owned by a deceased person (called a *decedent),* including real estate, cash, stock, bonds, and all other personal property. An estate also includes all debts and other legal obligations. When a person dies, his or her estate normally becomes subject to administration by a court to ensure that everything relating to the affairs of the deceased is assembled, accounted for, and distributed as the law directs.

The first step a court will take is to appoint an **executor** to oversee the estate throughout the probate procedure. A person who leaves a will usually has nominated a person to be appointed executor of the will. If there is no will, the court will appoint an administrator for the estate.

The executor or administrator (sometimes also referred to as the *personal representative)* administers the estate until all the deceased person's affairs are completed, including payment of any outstanding debts from the assets of the estate. Many states require that a notice of the death be published in a newspaper. This notice gives a date by which any parties having claims against the deceased must submit their claims to the court. Creditors whose claims are filed by the required date will be paid before the estate is closed and before any property is distributed to heirs. If the estate has insufficient money to pay the claims, then other assets, such as real estate or personal property, may be sold for cash to pay them. After all the claims have been paid, fees and costs settled, and remaining property distributed, the estate is closed. Until it is closed, an estate continues to have the right to conduct business like any other business entity. It can buy and sell property, borrow money, and create accounts. Banks conducting business with executors or personal representatives must assure themselves that any transactions entered into in the name of the estate have been authorized by the court. Bankers also must remember that a person acting on behalf of an estate—by signing loan documents, for example—assumes no personal liability in doing so if the commitments are within the powers granted by the court.

### Example

To pay certain claims against an estate, the executor seeks a $50,000 loan at the bank. The executor signs a note on behalf of the estate promising to repay the loan. When the note becomes overdue, the bank demands payment and is informed that the estate no longer has funds to pay the loan because stocks that it owns have severely declined in value. Because the estate, not the executor, is the party to the loan, the bank cannot seek payment from the executor.

### Estates of Persons Subject to Guardianship

Banks conduct business not only with the estates of deceased persons, but also with the estates of persons subject to guardianship. A **guardian** has legal authority to care for a **ward** or for the estate of a ward. A ward is a person who is legally incapable of making decisions. Minors (persons under the age of 18, in most states) and mentally incompetent persons typically are wards of a guardian.

A ward's estate may consist of real estate or personal property. The guardian manages this estate for the ward's benefit according to the requirements of state law. Because of the power a guardian has over a ward's estate, the appointment and conduct of a guardian are under court supervision. However, if the guardian and ward are parent and child, a *guardianship by nature* or *natural guardianship* is recognized and no court supervision is required while the child is a minor. The appointment of a guardian is effective until a minor ward becomes an adult or until the guardian dies, resigns, or is removed.

Guardians can be appointed to care for a ward's health and general welfare as well as for his or her financial affairs. Some courts prefer separate guardianships to protect a ward more fully.

A bank doing business with a guardian should obtain a copy of an official document appointing the guardian, such as a court order, or a summary document verifying the appointment, such as letters of guardianship. It is important to verify that the person transacting business for the ward has authority as a guardian of the ward's estate and is not merely the guardian of the ward's health and general welfare.

### Example

After informing the bank that he is the ward's guardian and offering as proof the letters of guardianship, a man withdraws $10,000 from the ward's savings account. However, he is guardian of the ward's health and general welfare only, as the guardianship letters clearly state. The bank is liable to the ward for the $10,000 withdrawal. The guardian had no right to make the withdrawal, because his guardianship does not extend to the ward's financial affairs. The bank is considered to know this fact because the bank was shown the letters of guardianship.

Guardians of wards' estates are considered fiduciaries. As such, they are required to manage estates with the utmost good faith and competence and to avoid promoting their own interests.

Within the exercise of their fiduciary duty to manage their wards' estates, and upon court approval, guardians can buy and sell property, invest, open and close bank accounts for the estate, and take any other action as long as it is the result of reasonable diligence and care.

### Example

The guardian of a woman's estate obtains a line of credit at the bank for the estate. The guardian requests draws under the line of credit to improve property of the estate from time to time. She sometimes requests that advances on the line of credit be deposited into her personal account. Through this act of self-dealing, the guardian has abused her *fiduciary duty* to the ward. As a result, a court could remove her as guardian and make her reimburse the ward's estate for the amounts she spent for her personal use. In addition, the bank should make sure that the advances on the line of credit are made for the benefit of the ward and not for the guardian *personally* to make sure that the loan is collectible from the ward's estate.

Guardians may also invest estate funds. As long as they are diligent and prudent in making the investments, guardians are not liable for losses. Guardians involved in investing must carefully review applicable state law, because many states restrict guardian investment powers to particular types of accounts and stocks.

### Example

On the advice of a reliable investment adviser, the guardian of an estate purchases stock in a corporation with the intention of producing dividend income for the estate. Under state law, the stock was acceptable for estate investment purposes. Unfortunately, the stock not only pays no dividends, but loses almost 50 percent of its value before the guardian finally sells it. As a result, the estate loses $20,000. Because this loss occurs despite the guardian's diligent and prudent actions, he is not personally liable for it and is not required to pay the estate for the loss.

## TRUSTS

A **trust** is an arrangement in which property is held in the name of one person (the **trustee),** who keeps and manages the property for the benefit of another person (the **beneficiary).**

A trust is created by a property owner who wants the property to be placed in trust. Reasons for placing property in trust often involve tax advantages or future security for a family member. To place property in trust means that the owner gives up his or her right to control the property and the right to use it for his or her own benefit. The trustee holds legal title to the property of the trust and has a duty to see that it is used for the benefit of the beneficiary.

Trusts are created and governed by state law. They usually are created by means of a document that declares that the property is being placed in trust and names the trustee and the beneficiary (or beneficiaries). A trust document generally specifies the time of termination, such as at the death of a beneficiary, and names the person to whom the property will go when it is no longer held in trust.

When dealing with a trustee, a bank needs to obtain a copy of the trust document to verify that the trustee has the power to conduct banking transactions. Unless a trust document states otherwise, trustees have power to borrow money for the trust. Still, it is prudent for a bank doing business with a trustee to review the trust document to be certain that the trustee has the appropriate authority to borrow money or open accounts for the trust. Moreover, bankers must remember that any loan document the trustee signs on behalf of the trust does not bind the trustee personally to repay the loan.

An *inter vivos trust* is a trust that is effective during the lifetime of the person who established it. A trust that becomes effective upon the death of the person who set it up is called a *testamentary trust.*

### Example
A man creates an *inter vivos trust* in which he places $100,000 worth of stock. The dividends from the stocks are to benefit his oldest son, who is disabled. The trustee named is a longtime friend of the father who is establishing the trust. The man also writes a will, which provides for creation of a *testamentary trust* into which all his assets will go at the time of his death. Income from the trust property will be used to support his widow. At her death, the testamentary trust will be terminated and its assets divided among all his children. In his will, the man appoints his bank as trustee for this testamentary trust.

A trustee's responsibility toward the money or property in a trust is similar to the fiduciary responsibility that a guardian has for the money and property the guardian manages for a ward. A trustee has a duty to make cautious, careful, and sensible decisions concerning the property in the trust. In addition, trustees must observe the conditions placed on them by the trust document, as well as the requirements imposed by state laws and court decisions.

If their chartering authority grants them trust powers, banks may act as trustees. People often prefer banks as trustees because, in addition to the laws that apply to all trustees, bank trust departments are subject to examination by regulatory agencies. These agencies focus on trust investments, the qualifications of trust officers, proper supervision by the board of directors, and compliance with strict recordkeeping standards.

## SURETIES

If a person needs to borrow money but is not creditworthy and has no collateral to offer the bank, he or she may find a surety to support the loan. A **surety** is a person who agrees to be equally liable with the borrower on the debt. The borrower is the principal debtor, whose promise to pay is cosigned by the surety. The lender in this arrangement is entitled to seek payment from either the surety or the principal debtor because both are considered to be legally committed to the loan agreement. The lender is not required to seek repayment from the borrower before pursuing the surety.

When when servicing and collecting loans with sureties, banks must be careful not to unintentionally release the surety from liability. It is more difficult to collect a loan from a surety if the bank's actions have inadvertently released or discharged the surety from the obligation to repay the debt. For example, sureties may be discharged from their duty to repay if the bank impairs their rights in any way. For example, if the bank releases collateral without receiving value for it, or fails to notify a surety if the debtor becomes delinquent in paying the debt, the bank may have difficulty collecting from the surety.

If the loan is properly documented and administered, both the surety and the principal borrower are considered to be primary debtors—and thus equally liable for the debt at all times. The surety has the right to receive all notices that the law requires the bank to send to the borrower. Demand letters, letters of acceleration, and foreclosure notices should be sent to the surety if they are sent to the principal borrower.

## GUARANTORS

Guarantors differ from sureties. While a surety is committed to repay the loan from the beginning, a **guarantor** does not become liable unless the debtor is unable to pay. The guarantor signs a document guaranteeing payment *if the debtor cannot pay,* while the surety signs the actual loan agreement as a primary debtor. A guarantor has a contingent liability. While guarantors usually agree to guarantee a certain loan for a borrower, banks often use continuing guaranty agreements that obligate the guarantor to be contingently liable for the debt even if it is renewed or increased. Most such agreements allow the bank great latitude to change the loan terms or release collateral without releasing the guarantor from liability.

## CONCLUSION

In this chapter we have considered a variety of legal entities that conduct transactions with banks. Bankers should recognize the legal formation and purposes of corporations, limited corporations, trusts, and estates, and how the differences among them affect documentation requirements for bank transactions.

Some legal entities are distinct personalities in their own right, entirely separate from the individuals who create them. Governments and corporations are examples of such legal entities. Their distinguishing features are that they have permanent existence independent of any individual person, and that no individual is personally liable for their debts. Other legal entities may have features that distinguish them from individuals, but they are not independent beings in the eyes of the law. Estates and trusts, for example, are not distinct legal personalities. Their existence is tied to the lives of individual wards or beneficiaries. Decedents' estates last only as long as it takes to complete the probate procedure.

Sureties and guarantors are not legal entities. These terms describe functions that are taken on by entities or individuals. The primary function of sureties or guarantors is to ensure that the debts of other entities or individuals are paid.

## QUESTIONS FOR REVIEW AND DISCUSSION

1. Who has the authority to bind a corporation?
2. What happens to the estate of a person who dies without a will?
3. Why is it important to thoroughly check the authority of a government entity before conducting business with it?
4. What does the guardian of an estate do?
5. What is a trust? Why are trusts created?
6. What is the difference between a surety and a guarantor?

## LEARNING ACTIVITIES FOR CHAPTER 5

### Multiple Choice

Choose the best answer for each question.

1. Ownership interest in a corporation is known as:

   a. corporate treasury notes
   b. corporate bonds
   c. stock
   d. power of attorney

2. A close corporation:

   a. raises money by issuing new stock and selling it to the public
   b. is a corporation whose stock is not generally traded in the securities markets
   c. is governed by Blue Sky laws
   d. is a corporation with fewer than 100 shareholders

3. All of the following are rights of shareholders *except:*

   a. to receive official reports on the condition of the corporation
   b. to bind the corporation in business transactions
   c. to bring suit against corporate officers and directors who abuse their responsibilities
   d. to elect directors, adopt and amend bylaws, and amend the articles of incorporation

4. Which of the following statements about directors of corporations is *not* true?

   a. They have extremely important responsibilities.
   b. They are involved in day-to-day corporate operations.
   c. They must be aware of and approve major transactions.
   d. They establish the corporation's policy and objectives.

5. A trust that becomes effective during a settlor's lifetime is called:

   a. a testamentary trust
   b. a lifetime trust
   c. an interactive trust
   d. an inter vivos trust

6. A guarantor is:

   a. liable on a debt from the beginning
   b. the same as a surety
   c. liable on a debt only after the debtor fails to pay
   d. a legal entity

### Completion

Fill in the blanks with the word or words that best complete the sentences.

1. The document through which investors found a corporation is called _____ _____ _____.

2. The persons who are appointed by the board of directors to run the corporation on a day-to-day basis are called _____.

3. The person holding title to property in a trust is called a _____.

4. The person for whose benefit property is held in trust is known as the _____.

5. The type of trust that goes into effect upon the settlor's death is called a _____ trust.

## Short Answer

Briefly answer each of the following questions.

1. What are Blue Sky laws?

_____

_____

_____

_____

2. Why does a registration statement and prospectus have to be filed when stock is publicly issued?

_____

_____

_____

_____

3. What do the officers of a corporation do? How do they get their jobs?

_____

_____

_____

_____

4. What is the benefit to the owners of a limited liability company?

_____

_____

_____

_____

5. What is the benefit to the owners of a professional corporation?

_____

_____

_____

_____

## True/False

Indicate whether each of the following statements is true or false.

T F 1. A corporation's debts and liabilities are confined to the corporation itself and do not extend to its owners.

T F 2. Most banks lending to close corporations require the major shareholders to cosign or personally guarantee the loans.

T F 3. A significant change in the terms of a loan can cause a surety to be discharged from the obligation to pay.

T F 4. Shareholders are personally liable for corporate obligations.

T F 5. A corporation's directors may be held liable for damages or losses the corporation suffers due to their negligence.

T F 6. A trustee is someone who has legal authority to care for the person and/or estate of someone who is incompetent.

T F 7. Both guardians and trustees are fiduciaries.

T F 8. A professional can limit his or her liability for negligence by forming a professional corporation.

# 6

# CONTRACTS

## LEARNING OBJECTIVES

After studying this chapter, you should be able to

- identify and discuss the necessary elements of a contract, including mutual assent and consideration
- describe elements in defective contracts, such as legal capacity and illegal objectives, which can render the contract void or unenforceable
- define and explain the purpose of the Statute of Frauds
- describe the conditions under which contractual rights may be transferred to third parties
- explain the primary and secondary rules of interpretation for contracts and note the effect of the parol evidence rule
- elaborate on the various excuses for nonperformance of a contact and on the conditions that might qualify as substantial performance
- define and use the legal and banking terms that appear in bold in the chapter text

## INTRODUCTION

A contract is a legally binding promise or agreement enforceable in court. Contracts are made to cover almost any legal agreement, including buying and selling, borrowing and lending, employment, providing services, and promising to do something in the future. Many banking transactions involve the use of contracts (exhibit 6.1).

Persons or entities who reach agreement and form a contract are called **parties** to the contract. Contracts usually are put in writing so that the parties can have a document that spells out the details of their agreement. But many contracts are not in writing and the parties' agreement may have no more formality than a handshake. Whether oral or written, valid contracts are legally enforceable.

When a dispute arises because one party fails to perform its duties under the contract or because the parties interpret their agreement differently, the parties may turn to the courts for enforcement or interpretation of the contract.

A contract specifies rights and duties to which the parties have legally committed themselves. Each party has a legal right to what the other promised, or to a **remedy** (usually money) if the other party fails to perform its obligations under the contract. The job of a court in contract enforcement cases is to analyze the agreement, deter-

mine the rights and duties of the parties, and decide what must be done to put the contract into effect. In performing its analysis, the court may discover that the agreement lacks certain requirements for a valid contract. If so, the law cannot make the agreement effective and the contract is not legally enforceable. This chapter discusses the requirements for a valid contract, how the parties' rights and obligations are determined and enforced, and factors that may make a contract unenforceable.

Uniform Commercial Code (UCC) Article 2 governs contracts that relate to the buying and selling of goods within the United States. The International Convention on the Sale of Goods governs contracts relating to the international buying and selling of goods. Contracts containing personal property leases are governed by UCC Article 2A. Real estate, service, and most other types of contracts are governed by common-law rules.

### Example

A bank buys several large potted plants for its main office and eight branch banks. The nursery that sells the plants contracts with the bank to send an employee each week to water, trim, and fertilize the plants. The contract for the purchase of the plants is governed by the UCC. The maintenance agreement is a service contract that is governed by common-law rules.

## ELEMENTS OF A CONTRACT

The two basic elements of a valid contract are: 1) the parties' mutual assent to terms and conditions of their agreement, and 2) consideration.

### Mutual Assent

**Mutual assent** means that each party to the contract understands the contract terms and agreements in the same way. The parties agree to the meaning of the contractual terms. This element of a contract is called a

---

| Exhibit 6.1 | Types of Contracts Typical in Banking |
|---|---|

Bill Paying Agreements
Credit Card Agreements
Deposit Agreements
Trust Agreements
Loan Agreements
Lock Box Agreements
Promissory Notes
Revolving Credit Agreements
Safe Deposit Box Contracts
Security Agreements
Trust Agreements

---

*meeting of the minds.* Mutual assent is conveyed when the parties communicate agreement by written or spoken words—or, in some situations, by the parties' conduct. Many contracts have been formed through an indication of mutual assent that occurs partly by written or spoken words and partly by actions or conduct.

### Example

A customer and a bank officer discuss the terms of certificates of deposit being offered at the bank. At some point the customer nods her head and says "That sounds good." The bank officer types some information into her computer and then, after the forms are printed, having marked signature lines with *X*s, gives them to the customer. The customer signs her name at each *X*. By words and conduct, these parties have mutually assented to the terms of the contract.

## Offer and Acceptance

To achieve mutual assent, an offer must be made and accepted. An **offer** is a proposal in which one party—the **offeror**—promises to do something if the other party—the **offeree**—will do something in return. What the offeror promises to do and wants the offeree to do in return constitute the terms of the proposed contract.

### Example

A bank offers to lend its customer $2,000 if the customer will promise to repay the money with interest in 90 days. The customer makes the promise by signing a promissory note (exhibit 6.2). At this point, both parties have committed to an enforceable contract.

The contract is created when the offer is accepted. **Acceptance** occurs when the offeree agrees to the terms and promises to meet the obligations spelled out in the contract. In the example of the customer who signed the promissory note, the

acceptance occurred upon the signing of the note.

A contract between two parties in which both parties make promises is called a **bilateral contract.** By contrast, in **unilateral contracts** only the offeree makes a promise. Acceptance occurs only when the act requested in the contract is performed.

### Example

A woman tells her neighbor's son that she will pay him $15 if he will mow her lawn. If he says "Okay, I'll do it tomorrow," his words do not constitute an acceptance of the terms of her offer and do not create a contract. The neighbor's son creates a contract when he actually mows the lawn (acceptance) and obligates the woman to pay the $15.

When an offer to purchase or sell goods is made, under the UCC the offeree may accept some of the offeror's terms and substitute others, or the offeree may accept all the offeror's terms and propose additional ones. The changed terms do not become part of the contract unless the offeror specifically accepts them.

### Example

A bank operates a banking Web site on the Internet. Through its Web site consumers may open accounts at the bank. The bank's site lists the types of accounts and the rates and fees applicable to each. The site also offers copies of the bank's policies and account agreements.

A consumer completes the new account form on the Web site and submits it to the bank. Shortly thereafter, the consumer mails an opening deposit to the bank. If the bank accepts the consumer's application and processes the funds, the bank has agreed to open the customer's account. However, the account is subject to the bank's rules and regulation, which may allow the bank or the customer to terminate the account under certain conditions.

## PROMISSORY NOTE

| Principal $101,500.00 | Loan Date 12-21-1999 | Maturity 12-21-2029 | Loan No | Call | Collateral | Account | Officer | Initials |
| --- | --- | --- | --- | --- | --- | --- | --- | --- |

References in the shaded area are for Lender's use only and do not limit the applicability of this document to any particular loan or item. Any item above containing "****" has been omitted due to text length limitations.

**Borrower:** JOE BORROWER
3200 "B" St.
Salem, OR 98765

**Lender:** Concentrex National Institution < CFI TEST BANK >
3225 National St
Portland, OR 97225

**Principal Amount: $101,500.00**　　　　**Initial Rate: 7.950%**　　　　**Date of Note: December 21, 1999**

**PROMISE TO PAY.** I ("Borrower") promise to pay to Concentrex National Institution < CFI TEST BANK > ("Lender"), or order, in lawful money of the United States of America, the principal amount of One Hundred One Thousand Five Hundred & 00/100 Dollars ($101,500.00), together with interest on the unpaid principal balance from December 21, 1999, until paid in full.

**PAYMENT.** Subject to any payment changes resulting from changes in the Index, I will pay this loan in 360 payments of $741.66 each payment. My first payment is due January 21, 2000, and all subsequent payments are due on the same day of each month after that. My final payment will be due on December 21, 2029, and will be for all principal and all accrued interest not yet paid. Payments include principal and interest. Unless otherwise agreed or required by applicable law, payments will be applied first to any unpaid collection costs and any late charges, then to any unpaid interest, and any remaining amount to principal. Interest on this Note is computed on a 365/365 simple interest basis; that is, by applying the ratio of the annual interest rate over the number of days in a year, multiplied by the outstanding principal balance, multiplied by the actual number of days the principal balance is outstanding. I will pay Lender at Lender's address shown above or at such other place as Lender may designate in writing.

**VARIABLE INTEREST RATE.** The interest rate on this Note is subject to change from time to time based on changes in an independent index which is the The Wall Street Journal July Rate (the "Index"). The Index is not necessarily the lowest rate charged by Lender on its loans. If the Index becomes unavailable during the term of this loan, Lender may designate a substitute index after notice to me. Lender will tell me the current Index rate upon my request. The interest rate change will not occur more often than each Month. I understand that Lender may make loans based on other rates as well. The Index currently is 5.825% per annum. The interest rate to be applied to the unpaid principal balance of this Note will be at a rate of 2.125 percentage points over the Index, resulting in an initial rate of 7.950% per annum. NOTICE: Under no circumstances will the interest rate on this Note be more than the maximum rate allowed by applicable law. Unless waived by Lender, any increase in the interest rate will increase the amounts of my payments.

**PREPAYMENT.** I agree that all loan fees and other prepaid finance charges are earned fully as of the date of the loan and will not be refunded to me upon early payment (whether voluntary or as a result of default), except as otherwise required by law. Except for the foregoing, I may pay without penalty all or a portion of the amount owed earlier than it is due. Early payments will not, unless agreed to by Lender in writing, relieve me of my obligation to continue to make payments under the payment schedule. Rather, early payments will reduce the principal balance due and may result in my making fewer payments. I agree not to send Lender payments marked "paid in full", "without recourse", or similar language. If I send such a payment, Lender may accept it without losing any of Lender's rights under this Note, and I will remain obligated to pay any further amount owed to Lender. All written communications concerning disputed amounts, including any check or other payment instrument that indicates that the payment constitutes "payment in full" of the amount owed or that is tendered with other conditions or limitations or as full satisfaction of a disputed amount must be mailed or delivered to: Concentrex National Institution < CFI TEST BANK >, 3225 National St, Portland, OR 97225.

**LATE CHARGE.** If a payment is 15 days or more late, I will be charged 5.000% of the regularly scheduled payment.

**INTEREST AFTER DEFAULT.** Upon default, including failure to pay upon final maturity, Lender, at its option, may, if permitted under applicable law, increase the variable interest rate on this Note to 4.125 percentage points over the Index. The interest rate will not exceed the maximum rate permitted by applicable law.

**DEFAULT.** I will be in default under this Note if any of the following happen:

**Payment Default.** I fail to make any payment when due under this Note.

**Break Other Promises.** I break any promise made to Lender or fail to perform promptly at the time and strictly in the manner provided in this Note or in any agreement related to this Note, or in any other agreement or loan I have with Lender.

**False Statements.** Any representation or statement made or furnished to Lender by me or on my behalf under this Note or the related documents is false or misleading in any material respect, either now or at the time made or furnished.

**Death or Insolvency.** Any Borrower dies or becomes insolvent; a receiver is appointed for any part of my property; I make an assignment for the benefit of creditors; or any proceeding is commenced either by me or against me under any bankruptcy or insolvency laws. Any creditor or governmental agency tries to take any of the property or any other of my property in which Lender has a lien. This includes taking of, garnishing of or levying on my accounts with Lender. However, if I dispute in good faith whether the claim on which the taking of the property is based is valid or reasonable, and if I give Lender written notice of the claim and furnish Lender with monies or a surety bond satisfactory to Lender to satisfy the claim, then this default provision will not apply.

**Defective Collateralization.** This Note or any of the related documents ceases to be in full force and effect (including failure of any collateral document to create a valid and perfected security interest or lien) at any time and for any reason.

**Collateral Damage or Loss.** Any collateral securing this Note is lost, stolen, substantially damaged or destroyed and the loss, theft, substantial damage or destruction is not covered by insurance.

**Events Affecting Guarantor.** Any of the preceding events occurs with respect to any guarantor, endorser, surety, or accommodation party of any of the indebtedness or any guarantor, endorser, surety, or accommodation party dies or becomes incompetent, or revokes or disputes the validity of, or liability under, any guaranty of the indebtedness . In the event of a death, Lender, at its option, may, but shall not be required to, permit the guarantor's estate to assume unconditionally the obligations arising under the guaranty in a manner satisfactory to Lender, and, in doing so, cure any Event of Default.

**Cure Provisions.** If any default, other than a default in payment, is curable and if I have not been given a notice of a breach of the same provision of this Note within the preceding twelve (12) months, it may be cured (and no event of default will have occurred) if I, after receiving written notice from Lender demanding cure of such default: (1) cure the default within fifteen (15) days; or (2) if the cure requires more than fifteen (15) days, immediately initiate steps which Lender deems in Lender's sole discretion to be sufficient to cure the default and thereafter continue and complete all reasonable and necessary steps sufficient to produce compliance as soon as reasonably practical.

## Termination of Offer

An offer cannot be canceled after it is accepted, because acceptance creates a contract. Until acceptance occurs, however, the offeror is generally free to withdraw—and thus terminate—the offer.

Once an offer has been terminated, the offeree no longer has the ability to accept it and form a contract.

Normally an offer may be terminated at any time before acceptance. One exception to this rule concerns offers to enter into unilateral contracts, when the

## Exhibit 6.2    Sample Promissory Note for a Variable Rate Loan

**PROMISSORY NOTE**
(Continued)                                                      Page 2

**LENDER'S RIGHTS.** Upon default, Lender may declare the entire unpaid principal balance on this Note and all accrued unpaid interest immediately due, and then I will pay that amount.

**ATTORNEYS' FEES; EXPENSES.** Lender may hire or pay someone else to help collect the loan if I do not pay. I will pay Lender that amount. This includes, subject to any limits under applicable law, Lender's attorneys' fees and Lender's legal expenses, whether or not there is a lawsuit, including attorneys' fees, expenses for bankruptcy proceedings (including efforts to modify or vacate any automatic stay or injunction), and appeals. If not prohibited by applicable law, I also will pay any court costs, in addition to all other sums provided by law.

**GOVERNING LAW.** This Note will be governed by and interpreted in accordance with federal law and the laws of the State of Oregon. This Note has been accepted by Lender in the State of Oregon.

**CHOICE OF VENUE.** If there is a lawsuit, I agree upon Lender's request to submit to the jurisdiction of the courts of Marion County, State of Oregon.

**RIGHT OF SETOFF.** To the extent permitted by applicable law, Lender reserves a right of setoff in all my accounts with Lender (whether checking, savings, or some other account). This includes all accounts I hold jointly with someone else and all accounts I may open in the future. However, this does not include any IRA or Keogh accounts, or any trust accounts for which setoff would be prohibited by law. I authorize Lender, to the extent permitted by applicable law, to charge or setoff all sums owing on the Indebtedness against any and all such accounts.

**COLLATERAL.** I acknowledge this Note is secured by a Mortgage dated December 21, 1999, to Lender on real property located in Marion County, State of Oregon, all the terms and conditions of which are hereby incorporated and made a part of this Note; and a Deed of Trust dated December 21, 1999, to a trustee in favor of Lender on real property located in Marion County, State of Oregon, all the terms and conditions of which are hereby incorporated and made a part of this Note.

**SUCCESSOR INTERESTS.** The terms of this Note shall be binding upon me, and upon my heirs, personal representatives, successors and assigns, and shall inure to the benefit of Lender and Lender's successors and assigns.

**GENERAL PROVISIONS.** Lender may delay or forgo enforcing any of its rights or remedies under this Note without losing them. I and any other person who signs, guarantees or endorses this Note, to the extent allowed by law, waive presentment, demand for payment, and notice of dishonor. Upon any change in the terms of this Note, and unless otherwise expressly stated in writing, no party who signs this Note, whether as maker, guarantor, accommodation maker or endorser, shall be released from liability. All such parties agree that Lender may renew or extend (repeatedly and for any length of time) this loan or release any party or guarantor or collateral; or impair, fail to realize upon or perfect Lender's security interest in the collateral. All such parties also agree that Lender may modify this loan without the consent of or notice to anyone other than the party with whom the modification is made. The obligations under this Note are joint and several. This means that the words "I", "me", and "my" mean each and all of the persons signing below.

**PRIOR TO SIGNING THIS NOTE, I READ AND UNDERSTOOD ALL THE PROVISIONS OF THIS NOTE, INCLUDING THE VARIABLE INTEREST RATE PROVISIONS. I AGREE TO THE TERMS OF THE NOTE.**

**I ACKNOWLEDGE RECEIPT OF A COMPLETED COPY OF THIS PROMISSORY NOTE.**

**BORROWER:**

X_____
    JOE BORROWER, Individually

Source: Concentrex Incorporated, Portland, Oregon.

---

offeree has begun but not completed the required performance. When an offer is made to enter into a unilateral contract and the offeree has started performance, the offeror loses the legal right to terminate the offer.

### Example

A woman tells her neighbor's son that she will pay him $15 if he will mow her lawn as soon as possible. Two days later, annoyed that the lawn has not yet been mowed, the woman calls her nephew and makes the same offer to him. He says, "Okay, I'll come tomorrow afternoon." The next morning, the woman looks out to see that her neighbor's son has arrived with a power mower and has started to work. Because the neighbor's son has started performance within a reasonable time after the offer, the woman cannot now cancel the offer. However, she can cancel the offer made to her nephew because he has not yet accepted by coming to mow the lawn.

An offer also may be terminated in other ways. The most obvious terminating event is failure to comply with a condition of the offer.

### Example

A bank offers to add $25 to new accounts opened with at least $1,000 during the month of May. A new customer with $1,000 arrives at the bank on May 31, having forgotten it was a Monday holiday that year, and finds the bank closed. Even if the customer comes back first thing on Tuesday, June 1, and complies with the other conditions, the offer will have terminated.

Other terminating events include the offeror's death or loss of legal capacity to make a contract; the death of a person or destruction of something essential for the performance of the proposed contract, or a newly enacted law that makes the proposed contract illegal.

### Example

A bank offers to purchase a competing bank from its shareholders. Before acceptance of the offer, the state where the banks are located enacts a law that prohibits banks from having more than one office. This new law terminates the offer because the proposed contract has become illegal.

## Consideration

A valid contract must meet the requirement of **consideration;** that is, both sides must provide something of value that represents their commitment to the bargain. Consideration is the "price" each party pays for the right to enforce the contract. However, consideration need not be monetary.

In a bilateral contract the parties provide consideration by exchanging legally binding promises. Taking on a legally binding obligation is sufficient consideration for the right to enforce the contract in court.

In a unilateral contract the parties provide consideration at different times. One party's consideration is actual performance of the act requested. When that is done the contract is formed and the other party's consideration (the promise to pay) becomes part of the contract.

Whether the parties exchange a promise for a promise or a promise for an act, the bargained-for exchange is the essence of consideration. Without this vital element no contract exists. A promise made with no request for something in exchange is called a **gratuitous promise.** It does not become a valid contract and cannot be enforced.

### Example

A boy knows that his elderly neighbor's lawn needs mowing and would like to mow it for her. He tells his neighbor that he will mow the yard on Saturday, right after baseball practice. He forgets his promise to mow the yard and agrees to attend a swim party after the practice. The neighbor finally has to call a lawn service to do the job. Because the boy's promise was gratuitous and had no consideration, there is no contract to enforce.

### Legal Value and Legal Detriment

Consideration must have legal value, which means it effects a change in a party's legal position. For example, a commitment to make monthly payments on a loan changes the borrower's legal position from that of someone who does not owe money to that of someone who does. A party also can change its legal position by giving up something, which is called suffering **legal detriment.** As the following example shows, legal detriment specifically involves

- giving up a legal right that one is entitled to exercise
- refraining from doing what one has a legal right to do
- agreeing to do something one has a right *not* to do
- giving up something one has a right to keep

### Examples

- A father promises his son that if the son will work and save at least $15 a week, the father will double whatever amount the son saves in one year. At the end of the year, the son has saved $800, thus creating a contract with his father. In reliance on the promise, the son has refrained from spending his earnings as he might have wished. This legal detriment to the son is the very thing that induced the father's promise. As such, it was effective consideration for the contract.

- A man promises his girlfriend that he will buy her a car. In reliance on this promise, she buys 25 tape cassettes, a car phone, and a membership in the American Automobile Association. She also arranges to install a small driveway and carport next to her house. These acts are not consideration for a contract because her legal detriment in doing these things has not been requested. There has been no bargained-for exchange. The man's promise, therefore, is gratuitous and cannot be enforced.

---

### Critical Terms

*Consideration* Something of value given to someone in exchange for that person's promise to do something.

*Gratuitous Promise* A promise to do something or to give something of value to someone without receiving anything in return.

*Promisee* A person to whom something is promised.

*Promisor* A person who promises to do something for someone else.

---

### Adequacy of Consideration

The law is unconcerned with whether the price paid as consideration is fair in the marketplace. Instead, the law addresses whether the consideration is **legally adequate.** The reluctance to use fair market price alone as a test of adequate consideration follows from the belief that people ought to be free to bargain without undue interference from the law.

As with many terms, the legal definition of *adequate* differs from the ordinary definition of the word. No specific test exists for the legal adequacy of consideration and courts base their decisions on the particular facts of each case. Generally, if a court determines that the consideration is inadequate, it will find that consideration is lacking entirely and the contract will not be enforced. Contracts rarely are held invalid for lack of consideration.

#### Examples

- A customer deposits $100,000 in a new savings account at a bank, which pays 3.5 percent interest per year. The competitive rate at other banks is 5 percent. The customer finds this out and asks to close the account and withdraw his funds. The terms of the contract prohibit early withdrawal, so the bank refuses. A valid contract exists in this situation. By paying even minimal interest for the deposit, the bank has given consideration.

- Knowing that a parcel of land contains oil, a man contracts with its owner, a poor and elderly widow, to pay $100 per acre to purchase the property. Comparable land is selling for $50,000 per acre. In such a case, a court would be likely to find that no contract exists because of the gross inadequacy of consideration.

## VOID, VOIDABLE, AND UNENFORCEABLE CONTRACTS

Some contracts that have the essential elements of mutual assent and consideration may still contain defects that make them unenforceable. Three types of defective contracts will be considered in this chapter: void, voidable, and unenforceable contracts.

If an agreement has an illegal purpose—one extreme example being "murder for hire" arrangements—it is considered an illegal agreement. Parties to illegal agreements often commit a crime just by entering into the illegal contract, so enforcement of the contract by the courts is not an option. Illegal contracts are **void.** A void contract creates no rights or enforceable duties for either party.

A **voidable contract** results when one of the parties lacks the legal capacity to enter into a contractual relationship. The party without legal capacity can rescind the contract by claiming lack of legal capacity.

A third type of defective contract involves promises that cannot be enforced unless they are in writing. These agreements are governed by the Statute of Frauds, which requires written proof of certain types of promises to prevent fraudulent claims concerning the parties' agreement.

## Legal Capacity

Parties must have the legal capacity to bind themselves to a contract when they enter into it. Over the centuries, the law has recognized that certain categories of people are unable to represent or protect their own interests. These people lack legal capacity and any contracts they enter into will not be legally binding. People regarded by law as lacking legal capacity include minors, the mentally incapacitated, and the intoxicated.

### Minors

The law protects young people because they generally are inexperienced and might be susceptible to control by others. This protection takes the form of limitations imposed on the enforcement of contracts made with minors. In many states, the age of majority is 18 years. Persons under the age of 18 years are deemed to be minors. Although they are free to enter into a contract, minors have the power to **disaffirm** the contract under most circumstances. Therefore, contracts with a minor are voidable. The minor has a choice either to perform the contract or to disaffirm his or her obligations under it.

If a minor disaffirms the contract, any property the minor has acquired under the contract (for example, money obtained from a bank under a loan agreement) must be returned to the other party. However, if the minor has spent or consumed the property, the other party cannot enforce its repayment or return.

Even if a minor has nothing left to return, if the minor disaffirms the contract the other party must return anything that was received from the minor under the contract. For example, if the minor gives a bank a legal claim on property as security for a loan and later disaffirms the loan agreement, the bank will be required to release its claim even if no payments have been made on the loan and the minor has spent the money. Clearly, doing business with a minor can be perilous.

A person who wants to disaffirm a contract because he or she is underage must do so while still a minor or within a reasonable time after reaching the age of majority. If the person does not disaffirm, but performs the contract for a reasonable time after reaching the age of majority, such performance is considered to be a validation of the contract. Once validated, a contract is no longer voidable.

A minor can be held liable for the reasonable value of *necessaries* furnished under contract. Necessaries are items required for existence, such as reasonable amounts of food, shelter, clothing, and medical care. A bank or other lender who lends a minor money to purchase necessaries can enforce repayment of the loan if the lender can prove that the money was used to purchase necessaries.

Even if minors claim a need for necessaries, lenders and others are well advised not to contract with them at all. No laws require anyone to do business with minors, even if the transaction involves necessaries. Those who decide to contract with minors should insist upon a surety or guarantor who will ensure performance of the obligation should the minor disaffirm. An alternative to securing a cosigner or guarantor is to conduct business with the minor's legal guardian.

A minor who misrepresents his or her age to obtain a loan or other contractual benefit is said by some courts to be prohibited from later disaffirming the contract on the basis of being a minor. Courts applying this principle usually do so only when 1) the minor is old enough to exercise discretion, 2) the conduct was intentionally fraudulent, and 3) the other party to the contract relied in good faith on the minor's misrepresentation.

## Mentally Incapacitated Persons

Persons who suffer from a mental incapacity fall into two categories regarding the legal capacity to contract—those with a court-appointed guardian and those without a guardian.

In the first category, the person suffering from the mental incapacity is referred to as a **ward.** A ward has no capacity to take on contractual obligations. A nearly universal rule of law holds that the appointment of the guardian serves to shelter the ward from contractual obligations. Any agreement into which a ward enters is an absolutely void (not merely voidable) contract. Once a guardian is appointed, all of a ward's property, interests, and power are the responsibility of the guardian, who has the sole power to contract in the ward's name for the ward's benefit.

Whether the party entering into an agreement with a ward knows of the legal incapacity or not is irrelevant. The agreement is void with or without such knowledge. Unlike a minor, a ward who enters into an agreement for necessaries cannot

be held personally liable to pay for them. However, the guardian has the power to convert the ward's transaction into a contract. If this occurs, the agreement becomes a contract enforceable against the ward's estate.

The second category includes persons who are mentally incapacitated but have no guardian. If no appointed guardian exists, it is likely that there has been no express finding that the person lacks mental competence. Mental incompetence varies so greatly in type and degree that the condition is difficult to determine. At one extreme, a person may be incompetent to enter into any transaction. At the other extreme, a person may be rational most of the time and only occasionally disabled. Whatever the degree, a person who is mentally incompetent at the time he or she undertakes a contractual obligation may disaffirm that contract.

Parties who claim mental incompetence at the time of transaction may disaffirm a contract only upon terms that are fair to the other party. Thus, if someone dealing with a mentally incompetent person knew or should have known of the disability, the courts generally treat the matter as they would one involving an infant. In other words, the court will consider that the party should have known better than to enter into a contract with the mentally incompetent person. However, if the party did not know and could not have been expected to know of the disability, the courts allow the contract to be disaffirmed only if the incompetent person first pays the value of anything received and consumed under the contract. In either situation, the incompetent person must pay for necessaries.

If the mentally incompetent person regains full mental capacity, he or she may disaffirm all contracts made while incompetent, within certain limitations. Failure to disaffirm a contract within a reasonable time after recovery may operate as a ratification that makes the contract enforceable.

### Intoxicated Persons

People who are judged mentally incompetent by reason of alcoholism or drug addiction and for whom guardians have been appointed are considered to be wards. If no guardian has been appointed, persons who are drunk or under the influence of drugs at the time of making a contract may disaffirm the contract in certain circumstances.

Current law holds that contracts made while a person is under the influence of drugs or alcohol are voidable if the condition was so extreme that it made the person incapable of understanding the nature and effect of the contract.

Upon becoming sober, the person previously under the influence of alcohol or drugs must promptly disaffirm a contract made while incapacitated. Otherwise, the person runs the risk that the contract will be considered ratified. Usually, a court will not permit disaffirmance based on intoxication unless an offer is made to give back or pay for any goods, moneys, or services received from the other party. If goods were destroyed or consumed during the period of intoxication, however, some courts permit disaffirmance without repayment. Disaffirmance also is allowed if it can be proved that the other party knew that the person was under the influence of alcohol or drugs when he or she entered into the contract.

## Illegal Objective

If the purpose or performance of an agreement is illegal, the agreement is unenforceable. Illegal agreements include

- agreements in unreasonable restraint of trade
- agreements harmful to the public interest or to the administration of justice
- agreements harmful to third persons
- wagering agreements
- agreements made illegal by statute

### Agreements in Unreasonable Restraint of Trade

The law disallows enforcement of contracts that unreasonably restrain trade or restrict competition. This includes contracts that unreasonably prevent a person from engaging in a business or profession, as well as agreements among business competitors to fix minimum prices, divide sales territories, limit production, or pool profits.

### Example

As part of an employment contract, a computer specialist signs an agreement promising that, if she leaves the company, she will not do similar work for any of its competitors for five years. Because this agreement would effectively prevent her from engaging in her profession for an unreasonable period of time, the agreement is illegal and cannot be enforced by the company.

### Agreements Harmful to the Public Interest

Agreements that disrupt or subvert the workings of government are illegal and unenforceable. Included in this category are agreements to

- pay bribes to elected officials for their votes
- pay for appointment to public office
- pay to obtain government contracts by corrupt methods
- pay public officials to perform duties that they are required by law to perform

### Agreements Harmful to the Administration of Justice

Examples of agreements harmful to the administration of justice include

- agreements that induce witnesses to give false testimony
- agreements by anyone, other than a court, to pay a juror

- agreements between attorneys and clients not to settle their cases on any terms, thus prolonging the litigation
- agreements not to prosecute a crime in return for payment

In connection with the last example, a bank's promise to someone whose loan application was fraudulent that the bank will not seek criminal prosecution in return for repayment of the money may or may not be considered harmful to the administration of justice. The court's decision will depend on how a state's law has evolved.

### Agreements Harmful to Third Persons

Unenforceable contracts to harm others include agreements that

- constitute fraud upon creditors or other third parties
- induce someone to breach a contract with a third party
- induce a fiduciary to violate his or her duties

#### Example

A trustee for a large trust is promised $100,000 by a developer if he will invest $2 million of the trust funds in a risky land venture. The trustee makes the investment, but then is not paid the $100,000. The trustee cannot enforce the promise because it was made in exchange for his violating his duty as trustee for personal gain.

#### Wagering Agreements

All gambling and other betting transactions are wagering agreements enforceable as contracts only in those states that permit them by statute. The enforceability of a lottery ticket as a contract depends on state law, which generally prohibits lotteries not licensed by the state—including even those lotteries whose proceeds are for charitable or civic purposes.

### Case for Discussion
*U.S. Nursing Corporation v. St. Joseph Medical Center*

In January 1993 U.S. Nursing entered into an agreement with St. Joseph Medical Center to provide nurses during a strike. The contract allowed either party to terminate on seven days' notice. If the hospital did not give seven days' notice, the contract provided that U.S. Nursing would be entitled to an additional seven days of pay. When the contract began, U.S. Nursing did not have a license from the state to operate a nursing agency. However, the agency began to supply nurses to St. Joseph and continued to do so while it attempted to obtain a license.

U.S. Nursing was unable to obtain a license. The state licensing agency notified the hospital that U.S. Nursing was not licensed and therefore unable to legally supply nurses to staff the hospital. The licensing agency further advised the hospital to immediately cease using the nurses from U.S. Nursing.

Fearing that a fine would be levied upon it, the hospital terminated the contract with U.S. Nursing and paid the company all amounts owed to it through the date of the termination. Because the notice required by the contract had not been given, U.S. Nursing demanded the seven days' additional payment. The hospital refused and U.S. Nursing filed suit.

At trial, the hospital argued that the contract was void because it was illegal for the company to perform its duties under the contract and that the hospital should not be held to the requirements.

The court ruled that the contract was unenforceable because it violated public policy. The public policy behind the nursing agency licensing statute was to ensure the quality of medical care to the citizens of the state. This policy took precedence over any and all conflicting contractual provisions.

**Questions for Discussion**
1. What other types of public policy might conflict with contract terms?
2. What could the parties have done to protect themselves against agreeing to an unenforceable contract?

### Agreements Made Illegal by Statute

Many states have statutes requiring that certain occupations and professions be practiced only by persons licensed by the state. These statutes usually provide that anyone engaging in such occupations or professions without a license cannot enforce an agreement relating to their unlicensed occupation.

### Usurious Agreements

Interest is money charged as payment for a loan of money. **Usury** is the collection of interest in an amount greater than that permitted by federal or state law. Most usury statutes set maximum interest rates according to the type of lender, borrower, or loan involved. In many states, loans made to businesses carry a higher interest rate than do consumer loans, and interest rates charged by financial institutions are higher than the rates allowed to private parties. While a few states set one maximum rate for all types of loans, most states do not. Thus, a lender must carefully review the law relating to each type of loan being considered.

#### Federal Law and Usury

The maximum interest rates available to banks traditionally have been governed by state law. Even rates for national banks have been tied primarily to state-set rates. Federal law provides that national banks may charge the rates available to other lenders within the state where the bank is operating. Banks' ability to use rates permitted to other lenders located in the same state is called the most favored lender doctrine. In some cases, such as for first lien mortgage loans, federal law preempts state law and all lenders may charge the interest rates allowed by federal law.

## STATUTE OF FRAUDS

Ideally, contracts should be in writing to assure the contracting parties that an agreement in fact exists. Certainly this is true of the contracts into which banks enter, because both the banks and their customers must have certainty when it comes to financial matters.

The law will not enforce the parties' agreement in some transactions unless a document exists to prove that the agreement is genuine. This rule of law originated over three centuries ago when the **Statute of Frauds** was enacted in England to prevent fraud and false testimony regarding oral contracts. The statute provided that certain types of contracts could not be enforced at all unless they were in writing. Statutes of frauds have been adopted in varying forms throughout the United States and interpreted through numerous court decisions.

### Contractual Promises Addressed by the Statute of Frauds

In most states, the Statute of Frauds requires the following types of contractual promises to be in writing in order for the contract to be enforced:

- contracts for the sale of land or any interest in land
- contracts for the sale of goods above a certain price, usually more than $500
- contracts that, by their own terms, cannot be performed within one year from the date of the contract
- promises to be responsible for another's debt

### Contracts for Sale of Land

To be enforceable, contracts creating or transferring any interest in real estate must be in writing.

#### Example

A man rents a small house owned by the woman who lives next door. After a year, he expresses an interest in buying the house. The owner makes an oral agreement that if he stays on as a renter for another year, she will sell him the house and apply the year's rental payments toward the purchase price. Eleven months later, the woman dies without a will. No document exists to confirm the agreement and thus make it binding on the woman's estate. The estate administrator can sell the house to anyone. If the administrator should agree to sell to the renter, the renter can not enforce the owner's oral agreement to apply rents to the purchase price.

### Contracts for Sale of Goods Above a Certain Price

The section of the original Statute of Frauds requiring written proof of contracts for the sale of goods above a certain price has been incorporated into the UCC. Under the UCC, contracts to sell or buy goods at a price of $500 or more must be in writing. Also, if modification to a contract involves a price change of $500 or more, even though such modification does not need to be exchanged for consideration under the UCC, it must be in writing to comply with the Statute of Frauds.

### Contracts that Cannot Be Performed Within One Year

If according to its own terms a contract cannot be performed within one year from the date of agreement, it is unenforceable if not in writing. The reasoning behind this is that contract terms should not be left merely to the memory of the parties if the contract might not be performed until long after the date of the agreement.

To come under the Statute of Frauds a contract must, by its own terms, be incapable of being performed within one year. For example, an employment contract made on December 15, 2000, relating to a period of employment from January 1 through December 31, 2001, must be in writing to be enforceable. Under its own terms the contract is incapable of being performed within one year from the date of agreement.

An oral agreement need not specifically refer to a completion date within one year to be enforceable. As long as the performance can be undertaken and possibly completed within one year, the agreement need not be in writing to be enforceable.

### Promises to be Responsible for Another's Debt

The Statute of Frauds makes general promises to be responsible for the debt or duty of another person unenforceable unless written proof of the promise exists. For example, statements such as "If he doesn't pay you, I will" or "I promise it will get done even if I have to do it myself," cannot be enforced unless the promises are put in writing.

Guarantees for large loans, where one party puts in writing its commitment to meet the loan obligation in the event of the primary debtor's default, are enforceable.

## Writings that Satisfy the Statute of Frauds

The document required to satisfy the Statute of Frauds need not be a formal contract. Statutory and case law require a document that sets forth essential terms of the agreement and is signed by the party whose promise is being enforced. The essential terms needed to satisfy the Statute of Frauds are the names of the parties, identification of the subject matter, and the consideration. Under the UCC the written proof of a contract for the sale of goods for $500 or more may be a memorandum signed by the parties, stating that the sale (or purchase) is agreed to and specifying the quantity of goods involved.

## Exceptions to the Statute of Frauds

Since passage of the original Statute of Frauds in 1677, courts and legislatures have recognized that application of the statute can have harsh results. Thus, court decisions and various laws provide in some situations for enforcement of oral contracts that would otherwise be unenforceable because of the Statute of Frauds.

Partial performance by the promisee will make an oral contract to convey an interest in land enforceable. For example, if an owner and buyer orally agree on the terms of sale and the buyer then partly performs by making payments and taking possession of the land or making valuable improvements to it, the owner's oral promise to sell (transfer the deed) is enforceable.

Under the UCC an oral contract for the sale of goods for $500 or more is enforceable if a party has partly performed, but only up to the value of what has been furnished by the performance.

In most cases a court will not automatically invoke the Statute of Frauds to nullify a contract. The party wishing to use the Statute of Frauds to void a contract must say so in its arguments before the court.

## CONTRACTS INVOLVING THIRD PARTIES

Under certain conditions contractual rights and obligations may be transferred to third parties. Transfer of rights (for example, the right to payment) is called **assignment.** Transfer of duties (obligations under the contract) is called **delegation.**

---

### Critical Terms

*Assignment* The transfer in writing by one person to another of the title to property, rights, or other interests.

*Delegation* Authorizing someone to perform an action on behalf of another person.

---

## Assignment of Rights

Unless a contract specifically disallows assignment, parties may assign their rights under the contract to third parties. When assignment takes place, the person to whom the assignment is made (the assignee) steps into the shoes of the assignor and acquires all of the assignor's rights under the contract. The assignor must ensure that the rights assigned are valid and enforceable. If it turns out the rights cannot be enforced, the assignee may sue the assignor for any loss suffered.

---

### Case for Discussion
*Crowne Bank v. Tri-State Airport Authority*

Builders, Inc. was selected by the Tri-State Airport Authority (TSAA) to construct a new control tower. To finance this project, Builders obtained a $500,000 construction loan from Crowne Bank, NA. As security for the loan, Builders assigned its interest in its contract with TSAA to the bank. This assignment was documented and recognized by TSAA.

In the contract TSAA agreed to pay Builders portions of the total amount on completion of various stages of the project. The contract also provided that Builders would receive a final payment for the balance due when the entire project was completed to the satisfaction of TSAA, and after Builders, Inc. had

---

furnished written proof that all subcontractors and suppliers had been paid in full.

When the project was completed, Builders submitted a request for the final payment. No mention was made of the fact that two subcontractors had not yet been paid and that $50,000 was due on Builders' construction loan. The two subcontractors failed to file a lien against Builders.

On the same day that the request for payment from Builders arrived, TSAA received notification from Crowne Bank that $50,000 was due under the assignment of the contract.

The subcontractors claimed that TSAA was under no obligation to pay Crowne Bank until Builders, Inc. had fully complied with the contract by paying all subcontractors and suppliers.

The court ruled in favor of Crowne Bank, stating that a contract must be interpreted in terms of the intentions of the two parties. To isolate one clause in the contract and to interpret it in favor of the subcontractors would be improper. When considered in light of the contract as a whole, the intent of the clause requiring full payment of all subcontractors and suppliers clearly was not intended to protect those who were not parties to the contract. Rather, the purpose of the clause was to protect TSAA against those who might later file liens or other claims against it.

## Questions for Discussion

1. Who were the beneficiaries in this contract?
2. What is a *third-party beneficiary?*
3. What actions could the subcontractors have taken to ensure that they were paid for work performed on this project?

The law does not permit assignment of a right if it will substantially change the promisor's risk or alter the character of the performance required. For example, contracts involving the right to receive personal services usually are not assignable. This is because of the likelihood that the performance rendered, if performed by another, will be too different from what the promisee bargained for.

### Examples

- ABC Software company agrees to license its operational software to the State National Bank for a period of five years. The contract calls for continual updates and maintenance service by ABC Software. State National Bank receives a license that allows it to run its operations on the software at all of its branches for the duration of the contract. ABC Software company is one of several companies writing and selling this type of bank operational software. Some of ABC's biggest competitors are owned by other banks. ABC places a nonassignment clause in its contract with State National so that if State National is purchased by another bank the contract with ABC will automatically terminate. ABC insists that no assignment of the contract will be valid without ABC's advance approval. Because ABC does not want its trade secrets potentially falling into the hands of a competitor, it uses the contract clause to prevent assignment by the bank.

- Bank President Milton Freemore is preparing for retirement. In honor of his years of service at the bank, the board of directors commissions a locally renowned artist, John Rosa, to paint Mr. Freemore's portrait. Mr. Rosa cannot assign his contract with the bank to another artist without the board's permission because the bank is expecting his particular skills and artistic abilities to be exercised in the performance of the contract.

A typical contract right that is assignable is the right to receive payment. Because it should not matter who receives the money, assignment of this right is no imposition on the promisor. The assignment does not increase the risk or change the character of performance.

The assignee should give notice of the assignment to the promisor to make sure that the promisor knows that performance must be made to someone other than the original promisee. If the promisor is unaware of the assignment and renders performance to the original promisee, the contract will no longer be in effect and the assignee will no longer have any right to the promisor's performance.

## Delegation of Duties

Just as contractual rights may be assigned, contractual duties may be delegated. Generally, duties may be delegated where no substantial reason can be shown why the delegated performance will not be as satisfactory as personal performance by the promisor. Thus, personal services contracts, in which the unique skills of the promisor are what was bargained for, cannot be delegated.

A promisor who delegates contractual duties is not released from responsibility. If the delegated performance is unsatisfactory, the promisor can be sued along with the person to whom the job was delegated. This rule protects the promisee and makes the delegation of performance possible and safe in most cases.

## Third-Party Beneficiaries

When the intention of contracting parties is that their contract will provide a benefit to a third party, the third party acquires rights under the contract as a **third-party beneficiary.**

If one party intends to give the other's promised performance as a gift to a third party, the third party is called a *donee beneficiary.* Donee beneficiaries become entitled under law to the promised performance. They have the same right to enforcement as an original party to the contract. The original promisee only has the right to enforce performance for the benefit of the donee beneficiary.

### Example

As a goodwill gesture, a bank decides to supply a neighborhood youth club with uniforms for its softball team. The bank contracts with a manufacturer to make 20 gray uniforms in a range of sizes, each with the team's name sewn in orange letters on the back. When the uniforms are delivered, there are only nine of them, all white, all the same size, and with the team's name misspelled. As donee beneficiary of the contract, the youth club has the right to sue the manufacturer for the money the bank paid. Alternatively, the club can enforce the contract as written and require the manufacturer to supply what was ordered.

When a person owes a debt and enters into a contract requiring another person to pay that debt, the person to whom the debt must be paid is called a *third-party creditor beneficiary.* A creditor beneficiary is entitled to seek payment from both the promisor on the contract and the original debtor, but can collect from only one of them.

## INTERPRETING CONTRACTS

The person who prepares a written contract tries to put the intentions of the contracting parties into words that express their entire agreement. The hope is that the words and phrases used will have the same meaning to all the parties and that each party will understand in the same way the rights and obligations under the contract. Unfortunately, that goal is not always met. After contracts are signed, conflicts often arise about what the written contract means and what the parties actually intended. The law has developed certain guidelines for lawyers, judges, and others who must interpret contracts to discover the true intentions of the parties. These guidelines are called the primary and secondary rules of contract interpretation.

### Primary Rule of Interpretation

Under the **primary rule of interpretation,** the words in a contract must be given their plain and usual meaning. This rule has three exceptions:

- Technical words, called *terms of art,* must be given their technical meaning.
- The usual meaning of words may vary according to their usage within the particular trade or locality.
- Words may not be given their plain meaning if doing so would contradict the intentions of the parties.

#### Example

A bank contracts to have wall-to-wall carpeting installed in the lobby. The contract as drafted by the contractor refers to carpeting for the ground floor. Under its plain meaning, the ground floor would include several areas where the bank never intended to install carpeting. If the term causes a dispute, a court will interpret the term according to the actual intention (the lobby), rather than its plain meaning (the entire first floor).

To be interpreted in a way that will carry out the intentions of the parties, the contract must be analyzed as a whole. Individual documents or clauses that together make up a contract should be read together. If the words themselves do not fully reveal the parties' intentions, circumstances leading up to the contract may be considered to shed light on the matter.

### Secondary Rules of Interpretation

If the meaning of the contract remains unclear after the primary rule of interpretation has been applied, the **secondary rules of interpretation** take effect. The secondary rules of interpretation are

- An interpretation that gives a reasonable meaning to all or the main provisions of the contract is preferred.
- A specific clause will prevail over a conflicting general clause.
- An interpretation that makes a contract valid and reasonable will be preferred over an interpretation that makes the contract unenforceable or harsh.
- Ambiguous language will be interpreted against the drafter of the contract.
- If a conflict exists between handwritten or typed provisions and provisions printed on a form, the handwritten or typed provisions will prevail.
- Related writings may be interpreted together.

### Parol Evidence Rule

When a contract is put in writing, the written document becomes the sole source of proof of the parties' intentions. The rules of interpretation apply only to the written document, which represents the parties' final agreement after the bargaining and negotiations have taken place. Courts do not want to hear details about the bargaining process when they analyze evidence of what the parties intended. Once a contract has been written and signed, details about earlier negotiations are regarded as irrelevant to the final agreement. Such evidence from outside the contract is called *parol evidence.*

The **parol evidence rule,** which has been incorporated in the laws of many states, developed under the common law. This rule holds that once parties have entered into a written contract, that contract is deemed to constitute a complete statement of their agreement and no evidence of earlier understandings or negotiations between the parties can be used to contradict or vary the terms of the written contract.

The parol evidence rule seeks only to prevent terms of the written contract from being contradicted or varied after the fact. Parol evidence can be introduced, however, to show a defect in the formation of the contract. For example, if the contract was induced by fraud or mistake, if it is illegal, or if a party lacks legal capacity, parol evidence can be offered as proof. Additionally, parol evidence can be used to explain ambiguous terms in a contract.

---

**Critical Terms**

*Breach*  The unexcused failure to perform an action promised in a contract.

*Remedy*  A legal means to enforce a right or correct a wrong.

---

## ENFORCING CONTRACTS

The parties perform their contract by doing exactly what they promised to do. The unexcused failure of a party to perform as promised is a **breach of contract.** If a contract is breached, the wronged party has a right to go to court and seek a remedy. The remedy may be either a court order requiring the other party to perform as promised or a judgment entitling the wronged party to payment *(damages)* as compensation for the breach.

Not every situation involving nonperformance is a breach. A party has breached a contract only if the failure to perform is without excuse and thus wrongful. Moreover, if a party has performed most—but not all—of the terms of the contract (that is, has rendered **substantial performance),** then the courts recognize that in some cases it would be unjust to hold that the contract has been breached by the lack of complete performance. Before a party's failure to perform can be considered a breach, the court must first determine if there are circumstances that excuse the nonperformance or require one party to accept the other's incomplete but substantial performance.

## Excuses for Nonperformance

A party is excused from the duty to perform a contract only for certain reasons or in certain circumstances. The duty to perform is so absolute in contracts that the promisor is required to seek any and all means to ensure the promised performance. Labor problems, increased costs, nonfunctioning equipment, personal problems, lack of time, even death is insufficient to override the other party's legal right to the promised performance or payment for the breach.

Nevertheless, some excuses will prevail over the other party's right to performance. If found by the court to exist, the excuses will discharge the nonperforming party's duty and release the party from the obligation to pay damages. Valid excuses for not performing as promised include legal impossibility, impracticability, frustration of purpose, and failure of a contract condition.

### Legal Impossibility

Legal impossibility of performance is different from personal impossibility. Legal impossibility in effect means "it cannot be done," whereas personal impossibility means "I cannot do it." Personal inability to perform is often a reason why contract duties are delegated to third parties. However, if performance is legally impossible, then the party's duty is discharged. Legal impossibility generally involves one of three situations: 1) the death or incapacity of a party necessary to the contract, 2) a new law that makes performance of the contract illegal, or 3) the destruction of something essential to the performance of the contract.

### Death or Incapacity of Necessary Party

A necessary party is one whose skill or particular knowledge is considered to be unique and is the essence of the contract. A third-party beneficiary might also be a necessary party if specifically designated in the contract as being the only intended beneficiary of the agreement. For example, if a man hires a tutor to teach his son Chinese, the death or incapacity of either the tutor or the son makes enforcement by the other party legally impossible.

### Illegality

Contract law does not require a person to perform illegal acts. If the parties contract to do something that becomes illegal under a subsequently enacted law, the parties are excused from their duties to perform. This type of impossibility is called *supervening illegality*.

### Destruction of Subject or Means of Performance

Destruction of an item that is the subject of the contract, or destruction of a means or source of performance that is specifically designated as such in the contract, will serve to discharge the promisor from the duty to perform.

#### Example

A tour group contracts for a bus and driver to take the group 17 miles up a mountain's only road so that they can enjoy the view at the top of the mountain. On the day of the trip, the group learns that a heavy rainfall the night before has damaged the road so that it is no longer passable. The local authorities have ordered the road closed. Because an essential means of performance designated in the contract has been destroyed, neither party is obligated to perform. The group is not required to pay for the driver's time, and the driver has no obligation to somehow get the group to the mountaintop.

### Impracticability

Under common law and the UCC, impracticability excuses nonperformance. Impracticability exists where a party is unable to perform because of unforeseen circumstances beyond the party's control, such as war or natural disasters. Impracticability also exists when, because of unforeseen events, a party's costs to perform become grossly increased beyond what either party anticipated when the contract was made. Increased costs that could or should have been anticipated, or costs that are more than the contract price but not significantly more, are not valid excuses for failure to perform a contract.

### Frustration of Purpose

Frustration of purpose will discharge contract duties. Under this doctrine, although the party is able to perform, the duty is discharged because something happens that the parties had no way of anticipating when they made the contract and that destroys the value or purpose of the contract.

### Failure of Condition

Parties often include provisions in their contracts that suspend a party's duty to perform if certain events do or do not occur. These provisions often are referred to as *conditions*.

### Example

A bank agrees to lend a man $5,000 to buy a car on condition that the car passes state safety and emissions inspections. Should the car fail inspection, the bank does not have to perform the contract.

Conditions may be created expressly or by implication. A condition that is described as such in the contract is called an *express* condition. *Implied* conditions can be established indirectly. For example, an agreement that calls for payment to be automatically debited from a customer's account creates an implied condition that the customer must open and maintain an account at the bank.

## Substantial Performance

Failure to perform a contract completely may be excused under the doctrine of **substantial performance,** which is designed to protect a party against loss of all rights and benefits under the contract. Substantial performance means that the major purpose of the contract has been achieved and the failure to perform involves only technical or unimportant omissions or defects.

### Example

A builder, under contract to build a house for $100,000, has completed the project except for some small defects in the plastering. These can be fixed for about $1,500. The builder does not have time to correct these defects because the time for performance has expired. The owner of the house refuses to pay on the contract because the clause regarding plastering has been breached. Even though the builder has not fully performed, thus breaching the contract, a court would require the owner to accept the house and pay full price minus a money allowance of $1,500 to fix the defects.

The doctrine of substantial performance may not excuse failure to perform completely if the failure is willful or negligent.

## REMEDIES FOR BREACH OF CONTRACT

When a contract is breached, the wronged party is entitled to be put in as favorable an economic position as the party would have enjoyed had the contract been performed. Courts provide this remedy by ordering the breaching party either to perform the contract or to pay compensation (damages) for the breach.

### Specific Performance

**Specific performance** is a doctrine that allows a court to compel the breaching party to perform specific terms of the contract. Courts often consider specific performance an impractical remedy for breach of contract because of the difficulty of actually forcing a party to perform contract obligations. The assumption is that if a party is forced to perform on a contract, the resulting product or service might well be below acceptable standards, and the wronged party could end up in a worse situation than existed before the contract was made. Only when money damages are inadequate compensation for the breach will the courts order specific performance as a remedy.

Contracts promising to sell land and real estate are considered to be in this category and are generally enforceable by specific performance.

### Damages

Statutes and case law generally divide **damages** into six categories: compensatory, consequential (special), punitive (exemplary), incidental, nominal, and liquidated. The UCC also provides for these damages (except for nominal damages) for the various types of breaches of contracts for the sale of goods.

## Compensatory Damages

Compensatory damages place the wronged party in the same economic position the party would be in had the breach not occurred. Compensatory damages usually are computed by measuring the difference between the value of the promised performance and the cost to the wronged party for substitute performance.

### Example

A farmer contracts to sell and deliver 500 bushels of potatoes to a restaurant for $1,200. The restaurant refuses to accept delivery, breaching the contract. If the farmer sues for damages, he is entitled to the difference between the contract price and the market price at which the potatoes can be sold to someone else. If the potatoes can be sold for $1,000, the farmer will be entitled to $200 in compensatory damages, thus placing the farmer in the same economic position he would have been in had the breach not occurred.

## Consequential or Special Damages

Loss of employment, loss of business credit, loss of customers, or other types of unusual losses that result indirectly from a breach of contract may be compensated with special or consequential damages. These are recoverable along with compensatory damages if the party seeking the damages can prove that the unusual loss was foreseeable when the contract was made.

### Example

A bank gives a loan applicant a commitment letter contracting to lend her $40,000 to purchase a piece of property on which she has an option to buy. In her application, she discloses that she is buying the property for resale to someone who has offered her $55,000 for it. Subsequently, the bank wrongfully breaches its commitment and refuses to lend the money. If the applicant can demonstrate to a court that her option to buy fell through because the bank failed to lend her the $40,000, she can receive $15,000 in consequential damages. This was her expected profit on the transaction, which the bank was aware of when it breached the contract.

## Punitive or Exemplary Damages

Punitive or exemplary damages are allowed in addition to compensatory damages as a way to punish the breaching party. Punitive damages seldom are awarded in commercial contract cases but may sometimes be awarded in certain noncommercial cases involving intentional wrongs. For example, if a bank wrongfully withheld a consumer's funds in a deposit account when the bank was aware that the consumer should have had access to the money, the bank might be subject to punitive damages.

## Incidental Damages

Incidental damages include expenses the nonbreaching party had to pay as a result of the breach of contract.

### Example

A farmer agrees to sell 500 bushels of potatoes to a restaurant, which refuses delivery. As a result, the farmer is forced to store the potatoes and hire an agent to resell them. In his action against the restaurant for breach of contract, the farmer will be entitled to compensatory damages and also to damages covering the incidental expenses caused by the breach. These include the storage costs, the agent's fee, and court costs.

## Nominal Damages

Every breach of contract entitles the wronged party to damages. As result of this principle, the wronged party is permitted nominal damages in cases where no actual financial loss is suffered or the amount is too indefinite for proof. Nominal damages are a token amount (perhaps a few dollars) given to show the world that the party—although unable to demonstrate financial loss—is correct in saying an interest was wrongfully invaded.

### Liquidated Damages

Parties to a contract often wish to avoid the difficulties and uncertainties that come with determining damages. Accordingly, they will agree in advance on what the damages will be in case of breach. Amounts specified under such an agreement are called *liquidated damages*. A liquidated damages clause in a contract is enforceable if the amount is reasonable.

#### Example

A hotel has large conference and banquet rooms and a staff that works exclusively on events staged in these rooms, which must be booked more than a year in advance. The hotel's booking contract includes a liquidated damages clause that applies when parties fail to cancel by a certain time (for example, when a wedding is called off after booking a large room, staff, or food).

### Mitigation of Damages

Once a contract has been breached, the nonbreaching party cannot just stand by without at least trying to keep damages to a minimum. In fact, the party is required by law to **mitigate damages.** That is, the nonbreaching party is required to do all that is reasonable to ensure that the amount of damages will be as low as possible. This doctrine was not developed to favor breaching parties but rather to prevent unnecessary economic waste. If the nonbreaching party does nothing to mitigate damages, the court will not award any damages that could have been avoided.

#### Example

A bank leases a building in a small shopping mall, which it uses as a branch office. With six months remaining on the lease, the bank vacates the building. The management of the mall takes no action to rent the building after the bank moves out. Several prospective tenants inquire about renting, but none is willing to pay as much as the bank had been paying. The mall wants to rent at that same rate, and so has no tenant at all for the six months. Because the mall has made no attempt to lessen the damages (the value of six months' rent), the mall will not be entitled to that amount if it sues the bank.

### Quasi Contract

The doctrine of **quasi contract** grants a contractual remedy in cases where no actual contract exists. In quasi contract a legal obligation is imposed on someone who receives a benefit without having promised to pay, but who is unjustly enriched if allowed to keep the benefit without paying. This doctrine developed out of a need to provide a remedy in such situations of unjust enrichment.

Not every enrichment is unjust. Similarly, not every unfair detriment to one party results in enrichment of another. Only where the two components come together may relief be ordered under quasi contract.

#### Example

A painter contracts to paint a house while the homeowner goes away for five days. By mistake, he paints the house next door, at which no one is home for the entire time he works. In this situation, the painter cannot expect to be paid for his efforts. Even though the neighbor has been enriched by the new paint job, the enrichment is not unjust because the neighbor never requested that the house be painted and knew nothing about the mistake at the time it was being made. Unjust enrichment would be found, however, if the neighbor had been home when the painter was working and had stood by without saying anything until the job was done.

### Situations Giving Rise to Quasi-Contractual Relief

Common situations involving unjust enrichment and allowing relief under the doctrine of quasi contract include

- contracts on which advance payment has been made but performance becomes impossible or unenforceable
- situations in which benefits have been given during an emergency
- situations involving mutual mistakes of fact, with benefits given unintentionally

### Impossibility or Unenforceability of Performance

Legal impossibility is a valid excuse for nonperformance of a contract. If advance payment has been made for performance that becomes impossible, that payment can be recovered under quasi contract.

Contracts in which performance is unenforceable usually arise in situations where a law (the Statute of Frauds, for example) provides the promisor with an excuse for nonperformance. The promisee can recover under quasi contract any benefits given to the promisor in connection with the contract.

### Benefits Given in Emergency

When a person receives a benefit during an emergency—for example, a doctor's volunteered care at the scene of a traffic accident—the law is divided as to whether the person giving the benefit may demand payment for it. Some courts presume that the person acting as a volunteer gives the benefit gratuitously. Under this presumption, any enrichment of the other party cannot be characterized as unjust, and no quasi-contractual relief is possible. Generally, if benefits are provided during an emergency, the particular circumstances involved will determine whether a quasi-contractual relationship came into effect.

### Mutual Mistakes of Fact

When parties negotiate an agreement that is prevented from becoming a contract because of a mutual mistake of fact, anything either one has given the other can be recovered in quasi contract. For example, if parties agree on the sale of an animal that, unknown to either party, has already died, a mutual mistake exists as to the existence of the subject matter of the contract. Any money that has changed hands can be recovered in quasi contract.

Mutual mistakes of fact also occur when money is paid or services rendered to the wrong person, or when too much money is paid mistakenly in a transaction. In these cases, the error can be remedied under quasi contract.

## CONCLUSION

Contract law encompasses virtually all private legal transactions involving the exchange of items of value. A contract can be as simple as a deposit account agreement between a bank and an individual customer or as complex as a multimillion-dollar merger agreement between giant corporations. Whether simple or complex, all contracts are formed, performed, or breached according to the same basic legal principles.

Parties to any contract must have the legal capacity to enter into the contract, their objective in doing so must be legal, they must mutually assent to the contract, and consideration must be given. Once a contract has been negotiated, the Statute of Frauds may require it to be in writing.

When a contract is in writing, the parol evidence rule provides certainty by binding the parties to their final written document. Under this rule, the parties may not propose contradictory understandings of negotiations that occurred before the contract was put in writing and signed. Although the parol evidence rule eliminates reference to prior negotiations when interpreting a written contract, it does not eliminate the need to interpret the actual words of the contract.

When a contract is performed fully according to its terms, problems generally do not arise. Unfortunately, not all contracts are so performed and the law has developed specific rules to define adequate and inadequate performance. When a contract has not been adequately performed, the wronged party is entitled to damages.

## QUESTIONS FOR REVIEW AND DISCUSSION

1. If a party is legally disabled but the disability is not outwardly manifested, will the party be excused from performing the contract?
2. Why is mutual assent a critical element of a contract?
3. If, after entering into a contract, a party indicates that he or she was under the influence of drugs, is the party bound to the contract?
4. If a person obviously agreed to pay too much for a product or service, will the law excuse payment?
5. Can an oral contract for the sale of land be enforced? Explain your answer.
6. What are the different types of third-party rights and obligations?
7. What does the term *delegation of duties* mean? Give an example.
8. What does the term *parol evidence* mean? Describe the parol evidence rule.
9. Under what circumstances would a court likely award punitive damages?
10. What are two types of damages and why would a court award them?
11. What is the doctrine of specific performance and why is it seldom invoked?
12. Why does a plaintiff have the duty to mitigate damages?

## LEARNING ACTIVITIES FOR CHAPTER 6

### Multiple Choice

Choose the best answer for each question.

1. A valid contract:
   a. specifies rights and duties to which the parties are legally committed
   b. is like a private law
   c. may be either written or oral
   d. all of the above

2. The mutual assent element of contracts is called:
   a. common ground
   b. common law
   c. meeting of the minds
   d. bilateral understanding

3. A contract that requires one person to perform an act in return for another person's promise to pay when the act is complete is called:
   a. a unilateral contract
   b. a bilateral contract
   c. mutual assent
   d. a gratuitous promise

4. Which of the following persons has the legal capacity to enter into a contractual relationship?
   a. a minor
   b. a senior citizen
   c. a mentally incapacitated person
   d. a person who is temporarily intoxicated

5. Types of contracts involving promises that cannot be enforced unless they are in writing are identified by:

   a. the Uniform Commercial Code
   b. state laws
   c. the statute of limitations
   d. the Statute of Frauds

6. A promise made with no request for something in return is:

   a. a contract
   b. a voidable contract
   c. a gratuitous promise
   d. an unenforceable contract

7. A contract with a minor is:

   a. void
   b. voidable
   c. enforceable
   d. against public policy

8. If one party agrees to give up a right that he or she can legally exercise, this is called:

   a. consideration
   b. legal detriment
   c. inadequate consideration
   d. void consideration

9. The collection of interest in an amount greater than permitted by statute is known as:

   a. petty theft
   b. gratuitous consideration
   c. usury
   d. fraud

10. Which of the following agreements is unenforceable because it is harmful to the administration of justice?

    a. an agreement that induces a witness to give false testimony
    b. an agreement to pay elected officials for their votes
    c. a wagering agreement
    d. an agreement in unreasonable restraint of trade

11. Transfer of contract obligations is:

    a. called *assignment*
    b. called *delegation*
    c. called *exchange of duties*
    d. legal but inadvisable

12. If one party intends to give the other's promised performance as a gift to a third party, the third party is called:

    a. a third-party creditor beneficiary
    b. the assignor
    c. the assignee
    d. a donee beneficiary

13. The primary rules of interpretation hold that:

    a. the words written in a contract must be given their plain and usual meaning
    b. a specific clause will prevail over a conflicting general cause
    c. ambiguous language will be interpreted against the drafter of the contract
    d. all of the above

14. The parol evidence rule holds that:

    a. only written contracts are valid
    b. ambiguous language is not permitted in written contracts
    c. the rules of interpretation apply only to oral contracts
    d. no evidence of earlier understandings can be used to vary the terms of a written contract

15. Which of the following situations constitutes a breach of contract?

    a. nonperformance due to illegality
    b. nonperformance due to nonfunctioning equipment
    c. nonperformance due to legal impossibility
    d. nonperformance due to impracticability

16. To which of the following types of contracts would the doctrine of specific performance most likely be applied?

    a. a contract for personal services
    b. a contract for services as a laborer
    c. a contract to sell land
    d. a contract involving a third-party beneficiary

17. Parol evidence can be offered as proof in which of the following cases?

    a. the contract was illegal
    b. one party to the contract lacks legal capacity
    c. the contract contains ambiguous terms
    d. all of the above

18. Damages that are computed by measuring the difference between the value of the promised performance and the cost to the wronged party for substitute performance are called:

    a. compensatory damages
    b. liquidated damages
    c. consequential damages
    d. punitive damages

19. Damages that are meant to punish the breaching party are called:

    a. compensatory damages
    b. liquidated damages
    c. nominal damages
    d. punitive damages

20. Damages that are granted because of special or unusual circumstances are called:

    a. compensatory damages
    b. incidental damages
    c. consequential damages
    d. punitive damages

**True/False**

Indicate whether each of the following statements is true or false.

T F 1. The remedy for a failed contract usually is money damages.

T F 2. Mutual assent is all that is needed to form a valid contract.

T F 3. Adequacy of consideration concerns whether the price paid as consideration in a contract is fair in terms of the marketplace.

T F 4. Minors are legally barred from entering into contractual agreements.

T F 5. Contracts that cannot be performed within one year are subject to the Statute of Frauds.

T F 6. A contract with a minor for necessities usually is enforceable.

T F 7. The right to receive payment usually is an assignable right.

T F 8. A promisor who delegated contractual duties is released from legal responsibility for performing those duties.

T F 9. Legal impossibility is a valid excuse for not performing as promised in a contract.

T F 10. Under contract law, a person cannot be required to perform an illegal act.

T F 11. Failure to perform a contract completely may be excused under the doctrine of substantial performance.

T F 12. Every breach of contract entitles the wronged party to damages.

T F 13. The duty to perform is so absolute in contracts that virtually every situation involving nonperformance is a breach of contract.

# 7

---

# PROPERTY

## LEARNING OBJECTIVES

After studying this chapter, you should be able to

- distinguish between real and personal property and discuss various ways that property can be transferred or obtained
- define *joint tenancy* and *tenancy in common* and explain the rights of the parties in these forms of multiple ownership
- explain types of property interests, including *possessory interest,* that give owners the right to possess and use property security interests and allow lenders to place liens on property to guarantee payment
- discuss the importance of proper and timely recording of real property interests
- define *bailment* and discuss a bank's role as the bailee in its safe deposit box services
- define and use the legal and banking terms that appear in bold in the chapter text

## INTRODUCTION

Most people think of property as something a person owns. In a legal sense, however, there is more to the definition. Property includes the rights and interests that accompany the ownership. For example, if a man owns a house, the house is his property. But suppose the man is renting the house? In that case the man does not own the house, but he does have a property interest in it.

Property interests define what legal rights a person has with respect to any property. The two most important rights with respect to property are the right to *possess* the property and the right to *use* it. Property interests are important to banks because banks are involved in holding their customers' property. Funds in deposit accounts and the contents of safe deposit boxes are property owned by the bank's customers. In addition, banks obtain an interest in property when they take security interests in or place liens against the property of their borrowers.

This chapter discusses how property is acquired. It also addresses how multiple owners with varying rights can together own property. As noted above, property owners can have differing rights to possess and use property. These rights are covered in detail, as are the rights of creditors to place liens on property to ensure repayment. The chapter also stresses the importance of proper and timely recording of interests in real property. The chapter concludes with a brief discussion of bailments, which are of particular interest to banks in their offering of safe deposit services to customers.

## REAL PROPERTY AND PERSONAL PROPERTY

All property can be classified as either real or personal. **Real property** consists of land and anything attached to land such as buildings, trees, or growing plants. **Personal property** is anything that is not real property. Personal property includes tangible and movable objects as well as intangible rights, such as those represented by a stock certificate or a patent.

Many objects can be either real or personal property, depending on their use. Consider trees. When trees are growing on real property, they are attached to it and are considered real property. After the trees are cut down and are no longer attached to the land, they become personal property. When the trees are milled into lumber and delivered to a vacant lot as building material, they still are personal property. But when the lumber is used to construct a building that is fixed on the lot, the lumber becomes real property. When the building is torn down and is no longer attached to the land, its various parts (including lumber) are transformed back into personal property.

---

### Critical Terms

*Deed* A legal document in which the owner of real property transfers it to another person.

*Adverse Possession* Gaining possession of property by openly taking possession of and control over the property for a specified number of years and in a manner that is adverse to the interests of the true owner.

---

## ACQUIRING OWNERSHIP

The most common way to acquire ownership of property is by transfer from the existing owner. Other means of acquiring ownership include producing new property, taking possession of existing property, and finding lost property.

### Transfer From Existing Owner

Ownership of property may be acquired from the existing owner by sale or by gift. If the property is a type that requires title documentation, such as real property or some types of personal property such as automobiles or corporate stocks, the title documents will be part of the sale or gift transaction.

Whether the transfer is by sale or gift, a **deed** must be included in transfers involving real property. A deed is a document that the owner of the real property must sign and give to the new owner as evidence that the transfer of ownership has actually occurred. In the deed, the owner describes the property and specifies the interest that is being transferred to the new owner. When the new owner receives the deed, the transfer of ownership is accomplished.

A bank that takes real property as collateral can only receive a lien from the rightful owner. Therefore, a bank often will require a legal opinion or title insurance policy to protect itself against the possibility that someone other than the true owner of the property is giving the lien. The title company or attorney researches the chain of title (the previous owners and how each transferred their interest to the next person in the chain) to make sure that the current owner is the one who is giving a lien to the bank.

### Gifts

A **gift** is a voluntary transfer of ownership by the property owner to someone else, without any payment or other consideration given in return. The owner who gives the gift is known as the **donor,** while the recipient of the gift is the **donee.** For a gift to be effective, three requirements must be met: 1) delivery of the property, 2) intent, and 3) acceptance.

First, the property must be delivered (or given) to the donee. If the gift is real estate or some other item that cannot be handed over physically to the donee, a document that is representative or symbolic of the property may be delivered instead. A deed or title, a savings account passbook, and keys to a safe deposit box that contains the actual gift all are items that can represent a gift.

Second, the donor must intend, upon delivery of the property, to give up ownership and transfer it completely to the donee. This intent can be expressed with words such as, "I want you to have this," or "This is for you." Statements such as, "Keep this for me while I'm away," or "Use this until you can get your own" do not express intent to give something as a gift and therefore do not transfer ownership. In addition, gifts given because the donor believes his or her death is imminent are considered conditional and may be revoked if the donor does not die of the cause expected, if the donee predeceases the donor, or if the donor revokes the gift.

The third necessary element of transfer of ownership by gift is acceptance by the donee. Once the donee has accepted the gift, ownership has been transferred—the donor cannot then change his or her mind and get the property back. Although acceptance of a gift is usually a certainty, in some situations a person might not want to receive a donation of property. Sometimes tax liabilities or environmental concerns will deter potential donees from accepting property offered as gifts. Ownership cannot be forced on anyone. Anyone can refuse a gift and thereby avoid ownership.

### Will or Inheritance

A will is a written declaration of a person's wishes regarding transfer of real or personal property after death. An effective will describes the property, states who is to receive it, and is signed by the owner. Although a will declares a person's intent to transfer ownership of property, the actual transfer of ownership does not occur until the owner dies. A will may exist for a long time before this event occurs. The owner may transfer ownership of any of the mentioned property after writing the will—in which case the will has no effect with respect to the property that has already been transferred. Executors, including banks in some cases, will be responsible to determine whether any property has been transferred before the decedent's death.

When an owner dies without a will, property ownership is transferred by operation of law to the owner's heirs. This process is called **intestate succession.** If no will exists, state law determines a person's heirs. Often these heirs turn out to be the same people who would have been the beneficiaries of a will had the decedent written one. In general, the deceased's spouse and children take the property, in proportions established by state law, with all children sharing equally. If there is no spouse or children, the property goes to the grandchildren—or, if there are no grandchildren, to siblings or parents of the decedent. If the decedent leaves no immediate family, his or her property goes to other relatives, depending on who is living and who has children living. If a decedent has no heirs at all, the property is left to the state in a process called **escheat.**

## Accession: Producing or Creating Property

Another way to obtain ownership of property is through accession. Accession is the process of creating property. A person who creates or produces property becomes its owner. If someone owns a bare piece of land and plants trees and crops or builds a house on it, that person has improved the real property by doing so. The addition to the property is called an *accession.* The owner of the bare land becomes the owner of the accession also. The same situation holds with personal property. If a person makes furniture in a workshop, owns a cow that produces milk, or owns a dog that produces a litter of puppies, the furniture, milk, or puppies (the newly created property) belongs to that person.

An exception to this rule involves property considered a work for hire. A person who creates or produces property as a work for hire—that is, as the product or byproduct of his or her employment by someone else—does not own the property.

The employer owns it. For example, a scientist who invents a device in the course of his or her employment at a software company will not own the device even though he or she created it. The software company owns the device because it was a work for hire.

## Taking Possession of Unowned Property

Abandoned property is the best example of unowned existing property. Abandoned property is property in which the owner has completely, voluntarily, and intentionally given up all rights and interests in the property. To become the owner of abandoned property a person must take possession with the intent of keeping it. Both personal and real property can be abandoned. It is easier to recognize abandoned personal property, however, because it is often left in such a way that makes it clear that no one has possession or control.

Some states have unclaimed-property laws declaring that possession, but not ownership, of abandoned property goes to the state until the owner or an heir reclaims it. Bank accounts that have had no activity for a prolonged time are an example of property in this category. These accounts are considered dormant and most states require that, after a specified period of time, the funds they contain be remitted to the state. Usually the state will publish a list of accounts (and other property) that has become dormant so that the true owner may reclaim it.

## Finding Lost Property

Personal property is lost when the owner cannot find it. The owner does not intend to give up possession or control of the property. Anyone who finds lost personal property and takes possession can assume ownership if the person who lost it is unknown and cannot be determined. This ownership is considered to be limited rather than absolute because if the true owner is able to locate the property, the finder must give it back. Except for that limitation, the finder becomes the property owner with valid rights against everyone but the true owner.

## Adverse Possession of Real Property

A person may acquire ownership of real property, including real property that appears to have been abandoned, by taking possession (using or living on the property) and acting as an owner (paying taxes, putting up fences, making improvements) for a certain number of years as set by state law. Usually the number of years required to adversely possess property is quite long—often 5 to 20 years. If these actions—known as **adverse possession**—are done openly, are obvious to everyone, and continue without interruption for the required number of years, and if the true owner never asserts a claim against the possessor for the entire time, the possessor acquires ownership and the owner loses it.

## MULTIPLE OWNERSHIP

Property can be owned by more than one person at the same time. When two or more persons own property together, their ownership is either *joint* or *in common*. Documents of ownership such as deeds, trust instruments, stock certificates, and many bank records use those terms, often with the word *tenant* attached, describing co-owners as **joint tenants** or **tenants in common.**

The difference between these two types of multiple ownership is the way the property passes upon the death of one of the owners. A joint tenant's ownership share disappears at death, leaving the surviving joint tenant as sole owner of the property. The right of a surviving joint tenant to keep the entire property upon the death of the other joint tenant is called the *right of survivorship*. In contrast, tenants in common each own a fixed fraction of the property so their shares do not disappear at death. The property left by a tenant in

common can be willed to another person. If the tenant in common dies without a will, the share goes to his or her heirs.

---

**Critical Terms**

*Joint Tenancy* Undivided ownership of a piece of property by two or more people, each of whom has the same degree of ownership in the property. The ownership cannot be divided, so after the death of an owner the other owners continue to own the property and to have the right to use it.

*Tenancy in Common* Common ownership of a piece of property by two or more people, each of whom owns a specified interest in the property. Each owner can leave his or her interest in the property to someone else when he or she dies.

---

While living, a joint tenant can transfer his or her ownership share by sale or gift. However, the joint tenant's right of survivorship cannot be transferred. In most states, a joint tenant's transfer of his or her share by sale or gift immediately converts the joint tenancy to a tenancy in common. That is, once the transfer occurs, the person who acquires the joint tenant's share becomes a tenant in common with the other co-owner(s), with no right of survivorship. A joint tenant's attempt to transfer the share by will has no effect, as the share will cease to exist at the moment of the joint tenant's death.

A form of joint tenancy called **tenancy by the entirety** always involves a husband and wife. Neither spouse in a tenancy by the entirety has the right to transfer his or her share except with the agreement of the other. Both spouses must join in a deed or other conveyance for the transfer to be effective. In many states, tenancy by the entirety has been abolished in favor of the husband and wife holding their property simply as joint tenants.

Banks need to be sure that the owners of deposit accounts designate how they hold the account so that upon the death of one account holder the bank knows the ownership status of the funds remaining in the account.

### Examples

- Juan and Nancy Hernandez open a joint checking account as *Juan or Nancy Hernandez, Joint Tenants.* If Juan dies, the money in the account reverts to Nancy. None of the funds go to Juan's heirs.

- Juan and Nancy Hernandez open a joint checking account as *Juan or Nancy Hernandez, Tenants in Common.* The deposit agreement shows that each one has a 50 percent interest in the funds in the account. If Juan dies, half of the funds in the account will be transferred according to the terms of his will. Nancy will remain the owner of the other half.

## PROPERTY INTERESTS

A **property interest** is a legal right to property. Property interests vary in the quality of rights they bestow on the owner. One type of property interest gives complete ownership of real property along with the ability to sell or dispose of it. Other types of property interests give the owner the right to use the property in specific ways but not the right to sell the property.

Multiple interests can exist in the same piece of property. For example, consider a piece of real property. One person might own the surface and have the right to use it or sell it. Another person might own the mineral rights to the same piece of property and have the right to extract minerals from the property. Still another person might have an *easement* interest in the property and have access to the property for a specific use. Utility companies often have easements to property in order to string wires for electrical services, lay pipe for natural gas or bury cable for telephone service.

A bank can have a lien only on the property interest specifically owned by the borrower. If the borrower has only a mineral interest in the property, the only lien that borrower can give to a financial interest is a lien on the mineral interest.

## Possession and Use

Several levels of property interests allow owners to possess and use real property in various ways. These property interests include

- fee interests
- life estates
- leaseholds

### Fee Interests

When an owner has the right to possess and use real property, the interest is called a **freehold.** Freehold means that no other person has superior rights in the property and there is no fixed or definite time at which the interest must come to an end. The owner's interest exists free of anyone else's right to interfere with it.

The highest freehold interest is called a **fee** (or sometimes *fee simple*). A fee interest in real property can last as long as the land itself. The fee interest passes from one generation to the next in a family forever, as long as no one sells the ownership.

### Life Estates

A lower level of interest in real property is the **life estate.** A life estate is created when the fee owner transfers property by deed or by will, giving the new owner the right to possess the property for the duration of his or her life. The person with the life estate is called a **life tenant** and has all the rights of the fee owner except the right to sell the property or pass it on to his or her heirs. As soon as the life tenant dies, the estate ends and the owner of the fee reacquires all rights to possession. This right to regain the property is called a *remainder interest.*

If the life tenant has damaged or destroyed the property, his or her estate may have to pay damages to the fee owner.

### Example

Mr. Jones wants to let his parents live in his condominium with all rights of ownership until their deaths. He does not, however, want the condominium to become part of his parents' estate when they die. To ensure that the condominium will either come back to him (if he is still alive) or to his children, Mr. Jones transfers the property by deed as a life estate. His parents have full possession of the condominium during their lifetime but cannot sell it or transfer it in their wills.

Suppose Mr. Jones predeceases his parents and his daughter wants to move into the condominium. The daughter has no right to do so as long as her grandparents are alive. She has inherited the remainder interest from her father, Mr. Jones, which gives her the right to possess the property only after the life estate is ended.

### Leaseholds

The next level of property interest is a **leasehold.** A **lease** is a contract in which the fee owner of the property grants to another party the right to possess and use the property for a specified time in return for payment. A property owner who grants the right to possess and use the property through a lease is is called a *lessor.* The party who gains the right to possess the property under a lease is called the *lessee.* The lessor owns the property but does not have the right to use or possess it during the time the lease is in effect. The lessee has a leasehold interest in the property.

Unlike a fee interest, a leasehold only provides the lessee with rights to the property for fixed time period—the duration of the lease. A leasehold does not convey ownership interest. Generally, lessees have the right to use the property just like a fee interest owner, except that they cannot damage or destroy the property. Lessees cannot transfer the ownership of the property, although they may have the right to transfer their leasehold interest.

Some leases, like commercial leases, are created for long time periods (sometimes in excess of 75 years) while others, like apartment leases, are for much shorter terms.

## Other Property Interests

Nonpossessory rights to use property also are transferable. For example, an owner might give mineral rights to a company to come onto the land to take and use its mineral products but not to possess the surface. Easements, or rights to access, are another type of nonpossessory property interest. An easement allows its owner to cross over a portion of another person's property for a specific purpose, such as to gain access to adjacent property if the owner has no other way to get there.

Owners of personal property also can grant the use of the property without possession. Income from corporate stock, for example, can be transferred to someone else while the owner retains ownership of the stock.

---

### Critical Terms

*Mortgage* A lien placed on real property.

*Lien* A legal claim against a piece of property to be used to obtain repayment if a debt is not paid as promised.

*Foreclosure* The exercise of a lienholder's rights upon the default by the landowner, whereby the lienholder takes possession of the real property pledged as collateral for a loan.

---

## SECURITY INTERESTS

Security interests in property serve to guarantee payment of a property owner's financial obligations, such as the obligation to repay a loan or to complete payments on a purchase. In return for a loan or extension of credit, lenders often require that the borrower pledge an interest in the borrower's property to secure the debt. If the borrower fails to pay a financial obligation when due, the borrower is in default. A security interest provides that, in the event of default, the holder of the interest can force a sale of the property to satisfy the obligation. Security interests generally are created by contract as part of the loan or sale transaction. Article 9 of the Uniform Commercial Code (UCC) covers security interests in personal property in nearly every state.

### Example

Two people come to the bank seeking loans. One person wants to buy a car, the second wants to put an addition on his or her house. For each of these loans, the bank will want an interest in the borrower's property as security for repayment. Most likely, property relating to the loan—the car and the house—will be used as security. Each borrower will be asked to sign documents promising to repay the loan and giving the bank an interest in the property that allows the bank to claim and sell the property should the borrower default on the loan.

A **lien** that is placed against particular real property to enforce payment of an obligation represents the lender's or creditor's security interest in the property. Liens are extinguished if the obligation is paid. Their only purpose is to ensure payment by giving lenders, creditors, and other lien holders the right, as a last resort, to require sale of the property so that the proceeds can be used to satisfy the unpaid obligation. Real estate liens are not governed by a uniform law. Security interests in personal property are governed by the UCC as explained in chapter 9. Real estate lien statutes vary from state to state and must be followed carefully in order for a lender to place a lien on the property.

## Mortgages

A common type of real estate lien is a mortgage. A **mortgage** is a legal document in which a borrower gives the lender a lien on property as security for repayment of the loan (exhibit 7.1). Mortgages often are issued in conjunction with loans for purchasing or improving real property. In return for the loan, the mortgage gives the lender (mortgagee) the legal right to take possession, acquire the fee, and sell the property if the borrower (mortgagor) fails to pay on time. The legal process by which this right is enforced is called **foreclosure** and varies among the states. Some states permit the mortgagee to sell the property upon default; others require the mortgagee to apply to the courts for permission to sell, which is granted after proper notice to the mortgagor (borrower) and to any others with interest in the property.

In some states a deed of trust is used instead of a mortgage to place a lien on real property (exhibit 7.2). Although somewhat different in a legal sense, the deed of trust and mortgage document both convey an interest in the real property to the lender. However, the interest can be possessory only if the borrower defaults and the lender has the property sold, according to the law.

In some states the borrower has the right to redeem the property to be sold at foreclosure only until the sale itself takes place. In other jurisdictions the borrower has the right to redeem the property for a time period after the sale occurs. The borrower redeems the property by paying the lender all the funds that are due under the promissory note, as well as all expenses the lender has incurred in getting the property ready for sale.

## Other Types of Liens

Security interests that give lenders a lien on the borrower's property are created by contract as part of the loan or credit transaction, but liens also can come into

## Exhibit 7.1    Sample Mortgage Document

**RECORDATION REQUESTED BY:**
Concentrex National Institution < CFI TEST BANK >
3225 National St
Portland, OR  97225

**WHEN RECORDED MAIL TO:**
Concentrex National Institution < CFI TEST BANK >
3225 National St
Portland, OR  97225

**SEND TAX NOTICES TO:**
Concentrex National Institution < CFI TEST BANK >
3225 National St
Portland, OR  97225

SPACE ABOVE THIS LINE IS FOR RECORDER'S USE ONLY

### MORTGAGE

THIS MORTGAGE dated December 21, 1999, is made and executed between JOE BORROWER, whose address is 3200 "B" St. , Salem, OR  98765 (referred to below as "Grantor") and Concentrex National Institution < CFI TEST BANK >, whose address is 3225 National St, Portland, OR  97225 (referred to below as "Lender").

GRANT OF MORTGAGE.  For valuable consideration, Grantor mortgages and conveys to Lender all of Grantor's right, title, and interest in and to the following described real property, together with all existing or subsequently erected or affixed buildings, improvements and fixtures; all easements, rights of way, and appurtenances; all water, water rights, watercourses and ditch rights (including stock in utilities with ditch or irrigation rights); and all other rights, royalties, and profits relating to the real property, including without limitation all minerals, oil, gas, geothermal and similar matters, (the "Real Property") located in Marion County, State of Oregon:

**Legal Description for Subject Property...**

The Real Property or its address is commonly known as  3200 "B" St. , Salem, OR  98765. The Real Property tax identification number is a125455s8e.

Grantor presently assigns to Lender all of Grantor's right, title, and interest in and to all present and future leases of the Property and all Rents from the Property. In addition, Grantor grants to Lender a Uniform Commercial Code security interest in the Personal Property and Rents.

THIS MORTGAGE, INCLUDING THE ASSIGNMENT OF RENTS AND THE SECURITY INTEREST IN THE RENTS AND PERSONAL PROPERTY, IS GIVEN TO SECURE  (A)  PAYMENT OF THE INDEBTEDNESS AND (B)  PERFORMANCE OF ANY AND ALL OBLIGATIONS UNDER THE NOTE, THE RELATED DOCUMENTS, AND THIS MORTGAGE. THIS MORTGAGE IS GIVEN AND ACCEPTED ON THE FOLLOWING TERMS:

PAYMENT AND PERFORMANCE.  Except as otherwise provided in this Mortgage, Grantor shall pay to Lender all amounts secured by this Mortgage as they become due and shall strictly perform all of Grantor's obligations under this Mortgage.

POSSESSION AND MAINTENANCE OF THE PROPERTY.  Grantor agrees that Grantor's possession and use of the Property shall be governed by the following provisions:

Possession and Use.  Until the occurrence of an Event of Default, Grantor may  (1)  remain in possession and control of the Property;  (2) use, operate or manage the Property; and  (3)  collect the Rents from the Property.  THIS INSTRUMENT WILL NOT ALLOW USE OF THE PROPERTY DESCRIBED IN THIS INSTRUMENT IN VIOLATION OF APPLICABLE LAND USE LAWS AND REGULATIONS.   BEFORE SIGNING OR ACCEPTING THIS INSTRUMENT, THE PERSON ACQUIRING FEE TITLE TO THE PROPERTY SHOULD CHECK WITH THE APPROPRIATE CITY OR COUNTY PLANNING DEPARTMENT TO VERIFY APPROVED USES AND TO DETERMINE ANY LIMITS ON LAWSUITS AGAINST FARMING OR FOREST PRACTICES AS DEFINED IN ORS 30.930.

Duty to Maintain.  Grantor shall maintain the Property in good condition and promptly perform all repairs, replacements, and maintenance necessary to preserve its value.

Compliance With Environmental Laws.  Grantor represents and warrants to Lender that: (1)  During the period of Grantor's ownership of the Property, there has been no use, generation, manufacture, storage, treatment, disposal, release or threatened release of any Hazardous Substance by any person on, under, about or from the Property;  (2)  Grantor has no knowledge of, or reason to believe that there has been, except as previously disclosed to and acknowledged by Lender in writing,  (a)  any breach or violation of any Environmental Laws, (b)  any use, generation, manufacture, storage, treatment, disposal, release or threatened release of any Hazardous Substance on, under, about or from the Property by any prior owners or occupants of the Property, or  (c)  any actual or threatened litigation or claims of any kind by any person relating to such matters; and  (3)  Except as previously disclosed to and acknowledged by Lender in writing,  (a)  neither Grantor nor any tenant, contractor, agent or other authorized user of the Property shall use, generate, manufacture, store, treat, dispose of or release any Hazardous Substance on, under, about or from the Property; and  (b)  any such activity shall be conducted in compliance with all applicable federal, state, and local laws, regulations and ordinances, including without limitation all Environmental Laws. Grantor authorizes Lender and its agents to enter upon the Property to make such inspections and tests, at Grantor's expense, as Lender may deem appropriate to determine compliance of the Property with this section of the Mortgage. Any inspections or tests made by Lender shall be for Lender's purposes only and shall not be construed to create any responsibility or liability on the part of Lender to Grantor or to any other person.  The representations and warranties contained herein are based on Grantor's due diligence in investigating the Property for Hazardous Substances.  Grantor hereby  (1)  releases and waives any future claims against Lender for indemnity or contribution in the event Grantor becomes liable for cleanup or other costs under any such laws; and  (2)  agrees to indemnify and hold harmless Lender against any and all claims, losses, liabilities, damages, penalties, and expenses which Lender may directly or indirectly sustain or suffer resulting from a breach of this section of the Mortgage or as a consequence of any use, generation, manufacture, storage, disposal, release

Note: This exhibit reproduces only page 1 of the sample mortgage document.

Source:  Concentrex Incorporated, Portland, Oregon.

## Exhibit 7.2    Sample Deed of Trust

**RECORDATION REQUESTED BY:**
Concentrex National Institution < CFI TEST BANK >
3225 National St
Portland, OR  97225

**WHEN RECORDED MAIL TO:**
Concentrex National Institution < CFI TEST BANK >
3225 National St
Portland, OR  97225

**SEND TAX NOTICES TO:**
Concentrex National Institution < CFI TEST BANK >
3225 National St
Portland, OR  97225

_____
SPACE ABOVE THIS LINE IS FOR RECORDER'S USE ONLY

### DEED OF TRUST

THIS DEED OF TRUST is dated December 21, 1999, among JOE BORROWER, whose address is 3200 "B" St. , Salem, OR  98765 ("Grantor"); Concentrex National Institution<CFI TEST BANK>, whose address is 3225 National St, Portland, OR  97225 (referred to below sometimes as "Lender" and sometimes as "Beneficiary"); and Trustee Name, whose address is 3212 Baker Blvd, Salem, OR  97145 (referred to below as "Trustee").

CONVEYANCE AND GRANT.  For valuable consideration, Grantor conveys to Trustee for the benefit of Lender as Beneficiary all of Grantor's right, title, and interest in and to the following described real property, together with all existing or subsequently erected or affixed buildings, improvements and fixtures; all easements, rights of way, and appurtenances; all water, water rights and ditch rights (including stock in utilities with ditch or irrigation rights); and all other rights, royalties, and profits relating to the real property, including without limitation all minerals, oil, gas, geothermal and similar matters, **(the "Real Property") located in Marion County, State of Oregon:**

**Legal Description for Subject Property...**

**The Real Property or its address is commonly known as  3200 "B" St. , Salem, OR  98765.  The Real Property tax identification number is a125455s8e.**

Grantor presently assigns to Lender (also known as Beneficiary in this Deed of Trust) all of Grantor's right, title, and interest in and to all present and future leases of the Property and all Rents from the Property.  In addition, Grantor grants to Lender a Uniform Commercial Code security interest in the Personal Property and Rents.

THIS DEED OF TRUST, INCLUDING THE ASSIGNMENT OF RENTS AND THE SECURITY INTEREST IN THE RENTS AND PERSONAL PROPERTY, IS GIVEN TO SECURE  (A) PAYMENT OF THE INDEBTEDNESS AND  (B)  PERFORMANCE OF ANY AND ALL OBLIGATIONS UNDER THE NOTE, THE RELATED DOCUMENTS, AND THIS DEED OF TRUST.  THIS DEED OF TRUST IS GIVEN AND ACCEPTED ON THE FOLLOWING TERMS:

PAYMENT AND PERFORMANCE.  Except as otherwise provided in this Deed of Trust, Grantor shall pay to Lender all amounts secured by this Deed of Trust as they become due, and shall strictly and in a timely manner perform all of Grantor's obligations under the Note, this Deed of Trust, and the Related Documents.

POSSESSION AND MAINTENANCE OF THE PROPERTY.  Grantor agrees that Grantor's possession and use of the Property shall be governed by the following provisions:

Possession and Use.  Until the occurrence of an Event of Default, Grantor may  (1)  remain in possession and control of the Property;  (2) use, operate or manage the Property; and  (3)  collect the Rents from the Property.  The following provisions relate to the use of the Property or to other limitations on the Property.  THIS INSTRUMENT WILL NOT ALLOW USE OF THE PROPERTY DESCRIBED IN THIS INSTRUMENT IN VIOLATION OF APPLICABLE LAND USE LAWS AND REGULATIONS.  BEFORE SIGNING OR ACCEPTING THIS INSTRUMENT, THE PERSON ACQUIRING FEE TITLE TO THE PROPERTY SHOULD CHECK WITH THE APPROPRIATE CITY OR COUNTY PLANNING DEPARTMENT TO VERIFY APPROVED USES AND TO DETERMINE ANY LIMITS ON LAWSUITS AGAINST FARMING OR FOREST PRACTICES AS DEFINED IN ORS 30.930.

Duty to Maintain.  Grantor shall maintain the Property in good condition and promptly perform all repairs, replacements, and maintenance necessary to preserve its value.

Compliance With Environmental Laws.  Grantor represents and warrants to Lender that:  (1)  During the period of Grantor's ownership of the Property, there has been no use, generation, manufacture, storage, treatment, disposal, release or threatened release of any Hazardous Substance by any person on, under, about or from the Property;  (2)  Grantor has no knowledge of, or reason to believe that there has been, except as previously disclosed to and acknowledged by Lender in writing,  (a)  any breach or violation of any Environmental Laws, (b)  any use, generation, manufacture, storage, treatment, disposal, release or threatened release of any Hazardous Substance on, under, about or from the Property by any prior owners or occupants of the Property, or  (c)  any actual or threatened litigation or claims of any kind by any person relating to such matters; and  (3)  Except as previously disclosed to and acknowledged by Lender in writing,  (a)  neither Grantor nor any tenant, contractor, agent or other authorized user of the Property shall use, generate, manufacture, store, treat, dispose of or release any Hazardous Substance on, under, about or from the Property; and  (b)  any such activity shall be conducted in compliance with all applicable federal, state, and local laws, regulations and ordinances, including without limitation all Environmental Laws.  Grantor authorizes Lender and its agents to enter upon the Property to make such inspections and tests, at Grantor's expense, as Lender may deem appropriate to determine compliance of the Property with this section of the Deed of Trust.  Any inspections or tests made by Lender shall be for Lender's purposes only and shall not be construed to create any responsibility or liability on the part of Lender to Grantor or to any

Note: This exhibit reproduces only page 1 of the sample deed of trust.

Source:  Concentrex Incorporated, Portland, Oregon.

existence by operation of law. Some of the most common types of liens that arise by statute or legal process are the following:

- **Mechanic's** or **construction liens**—In commercial situations, when someone performs work or furnishes materials for the construction of a building, that person acquires a right to impose a lien on the real property as a means of ensuring payment.
- **Judgments** or **judicial liens**—Liens also may be placed on an owner's property as a result of a court judgment in a lawsuit against the property owner.
- **Federal tax liens**—The Federal Tax Lien Act provides methods for the federal government to collect delinquent taxes, including the seizure and sale of taxpayer property.

Liens that arise by statute or legal process do not require a voluntary transfer of rights by the property owner. However they arise, liens have a significant effect on the owner's ability to sell or otherwise control the use of property subject to a lien.

## RECORDING REAL-PROPERTY INTERESTS

Whenever someone acquires an interest affecting the title to real property, the interest should be entered in the public land records of the county or other jurisdiction in which the property is located. This procedure is called **recording.** Every piece of real property in each jurisdiction has a public record containing a description of the property and information on who owns it, who has interests in it, whether any liens exist, and other information. New information is added to the record only if those who acquire interests in the property go to the appropriate government office to have their interests recorded. Recording an interest in land is the primary way of giving notice to the world that the interest exists. This notice protects everyone who holds an interest or is in the process of acquiring one.

As lenders and mortgagees, banks have a particular responsibility to be aware of the importance of land records and recording procedures. It is in the bank's interest to know the status of the title to real property on which it plans to take a mortgage. The bank should check the deed and other title information filed in the land records. If the mortgagor does not actually own the property, a mortgage on it will have little value as a security interest for the bank. For example, someone with only a leasehold or a life estate has no power to transfer to the bank the right to have the property sold upon default of loan payments. The most the bank could acquire from such a mortgagor is a right to the lease or the life tenancy. While the bank could sell these interests if the mortgagor defaulted, their value might not cover the loan.

Even with a mortgagor who is sole owner of the property, a bank must check the land records to determine the status of the property. Borrowers sometimes use their real property to secure more than one loan. The bank will want to know if an applicant's property has an existing mortgage that would make the bank's own mortgage less valuable. For example, if an existing recorded mortgage secures a large loan from another lender, the amount of that loan would be paid first in the event of foreclosure on either mortgage. After payment on the first mortgage, the remaining proceeds from the sale might be insufficient to pay off the bank's mortgage.

Recording serves the purpose of giving notice of an interest in property and establishing the priority, or ranking, of that interest in relation to any other interests. **Priority** means that when two parties hold similar interests, one of them may exercise the rights involved before the other one.

For example, two mortgagees of the same property would each want to have priority in a foreclosure proceeding to ensure full recovery of their loans. Priority would go to the one whose mortgage was recorded first, whether or not that mortgage preceded the other in time. The time of recording is what establishes the priority of multiple claims to interests in property.

Failure to promptly record an interest in property not only affects the priority of one's claim, but also may render the interest completely ineffective. Property law includes the concept of a **bona fide purchaser.** This is someone who, in good faith and for valuable consideration, acquires an interest in property without having notice of any outstanding or prior interests. If a prior interest has been recorded, the record gives notice to all—so no one who later acquires an interest can claim to be a bona fide purchaser without notice. If an interest is not recorded, no assurance exists that persons who may later acquire interests in the same property will have notice of the interest. If they are bona fide purchasers, their rights in the property will be superior to all prior rights of which they had no notice.

### Example

A woman sells her small vacation cottage to a man for $25,000 cash. She gives him a deed, which he puts in his briefcase. He then hurries off to the airport to catch his flight home, 400 miles away. He plans to drive back in a month to record the deed and move into the cottage. Two weeks before he comes back, the woman sells the cottage to someone else, also for cash. This person has checked the land records and found no recorded interests or any indication that the woman is not the owner of the cottage. Thus, the second buyer is a bona fide purchaser for value, without notice of any prior interests in the property. The bona fide purchaser records her interest right away, which cuts off the first buyer's unrecorded interest. His only remedy is to seek out the original owner and get his money back.

## BAILMENTS

A **bailment** exists when the owner of personal property delivers the property into someone else's possession for a specific purpose. The purpose may be to improve the property, as when one leaves a suit of clothes with a dry cleaner or a car with a garage for repairs. The purpose may be for transporting the property from one place to another, as when one turns a package over to a courier service or transport company. Or the purpose may be for safekeeping, as when one leaves property in a storage warehouse or places valuables in a hotel safe. In a bailment relationship, the ownership of personal property is in one person (the bailor) while another (the bailee) has the right to possess the property for the specific purpose. Bailees have a duty of care with respect to the articles in their possession and must surrender the same property when the bailment ends.

In many states, banks are considered to be bailees of the property that customers keep in safe deposit boxes. As the bailee, a bank receives payment in return for providing a place of safekeeping for personal property of the customer. Unlike most bailees, a bank is usually unaware of the type of personal property within its custody; but that does not alter the bank's duty of care.

The bank must exercise **ordinary care** in regard to property in its safe deposit boxes. Ordinary care is that degree of care that a reasonable person would exercise in similar circumstances. This standard of care governs construction of the bank's building and the suitability of its safe deposit operation. To exercise ordinary care banks must ensure that their buildings and procedures protect the safe deposit boxes from theft.

**Example**

A customer who has placed several valuable items in a safe deposit box loses her purse containing the key to her box and her bank statement. A man finds her purse, goes to the bank, and is permitted access to the box without identification. Checking identification is part of the bank's written policy for access to safe deposit boxes. In this situation, the bank has failed to exercise ordinary care for the customer's property because it has failed to abide by its own policy. The bank will be held liable to the woman for losses that result from its negligence.

Bailees often use contracts to limit the duty of care they owe to customers. Some banks' safe deposit contracts with customers state that the relationship is not a bailment or include specific limitations of the responsibilities assumed by the bank. Most courts will honor contractual limitations of bailee duties unless the bailee attempts to avoid liability for willful acts. Contracts for safe deposit boxes usually include language disclaiming liability for any loss except loss caused by the bank's willful conduct.

A customer who fails to take possession of personal property at the end of the bailment is considered to have abandoned the property. This is the case with safe deposit boxes that are not renewed when the rental agreement expires. State laws usually include rules for notifying customers that the contents of boxes will be sold at a public auction unless the property is reclaimed during a particular period and overdue charges are paid in full.

## CONCLUSION

Property is a basic concept in the law. Banking transactions involve the property of the bank's customers. As custodians, banks have possession of their customers' money and other personal property, have title to their trust property, and manage their investments and retirement funds. As lenders, banks have interests in their customers' homes, cars, and business equipment. Bankers must be aware of the laws that govern their actions when they take possession of their customers' property or when they obtain an interest in it to secure a loan.

## QUESTIONS FOR REVIEW AND DISCUSSION

1. What is the difference between real and personal property?
2. Can property ever change its status from real to personal or vice versa? Explain.
3. What are the requirements for transfer of ownership by gift?
4. What are some of the different types of property interests? Which types have less than full ownership rights?
5. What are some of the types of liens that can be placed on real property?

## LEARNING ACTIVITIES FOR CHAPTER 7

### Multiple Choice

Choose the best answer for each question.

1. Which of the following would be an example of personal property?

   a. standing trees
   b. growing plants
   c. a building
   d. a stock certificate

2. Fred and Bob are brothers and together own a bank account as joint tenants. If Fred dies, who will own the funds in the account?

   a. half will go to Fred's heirs and half will go to Bob
   b. Bob
   c. Fred's heirs
   d. half will go to Fred's heirs and half will go to Bob's heirs

3. The type of lien that may be placed on an owner's property as a result of a court judgment against the owner in a lawsuit is called a:

   a. mechanic's lien
   b. mortgage
   c. chattel lien
   d. judicial lien

4. Failure to promptly record an interest in property can:

   a. affect the priority of one's claim
   b. render the interest completely ineffective
   c. result in a judgment lien
   d. result in adverse possession

5. The holder of a life estate on a piece of real property:

   a. can pass this interest in the property on to heirs
   b. has a right to possess the property for life
   c. may sell the property
   d. has no real rights to possession of the property

6. Rental of a safe deposit box is an example of the bank's role as a:

   a. donee
   b. lessee
   c. bailee
   d. lessor

**Completion**

Classify the following property as either real (r) or personal (p).

1. _____ a house built on a lot in the city
2. _____ the lights attached to an industrial plant
3. _____ playground equipment anchored to cement building piers on the property of a church
4. _____ a swing-set placed in the backyard of a family
5. _____ stock certificates in a safe deposit box
6. _____ cash in the owner's wallet
7. _____ oak trees growing on a residential lot
8. _____ a patio cover attached to the roof of a house
9. _____ shrubs and plants growing in large pots on the porch of a house
10. _____ a swimming pool built into the backyard of a residence

# 8

# CONSUMER LENDING

## LEARNING OBJECTIVES

After studying this chapter, you should be able to

- explain the relationships between the consumer protection statutes and the regulations that implement them
- list the main provisions of the Truth in Lending Act and the protections offered to consumers by the Equal Credit Opportunity Act
- state the basic requirements of the Fair Credit Reporting Act and the Consumer Leasing Act
- discuss how the Fair Debt Collection Practices Act and the Credit Practices Rule affect bank procedures
- explain the purposes for the Real Estate Settlement Procedures Act, the Flood Disaster Protection Act, and the Fair Housing Act
- define and use the legal and banking terms that appear in bold in the chapter text

## INTRODUCTION

Consumer credit is credit extended to a borrower for personal, family, or household purposes. Until the late 1960s, the only laws protecting consumers in their credit transactions were state laws that set ceilings on interest rates. These **usury** laws were the original consumer credit protection statutes.

With the tremendous increase in consumer credit transactions after World War II, regulation in this area began to receive more attention from state governments. Legislation was enacted in the states on a piecemeal basis, depending on the type of credit and the identity of the creditor and borrower. In many states this fragmented approach produced separate regulatory schemes for retail credit, automobile credit, home-improvement credit, and direct consumer lending by banks.

By the 1960s consumer credit had become popular in every state. However, an increase in the number of creditors that were not honest and fair dealing also had occurred. Some creditors charged exorbitant interest rates. Others calculated the costs in complex ways so that it was impossible for the customer to determine the real cost of the credit. In response, Congress and state governments began to review the legal protection available to consumers in the lending process. In 1969 a uniform consumer credit law was drafted. This law, the Uniform Consumer Credit Code (UCCC), provides consumers with a wide array of rights when obtaining credit for personal purposes. The UCCC restricts interest rates, late charges, garnishment actions, and deficiency judgments. Although its drafters envisioned that the UCCC would be as popular as the UCC, seven states and Guam enacted the UCCC into law.

Apart from the UCCC, Congress began enacting other consumer lending protection laws in the late 1960s. These laws required disclosures, governed the use of consumer credit reports and prohibited discrimination in lending.

As noted in chapter 1, laws enacted by Congress usually are assigned to a federal banking regulatory agency for implementation and oversight. Agencies such as the Federal Reserve or the OCC write regulations that contain more specific requirements than the laws themselves. The regulations written by the Federal Reserve are usually designated by a letter of the alphabet, such as Regulation Z or Regulation B. Where applicable, along with information about the federal laws that regulate consumer lending, this chapter will present information about the implementing regulations.

## TRUTH IN LENDING ACT

Reacting to the lack of consumer credit protection laws in some states and the lack of uniformity among existing laws, Congress passed the Truth in Lending Act (TILA) in 1968. This law affects lenders throughout the United States, requiring certain standard disclosures, uniform terminology and computation of costs, and simplified explanations of many of the fine-print terms in creditors' documents. The Federal Reserve Board's Regulation Z implements this law. The Federal Reserve has also written an official Federal Reserve Board staff commentary to Regulation Z to further explain the law's requirements.

### Coverage

TILA is a consumer protection law. With few exceptions, it applies only if the transaction involves consumer credit for personal, family, or household purposes. For example, suppose a bank lends its customer money for use in the business she runs in partnership with her husband. For purposes of TILA, this loan is not a consumer loan because it is not for consumer purposes. Loans for business purposes are not covered by TILA, so the bank need not comply with TILA requirements when making this particular loan.

TILA covers only consumer loans that are for $25,000 or less, provided that the loan is not secured by real estate. Therefore, a loan for $35,000 made to a consumer to purchase a family vehicle would not be covered by TILA. The creditor is free to provide the typical TILA disclosures but is not required to do so.

Real estate loans made for consumer purposes have no TILA dollar limit. In other words, any consumer-purpose real estate loan for any amount is covered by TILA. So a loan made to consumers to purchase their principal dwelling *will* be covered by TILA even if the house may cost several hundred thousand dollars.

## Requirements

TILA requirements cover disclosures, including special disclosure requirements for open-ended credit arrangements and credit card relationships; the composition of finance charges; the calculations used to determine the annual percentage rate; the consumer's right of rescission in certain types of transactions; and fair credit billing.

### Disclosures

If a credit transaction is covered by TILA, creditors must make a number of disclosures. A **disclosure** is notice to a consumer borrower pertaining to the credit terms and containing other facts relevant to the loan. Necessary disclosures are determined by whether the credit being extended is open-ended or closed-ended. **Open-ended credit** involves repeated credit extensions on a revolving basis, like a credit card. **Closed-ended credit** involves a one-time credit advance.

TILA requires disclosure of the finance charge and annual percentage rate in transactions involving both types of credit. The **finance charge** is the consumer's cost for the loan in dollars and cents. The **annual percentage rate** is the per-year cost calculated as a percentage of the loan amount. These two disclosures are the heart of TILA's objective that disclosure of credit costs be uniform throughout the United States. In requiring that these charges be calculated and disclosed uniformly, Congress assumed that consumers could then make intelligent choices among the terms offered by various lenders. Exhibit 8.1 presents an example of a disclosure form for a closed-ended installment loan.

### Finance Charge

A loan's finance charge is composed of the various charges a consumer pays for the credit being extended. Regulation Z is very specific about loan finance charges, which can include interest, service charges, transaction charges, certain insurance premiums, and loan fees.

#### Example

Citizens Bank lends $1,000 to its customer to purchase a used car for his family. The customer is to repay the loan in one payment at the end of one year. The interest rate is 15 percent. In addition, the bank charges a $20 loan fee. In this example, the customer pays $150 in interest. That figure plus the loan fee of $20 results in a finance charge of $170.

### Annual Percentage Rate

A loan's annual percentage rate is the finance charge expressed as a percentage per year of the loan. The annual percentage rate must be determined according to calculations defined in Regulation Z. In the previous example, the annual percentage rate of the loan is 17 percent. If a finance charge includes anything besides interest, the annual percentage rate will be greater than the interest rate. Continuing the previous example, if a $10 application

## Exhibit 8.1 Sample Disclosure Form for Closed-Ended Installment Loan

Friendly Bank & Trust Co.
700 East Street
Little Creek, USA

Lisa Stone
22-4859-22
300 Maple Avenue
Little Creek, USA

| ANNUAL PERCENTAGE RATE<br><br>The cost of your credit as a yearly rate. | FINANCE CHARGE<br><br>The dollar amount the credit will cost you. | AMOUNT FINANCED<br><br>The amount of credit provided to you or on your behalf. | TOTAL OF PAYMENTS<br><br>The amount you will have paid after you have made all payments as scheduled. |
|---|---|---|---|
| 12% | $675.31 | $5,000 | $5,675.31 |

You have the right to receive at this time an itemization of the amount financed.

❑ I want an itemization.     ❑ I do not want an itemization.

Your payment schedule will be:

| Number of Payments | Amount of Payments | When Payments Are Due |
|---|---|---|
| 1 | $262.03 | 6/01/01 |
| 23 | $235.36 | Monthly beginning 7/01/01 |

Late Charge:  If payment is late, you will be charged $5 to 10 percent of the payment, whichever is less.

Prepayment:  If you pay off early, you _ may _ may not have to pay a penalty.

Required Deposit:  The annual percentage rate does not take into account your required deposit.

See your contract documents for any additional information about nonpayment, default, any required repayment in full before the scheduled due date, and prepayment refunds and penalties.

_____

*means an estimate

fee is required in addition to the $20 loan fee and $150 interest, the APR would be 18 percent ($150 + $20 + $10 = $180, or 18 percent of the $1,000 loan).

### Open-Ended Credit

Open-ended credit involves repeated credit extensions on a revolving basis. Typical open-ended credit programs include credit cards, checking accounts with overdraft privileges, and retail charge accounts.

Required disclosures may vary according to the open-ended credit plan chosen by the consumer. Certain disclosures must appear together in a prominently featured area. These disclosures may also be presented as a separate document. Disclosures that are not required to be presented together must appear elsewhere in the loan documentation.

In addition to the finance charge and annual percentage rate, other types of disclosures may be required for open-ended credit, depending on the type of credit being offered or requested. Under the Fair Credit and Charge Card Disclosure Act of 1988, creditors that send unsolicited applications and solicitations for card accounts must provide consumers with standard disclosures explaining basic terms. Regulation Z gives creditors examples of several model forms for this purpose.

For all open-ended consumer credit accounts, TILA requires the bank or other creditor to make an **initial disclosure statement.** This disclosure must be provided before the consumer's first transaction under the terms of the account. Its purpose is to inform the consumer in advance about costs and other obligations the consumer will incur if the account is ever used. The initial disclosure statement also gives information on when a finance charge will be imposed and how it is to be calculated, and contains a description of fees.

**Periodic disclosure statements** reflecting transactions in the account during each billing cycle are required throughout the life of the account to inform the consumer in advance about costs and other obligations the consumer incurs as the account is used. These disclosures reveal the actual costs of the credit used by the consumer. Periodic disclosures include the amount of the debt, how the debt was incurred, payments made on any balances, and the annual percentage rate.

### Rescission

TILA is not just a disclosure law. Congress wanted to protect consumers who may put their homeownership at risk by using the equity in their homes to obtain credit. A creditor agreement may give creditors a **security interest** in the consumer's home to ensure repayment of a debt, and if the consumer fails to repay the loan, the creditor may then repossess or foreclose on the home. TILA not only protects consumers by requiring the bank to disclose the security interest and its potential consequences, it also provides consumers a cooling off period, during which the consumer may unilaterally *rescind,* or cancel, the loan. Under TILA, **rescission** is available only for consumer credit agreements that give the creditor a security interest in the consumer's primary residence. The right of rescission does not apply to the initial loan used to purchase the home.

Creditors must follow precise steps when the TILA right of rescission applies. The creditor must provide the Notice of Right to Cancel to each consumer when the initial statement is given to the consumer and any time a security interest is added or increased. Regulation Z provides model forms for notices of the right to cancel applicable to open-ended credit plans. Consumers have until midnight of the following third business day (including Saturday) to rescind the credit agreement. Rescission occurs when the consumer notifies the bank in writing that he or she is canceling the transaction. The bank may not fund the loan until the rescission period expires.

If for any reason the notice of right to cancel has not been provided with the initial disclosure statement, or if substantial errors appear in either document, the time allowed for rescission is extended to three years.

If a consumer chooses to exercise the right of rescission, the creditor must void the entire credit transaction within 20 days of receiving notice, including canceling the lien or security interest on the home and refunding all amounts paid by the consumer as a part of the loan process, even if such payments were not made to the bank for services rendered.

Once the creditor has voided the transaction and repaid any funds expended, the consumer must return to the creditor any part of the loan proceeds that has been funded. For example, a $20,000 loan would require that the consumer return $20,000; the creditor would have to return any interest payments that have been made.

### Example

Bob and Jennifer Wood apply for a home improvement loan from ABC Bank. ABC prepares the loan documents internally but requires the Woods to purchase an appraisal and an updated title policy to cover the loan. ABC instructs the appraiser of its requirements and the Woods pay the appraiser $125 for the appraisal. The loan documents are completed and closed at the title company, where the Woods pay a total of $225 for the policy and settlement services. The Woods are provided a Notice of the Right to Rescind, and a check is issued but not disbursed pending the expiration of the three-day right of rescission. The settlement occurs on Tuesday evening and the title company files the documents on Wednesday morning with the county register of records and issues its policy. On Thursday the bank receives a cancellation

notice from Mrs. Wood. The bank has 20 days to release its interest in the Woods's home and must, within that time period, repay them for the cost of the appraisal, the settlement services, and the title policy. Once the release has been filed and the payment of $350 made to the Woods, the bank has fulfilled its obligation and may collect any funds previously disbursed to them. In this case, because the check was not disbursed there are no funds to be collected and the transaction has been canceled.

---

### Critical Terms

*Rescission* Cancellation of a contract or legally binding agreement.

*Security Interest* A lender's right to seize a consumer's property if he or she fails to repay a loan or credit obligation.

*Initial Disclosure Statement* Written notification of the credit terms and other facts about a loan agreement that must be given to consumers before the closing of their loan.

---

### Credit Cards

Whether used for consumer or commercial purposes, credit cards come within the scope of TILA, which regulates both their issuance and a cardholder's liability for their unauthorized use. A **credit card** is any card, plate, coupon book, or other device presented to obtain money, property, labor, or services on credit.

Under TILA credit cards may be issued only in response to an application or request, or as a renewal of an already-issued card. **Unauthorized use** is the use of the credit card by a person who has no permission to do so, in a transaction that provides no benefits to the cardholder. A cardholder's liability for unauthorized use of a credit card is either the amount of credit obtained with the card before the cardholder notified the issuer of the unauthorized use or $50, whichever is less. A cardholder's liability up to $50 is conditioned upon the card issuer's having given the cardholder

- adequate notice of the cardholder's potential liability for unauthorized use
- an address or telephone number to which notices of unauthorized use, theft, or loss may be reported
- a card that contains a way to identify the cardholder or authorized user

If any of these three conditions to a cardholder's liability is not satisfied, the cardholder's liability—even for $50—cannot be enforced.

### Example

Joe Barton's credit card is stolen and the thief charges $500 worth of merchandise on it. The card issuer had never notified Barton that his liability for unauthorized use could not exceed $50. Under TILA, Barton's maximum liability of $50 for the unauthorized use of the card cannot be enforced because the issuer failed to meet one of the conditions governing enforcement of cardholder liability. Joe Barton has no liability for reimbursing the card issuer for the unauthorized use of his card.

TILA permits cardholders to withhold payment from card issuers when purchases made with the card for consumer purposes turn out to be unsatisfactory. To exercise this right, the cardholder must first attempt in good faith to resolve the dispute with the merchant. The cardholder must then notify the card issuer of the dispute if it cannot be settled. However, with limited exceptions, the cardholder cannot withhold payment from a card issuer if the disputed amount is $50 or less, or if the disputed transaction occurred at a location outside the cardholder's state or more than 100 miles from the cardholder's address. During any period of dispute, the card issuer cannot report the cardholder as delinquent in making payments to the account.

TILA does not allow bank card issuers to offset consumer credit card debts using the consumer's deposit account with the bank. If a cardholder's debt is for other than consumer purposes, this ban does not apply. Unless state law holds otherwise, a cardholder's deposits with the bank may be used to offset a delinquent *nonconsumer* credit card debt.

### Advertising

TILA's requirement that consumer credit costs be disclosed in uniform and understandable terms also applies to advertising. TILA interprets a **credit advertisement** to mean any commercial message in any medium that directly or indirectly promotes a credit transaction.

The content of an advertisement is within the lender's or advertiser's discretion unless it contains *triggering terms* (exhibit 8.2). A triggering term is a term which, by itself, could be misleading. Such a term triggers additional disclosures. Therefore, an advertisement containing a triggering term must include certain additional disclosures. What constitutes a triggering term and the content of the required disclosure will depend on

---

| **Exhibit 8.2   Regulation Z Advertising Rules—Triggering Terms** |
| --- |
| Triggering terms for advertising consumer credit products include <br><br> • the amount or percentage of any downpayment <br> • the number of payments or period of repayment <br> • the amount of any payment <br> • the amount of any finance charge |

whether the ad is for open-ended or closed-ended credit. Each use of a triggering term in advertising without the required disclosure is a violation of TILA. Lenders and those parties responsible for lenders' advertising programs should carefully review these TILA requirements.

### Fair Credit Billing

With the onset of the computer age in the 1960s came computerized billing, which resulted in numerous complaints that creditors were not responding to problems that consumers had with billing errors. In 1974 Congress amended TILA to include the Fair Credit Billing Act. The Fair Credit Billing Act is aimed only at billing errors in open-ended credit accounts. Regulation Z defines *billing errors* to include

- periodic statements that misidentify an extension of credit, give insufficient identification, omit information, give erroneous information about amounts or individuals involved, or reflect the use of credit by unauthorized persons
- requests by the consumer for explanation or clarification
- assertions that property or services reflected in a periodic statement or accompanying documents were not delivered or accepted according to an underlying agreement
- failure to deliver a periodic statement within the prescribed time

The Fair Credit Billing Act provides a procedure for consumers to follow in order to correct what they believe to be billing errors. To preserve his or her rights under the Fair Credit Billing Act, a consumer must notify the creditor of the error in writing within 60 days of receiving a periodic statement that contains the alleged billing error.

#### Example
On October 5, Joan receives a periodic statement from the bank pertaining to her overdraft checking account. The statement contains a finance charge for an overdraft check that Joan is sure she did not sign. On October 20, Joan sends a written notice of the error to her bank. In this situation Joan has acted in a timely fashion to claim a billing error, and the bank must comply with Fair Credit Billing Act procedures to review the allegation.

The first step in a creditor's response to an alleged billing error is a written acknowledgment to the customer that it has received the notification of billing error. This written acknowledgment must be sent within 30 days of the bank's receipt of the customer's notification of the billing problem. Within two complete billing cycles, but in no case more than 90 days from the date the bank receives notice of the alleged billing error, the dispute must be resolved.

Resolution of the alleged billing error may involve any one of the following three possibilities:

- agreement with the customer that an error has occurred and correction of the error
- agreement with the customer that an error has occurred, but a claim that the error is different from the amount alleged by the customer and a corresponding adjustment to the account
- denial that an error has occurred

If the creditor denies or adjusts the alleged error, the creditor must provide a written explanation to the customer along with any supporting documentation the customer requests.

A creditor cannot collect any disputed amounts during the investigation period. Nor may a creditor report to any third parties during this period that the disputed amount is delinquent. If the creditor determines at the conclusion of the resolution procedure that the customer owes all or part of the disputed amount, the creditor can insist on payment of the amount but must still allow for any grace periods provided in the loan agreement.

Once the creditor has completed the procedure for resolving a billing error, it has no further obligation to withhold collection efforts, even if the customer is dissatisfied with the creditor's answer. However, if after the resolution process has been completed the customer notifies the creditor that a dispute still exists, information to that effect must accompany any reports the creditor makes to third parties that the account is delinquent. The creditor also must notify the customer of the name and address of each third party to whom it has reported the delinquency.

To ensure that customers are aware of their rights under the Fair Credit Billing Act, creditors offering open-ended credit must disclose their procedures for resolving billing-error disputes. Initial disclosure statements for open-ended credit must describe—either within the disclosure statement itself or in an accompanying document—the billing-error procedure in a form suggested by Regulation Z. To ensure that customers continue to understand their rights in resolving disputes over billing errors, creditors must send each customer either a long billing-error disclosure form each year or a short billing-error disclosure form with every periodic statement.

A creditor that fails to comply with the procedure for resolving billing errors forfeits the right to collect payment of the disputed amount (or $50 minimum). In addition, any violation of FCBA billing-error provisions may result in the creditor's further liability for civil and regulatory penalties.

## Enforcement

Criminal, civil, and regulatory penalties help ensure compliance with TILA. Criminal penalties can result from intentionally violating either the act or Regulation Z. Conviction for such an intentional violation can lead to a fine or imprisonment, or to both.

Civil penalties also may be imposed for certain violations of TILA disclosure requirements. These penalties include actual damages, plus twice the amount of any finance charge (not to exceed $1,000), plus court costs and attorney fees.

Sometimes a single court action may be brought against a card issuer on behalf of all or a group of its customers. This type of lawsuit is called a **class action.** Class action penalties against a creditor allow for damages of 1 percent of its net worth or $500,000, whichever is less. The amount of damages awarded in a class action can be adjusted according to such factors as the frequency of the violations, the creditor's resources, the extent to which the violations were intentional, the number of people harmed by the violations, and the actual harm suffered.

A creditor whose disclosure of a charge is incorrect may escape liability under TILA if, within 60 days of discovering its error, it notifies the affected consumer of the error and adjusts the consumer's account to ensure that the charges paid are no greater than what was disclosed. However, this 60-day defense cannot be used if, before the creditor makes the correction, the consumer has brought a court action or has given the creditor written notice of the error.

A bank or other creditor violating TILA also will escape liability if it can prove that the violation as unintentional and resulted from a bona fide error despite procedures designed to avoid any such error. Examples of bona fide errors include those involving computer malfunctions and clerical or printing errors.

Consumers who choose to sue a creditor for a TILA violation must do so within one year after the violation occurs. In cases where a creditor sues a consumer—for failure to repay a loan, for example—the consumer may counterclaim against the creditor for the TILA violations even if the one-year period has expired.

Regulatory agencies, such as the Federal Reserve Board, FDIC, OCC, OTS, and National Credit Union Administration (NCUA) also may impose penalties on creditors for TILA violations. These and other regulatory agencies all have authority to enforce TILA.

Regulatory agencies have chosen to enforce TILA in various ways. Agencies that supervise financial institutions conduct compliance examinations. Other agencies respond to specific consumer complaints about violations. Still other agencies stress educational programs for the creditors over which they have oversight authority. All of the regulatory agencies have **restitution powers** that enable them to order creditors to return overcharges to consumers. In some cases, these refunds to consumers have amounted to many thousands of dollars for disclosure errors involving annual percentage rates, finance charges, and insurance.

## EQUAL CREDIT OPPORTUNITY ACT

The **Equal Credit Opportunity Act (ECOA)** prohibits discrimination in credit transactions based upon the applicant's or customer's sex, marital status, age, race, color, religion, national origin, receipt of income from public assistance, or past exercise of a right under the federal Consumer Protection Act. The Federal Reserve Board adopted Regulation B to implement ECOA's provisions. The Board also issued an official staff commentary.

### Coverage

ECOA applies to all types of credit, including consumer and business credit, although the notice requirements are different for large business customers than for consumers. The act defines **creditors** as those who in the course of their business regularly participate in decisions on whether to grant credit.

### Requirements

ECOA requirements affect creditors at the advertising and credit application stages and include specific notifications for loan approvals or denials, and for appraisal notices.

#### Application Information Restrictions

ECOA affects creditors at the advertising and credit application stages. In the latter stage it regulates the information a creditor may request from an applicant. This restriction also extends to application forms. Applications cannot seek any information that would reveal protected characteristics of the applicant. The intent of the regulation is to avoid the possibility or the perception that credit decisions are based on one or more of these protected characteristics rather than on the applicant's creditworthiness.

Generally, a creditor seeking information for the purpose of extending credit cannot ask an applicant's race, religion, color, or national origin. (Although the sex of an applicant cannot be asked directly, the application form may use optional courtesy titles such as Ms., Mrs., Mr., or Miss.) Birth control practices, family planning, ability to bear children, and child-rearing intentions are additional topics creditors cannot discuss with any applicant.

Under ECOA a creditor may inquire about an applicant's marital status if the applicant is relying on income from alimony, child support, or separate maintenance payments to establish creditworthiness. Requesting marital status also is permissible if the applicant lives in a community property state or is pledging property as security for the credit. In asking about marital status, the application may use only the terms *married, unmarried,* and *separated.* The application form must state that applicants are not required to reveal information about alimony, child support, or separate maintenance if they are not relying on this income to establish creditworthiness.

An application may ask an applicant's age, as well as whether any part of his or her income comes from public assistance. However, the bank may consider age only if it is related to some other pertinent element of creditworthiness, such as the ability to enter into a contract if the person is a minor. Public assistance income may be considered only in regard to the likelihood that the income will continue.

### Credit Evaluation Restrictions

In deciding whether to extend credit, a lender may use any information it receives about an applicant from whatever source, so long as the information is not used to discriminate on a **prohibited basis.**

ECOA permits creditors evaluating an applicant's creditworthiness to use an empirically derived credit-scoring system or a judgmental system. Credit-scoring is a numerical rating system that uses statistical information. A judgmental system is any other system a creditor may use to determine the creditworthiness of an applicant.

If a creditor uses an empirically derived credit-scoring system, it may assign constant values to particular age categories so long as being older than 62 is not considered a negative. It is permissible under ECOA for creditors to favor applicants age 62 and older.

If an applicant wishes a creditor to consider income from alimony, child support, or separate maintenance payments in its evaluation, the creditor must do so. However, as with any other source of income, the creditor has the right to consider its reliability. This may require the creditor to review the court decree ordering payment, the history of the payments, the procedures available to the applicant for compelling payment, and the creditworthiness of the payor.

The creditor must give part-time income the same consideration as full-time income.

That is, an applicant receiving $22,000 per year from part-time employment cannot be evaluated differently from one earning the same amount in a full-time job.

If a creditor considers the applicant's credit history, all accounts that the applicant is contractually liable for or permitted to use must be considered. The creditor must also consider information provided by the applicant that indicates the credit history is incorrect. If the applicant requests it, the creditor must consider credit reports in the name of the applicant's spouse or former spouse if the credit history reflects upon the applicant's creditworthiness. For example, a divorced applicant who had little, if anything, to do with his or her former spouse's failure to repay a joint credit account has the right to present evidence to that effect to the creditor considering the application. At the same time, if the divorced applicant helped establish a good credit history for a current or former spouse but was not a joint holder of the account, the applicant has the right to ask the creditor to consider that good repayment record in the evaluation.

Before ECOA, many married female applicants were unable to furnish a separate credit history because creditors routinely indexed the credit a woman had obtained jointly with her husband in the husband's name alone. To ensure complete credit histories for married women, ECOA requires creditors who furnish credit information to give the names of both spouses on accounts for which both are liable. Similarly, when furnishing credit information to consumer reporting agencies, creditors must provide the information in such a way that the agencies will be able to furnish the information in each spouse's name. In addition, creditors responding to inquiries about a married customer's credit record must furnish that information in the name of the particular spouse about whom the information is requested.

### Notification Requirements

ECOA notification requirements cover approvals, denials, and appraisal notices. All notifications must follow fair lending guidelines.

#### Approvals

After the creditor receives an application and evaluates the applicant's creditworthiness, the next step is to notify the applicant of its decision. ECOA requires notification within 30 days of the creditor's receipt of a completed application. If a creditor approves the application and grants credit to the applicant, written, verbal, or implied notice of the approval is all that is required.

#### Denials

If the creditor denies the consumer's application, the creditor must send a written **adverse action notice** within the 30-day period (see exhibit 8.3). ECOA prescribes the content of the adverse action notice and the Federal Reserve Board has drafted model forms to assist creditors in this matter. The notice must include

- the statement of the action taken (the loan request was denied)
- the name and address of the federal agency regulating the creditor
- a paragraph summarizing ECOA's purpose and scope
- a statement informing the applicant of the reasons for the credit denial or, if the creditor chooses, informing the applicant that the reasons for denial may be obtained upon request from the creditor

ECOA also requires adverse action notices to be sent to applicants

- who refuse to accept a counteroffer from a creditor
- who fail to complete their applications (unless a notice of incomplete application is sent instead)

- whose open-ended accounts are terminated or adversely changed

Any consumer whose credit card is terminated or whose overdraft checking plan's credit limit is reduced should thus receive a notice of adverse action within 30 days of such action.

#### Appraisal Notices

The ECOA also requires creditors to give a notice that the applicant has the right to request a copy of an appraisal on any loan to be secured by a one- to four-family dwelling. This notice does not have to be given if the creditor routinely provides copies of the appraisals to applicants. The appraisal notice must be given within 30 days of the receipt of the application.

#### Fair Lending Guidelines

In the early 1990s ten federal agencies responded to perceived growth in the number of cases in which lending institutions were found to have discriminated against protected classes of consumers. Their response took the form of the Joint Policy Statement on Fair Lending. While this policy statement is not officially a part of Regulation B, it does clarify potential types of discrimination. The three types of discrimination addressed in the Joint Policy Statement are

- overt evidence of discrimination, in which a lender blatantly discriminates against an individual or class of persons or expresses discriminatory preferences

    **Example**
    Lending officer *A* makes the following statement: "I hate making loans to pregnant women but I know I am required by law to do it, so I do." This is expression of a discriminatory preference.

- evidence of disparate treatment, in which a lender's treatment of a person or class of persons is based on

## Exhibit 8.3  Adverse Action Notice

*Adverse Action Notice*

1. Date: _____

2. Applicant's Name: _____

3. Description of Account, Transaction, or Requested Credit: _____

4. Description of Action Taken: _____

5. Part I—PRINCIPAL REASON(S) FOR CREDIT DENIAL, TERMINATION, OR OTHER ACTION TAKEN CONCERNING CREDIT. This section must be completed in all instances.

a. __ Insufficient number of credit references provided

b. __ Unable to verify credit references

c. __ Temporary or irregular employment

d. __ Unable to verify employment

e. __ Length of employment

f. __ Income insufficient for amount of credit requested

g. __ Excessive obligations in relation to income

h. __ Unable to verify income

i. __ Length of residence

j. __ Temporary residence

k. __ Unable to verify residence

l. __ No credit line

m. __ Limited credit experience

n. __ Poor credit performance with us

o. __ Delinquent past or present credit obligations with others

p. __ Garnishment, attachment, foreclosure, repossession, collection action, or judgment

q. __ Bankruptcy

r. __ Value or type of collateral not sufficient

s. __ Other, specify: _____

6. Part II—DISCLOSURE OF USE OF INFORMATION OBTAINED FROM AN OUTSIDE SOURCE. This section should be completed if the credit decision was based in whole or in part on information that has been obtained from an outside source.

- Our credit decision was based in whole or in part on information obtained in a report from the consumer reporting agency listed below. You have a right under the Fair Credit Reporting Act to know the information contained in your credit file at the consumer reporting agency. The reporting agency played no part in our decision and is unable to supply specific reasons why we have denied credit to you.

- Name: _____

- Address: _____

- Telephone Number: _____

- Our credit decision was based in whole or in part on information obtained from an outside source other than a consumer reporting agency. Under the Fair Credit Reporting Act, you have the right to make a written request, no later than 60 days after you receive this notice, for disclosure of the nature of the information.

If you have any questions regarding this notice, you should contact:

- Creditor's Name: _____

- Creditor's Address: _____

- Creditor's Telephone Number: _____

NOTICE: The federal Equal Credit Opportunity Act prohibits creditors from discriminating against credit applicants on the basis of race, color, religion, national origin, sex, marital status, age (provided the applicant has the capacity to enter into a binding contract); because all or part of the applicant's income derives from any public assistance program; or because the applicant has in good faith exercised any right under the Consumer Credit Protection Act. The federal agency that administers compliance with this law concerning this creditor is (name and address as specified by the appropriate agency).

a prohibited basis, whether or not such treatment was intentional

### Example

Lending Institution *B* has two home improvement loan programs. Program #1 is one in which borrowers have a five-year note with a balloon. Payments are based on a 15-year amortization. The interest rate is based on the lender's prime rate. Program #2 is a fully amortizing installment loan program with coupon books and a higher interest rate. More than 90 percent of the African-American customers with home improvement loans at this institution are in Program #2. Although the lender has no formal or informal policy that requires lenders to place African-Americans in the second program, its practice may indicate disparate treatment because there is no other reason to account for the way the customers are distributed between the programs.

- evidence of disparate impact, in which a lender's policy or practice, although applied equally to everyone, has a disproportionate, adverse impact on a protected class of persons.

### Example

Lending Institution *C* has a policy that it will not make loans in an amount less than $5,000, due to the cost of making loans in lesser amounts. Lending Institution *C's* policy may constitute disparate impact since a disproportionate number of women and other protected classes would benefit from the lower lending amount. This may not be illegal discrimination. Institution *C* must conduct a cost-benefit analysis to determine whether the loans less than $5,000 are truly cost-prohibited. If so, Institution *C* should attempt to find a less discriminatory alternative, such as open-ended lines of credit attached to checking account, for example, to cover smaller loans. If there is no less-discriminatory alternative and Institution *C's* policy is justified by a business necessity, then the practice is not illegal discrimination.

## Enforcement

Banking regulatory agencies enforce compliance with ECOA. If a creditor is found to be discriminating against a person based on a prohibited basis, the agencies have the power to refer the institution to the Department of Justice for prosecution. In most cases however, the agency and the institution work out an agreement whereby the institution will set aside funds and will solicit loans from persons who were the recipients of the creditor's discriminatory actions. In some cases the institution also agrees to pay fines and establish formal training programs or monitoring programs to make sure the discrimination does not happen again.

Civil remedies are available to individuals harmed by ECOA violations. Unlike the TILA provisions for minimum damages based on findings of civil liability, ECOA provides for damages only in cases where there is actual injury or such serious wrongful conduct by a creditor that punitive damages are justified. **Punitive damages** are amounts imposed as punishment for a serious and willful violation of a civil law. ECOA violations also expose creditors to class actions that, if successful, can result in damages of up to 1 percent of a creditor's net worth or $500,000, whichever is less.

## CONSUMER LEASING ACT

Passed by Congress in 1977, the Consumer Leasing Act requires that consumers receive uniform disclosures of financial terms when leasing consumer property. While the implementation of this law was first placed in Regulation Z, the Consumer Leasing Act is now implemented by Regulation M.

A **consumer lease** is defined as a lease of personal property for a term of four months or more for which the consumer's total obligation will not exceed $25,000. The lessee must be a consumer—that is, a natural person who will use the leased property for personal, family, or household purposes. The Consumer Leasing Act does not cover leases for agricultural, business, or commercial purposes.

A lessor is defined as someone who is regularly engaged in the business of offering or arranging consumer leases. Lessors must make certain disclosures in advance of any consumer lease transaction. The required disclosures include

- a description of the leased property
- the amount and schedule of lease payments
- fees
- warranties
- security interests and termination provisions
- disclosures regarding responsibility for amounts due when the lease expires

To help lessors the Federal Reserve Board has accompanied Regulation M with three model forms for lease disclosures, which lessors may adapt to their own use. The law also regulates the advertising of consumer lease arrangements. Lease arrangements that are advertised must actually be available. Certain triggering terms in advertisements, such as the amount of a payment, require lessors to furnish more complete information.

## FAIR CREDIT REPORTING ACT

The Fair Credit Reporting Act (FCRA) is part of the federal Consumer Protection Act. Its objective is to ensure consumers that records of their credit transactions are accurate and are used only for certain purposes.

---

### Case for Discussion
*Miller v. Midway Bank and Trust*

Bill Miller applied to Midway Bank and Trust for a bank credit card. His application was approved and Midway offered him the option of receiving a supplementary card for his wife, Joan. Joan did not have a credit card of her own, so Bill thought this would be a good opportunity for her to get one. According to the bank's rules, Joan was personally liable for all purchases made with her card, which had an account number different from Bill's and which required a separate annual fee.

A few years later Bill died unexpectedly. Midway abruptly canceled Joan's card without giving prior notification. The bank did this in accordance with its policy of automatically terminating accounts of supplementary cardholders upon the death of the primary cardholder.

Joan immediately contacted her attorney to sue Midway Bank and Trust, claiming that this policy was in violation of the Equal Credit Opportunity Act because it discriminated on the basis of marital status. The facts also showed that the bank invited Joan to apply for a new credit card as a primary cardholder, and that her application had been approved.

The court ruled that the bank's policy violated Equal Credit Opportunity Act (ECOA) regulations because the termination of the supplementary card was based solely on a change in marital status of a person who was personally liable on an open-ended credit card account. However, the court ruled that under ECOA it is acceptable for a bank to require reapplication for a credit card after a change in marital status.

**Questions for Discussion**
1. What should the bank have done to avoid violating the ECOA?
2. What procedures could the bank follow in the future to avoid this kind of ECOA violation?

## Coverage

FCRA regulates the content, purpose, and use of **consumer reports.** Consumer reports include information that consumer reporting agencies communicate by written, oral, or other methods regarding a consumer's creditworthiness, credit standing, credit capacity, character, general reputation, personal characteristics, or mode of living. This information can be supplied for a variety of permissible purposes that include

- determining a consumer's eligibility for credit or insurance for personal, family, or household purposes
- determining a consumer's eligibility for employment
- purposes outlined by court order
- purposes to which a consumer agrees in writing
- determining a consumer's eligibility for a license or other benefit granted by a government unit that by law requires consideration of an applicant's financial status or responsibility
- legitimate business needs for the information in connection with a business transaction initiated by the consumer

Besides supplying information for these permissible purposes, **consumer reporting agencies** may furnish to government agencies information about a consumer's name, address, former addresses, places of employment, or former places of employment without the need for the government agency to reveal how the information will be used.

### Exemptions

If a report does not contain information provided by a third party, it is not a consumer report. Institutions or persons who communicate to third parties only their own credit experience with a consumer are not considered consumer reporting agencies and need not comply with FCRA.

### Example

State Bank receives an application for a consumer loan from Homer Simpson. The bank contacts Third National Bank and requests any information it has on Simpson. Third National relates its own credit history with Simpson and shares the contents of a credit report in Simpson's file. The credit report was prepared by a consumer reporting agency. Third National must comply with FCRA requirements for consumer reporting agencies because it has provided information to State Bank from a third party. Had Third National shared only its own experience with Simpson, FCRA requirements would not apply.

FCRA regulates both how consumer reporting agencies must prepare and disseminate consumer reports and the procedures for ensuring the accuracy of those reports. The act does not regulate entry into the business of consumer reporting. The licensing of individuals or entities that wish to start consumer reporting agencies is left to state law.

## Requirements

FCRA requirements address the content and furnishing of consumer reports, as well as the consumer's rights to review such reports.

### Content of Consumer Reports

Whether or not the preparers or users of consumer reports would consider the following information relevant, consumer reports cannot relay any of the following information except under limited circumstances:

- bankruptcies occurring more than ten years before the date of the report

- lawsuits and judgments more than eight years old
- tax liens, bad debts, records of criminal activities, or any other adverse information more than seven years old

These limitations do not apply if the report is on someone seeking a loan over $150,000 or a position of employment paying $75,000 or more annually.

### Furnishing of Consumer Reports

Consumer reporting agencies must have procedures designed to avoid furnishing reports that are not for the specific purposes previously outlined. Procedures must include requiring users of the reports to identify themselves and to certify the particular use to which the reports will be put. Certification of use is not required when consumer reporting agencies respond to government requests for a consumer's name, address, former addresses, employment, and former employment.

Except for investigative consumer reports for employment purposes, consumer reports can be prepared without the consent of consumers and furnished to users without notifying consumers. **Investigative consumer reports** are products of personal interviews with individuals who know of the consumer's character, general reputation, personal characteristics, or mode of living.

Because of their extremely subjective and personal nature, investigative consumer reports cannot be ordered (except for purposes of employment for which the consumer has specifically applied) unless certain disclosures are made to the consumer. The disclosures, which must be in writing and delivered within three days after the report is ordered, must inform the consumer that he or she has a right to request a complete and accurate description of the nature and scope of the investigative report. If the consumer submits a written request for this information, it

must be furnished within five days. When the entity ordering an investigative consumer report satisfies the disclosure requirement, the report can be prepared and furnished whether or not the consumer consents.

### Consumer's Rights to Review Reports

When a consumer so requests, consumer reporting agencies must disclose all information (except medical information) in their files on the consumer, the sources of the information, and the identity of the recipients of any reports furnished within the previous six months (unless the report was requested for employment purposes, in which case the period is two years).

Consumer reporting agencies may impose a reasonable charge—up to $8.00—for providing this information as long as the consumer is informed of the charge in advance. If the consumer's request to see a file is made within 30 days after the consumer has been notified that—based on a consumer report—credit, insurance, or employment has been denied or the consumer's credit rating is in jeopardy, then the consumer reporting agency must provide a free copy of the report to the consumer.

### Disputing the Accuracy of Consumer Reports

FCRA specifically requires consumer reporting agencies to follow reasonable procedures to assure maximum possible accuracy of the information concerning the individual about whom the report relates. Furthermore, the act gives consumers the right to dispute the completeness and accuracy of reports directly to the agency. Unless the agency reasonably believes a consumer's dispute to be frivolous or irrelevant, it must reinvestigate and record the current status of the disputed information, usually within 30 days of the consumer's request. If the reinvestigation reveals the disputed information to be inaccurate or no longer verifiable, the consumer reporting agency must delete that information from the consumer's file.

However, if after reinvestigation the consumer reporting agency finds the disputed information to be accurate and verifiable and does not delete it from the consumer's file, the consumer may submit a brief statement describing the dispute for inclusion in the agency's file. Once the statement is filed, the agency must note its existence in subsequent consumer reports unless it reasonably believes the statement to be frivolous or irrelevant.

Whenever a consumer reporting agency deletes information that is inaccurate or cannot be verified, or receives a consumer's statement disputing information in the file, the agency must notify the consumer that upon request the agency will inform those who have received consumer reports (within two years for employment purposes and within six months for all other purposes) that the information has been deleted or is disputed. If the consumer requests that notification be sent to previous recipients of credit reports, the consumer reporting agency may impose a reasonable charge for the notification.

### Users of Consumer Reports

Although the greatest burdens imposed by FCRA fall on consumer reporting agencies, users of consumer reports also are regulated by the act. Unless an investigative consumer report is involved, a consumer need not be notified when a report is prepared or distributed regarding the consumer. However, if a user denies or increases the terms for consumer credit because of a consumer report, or denies employment because of a consumer report, the user must notify the consumer of the adverse action and disclose to the consumer the name, address, and toll-free telephone number of the consumer reporting agency that made the report. This disclosure also must state that the consumer

reporting agency did not make the decision to take the adverse action and is not able to provide the consumer with the reasons for the adverse action. Users also must disclose when information has been obtained from other sources and used in the adverse decision.

### Enforcement

Federal regulatory agencies that enforce FCRA include all the agencies that regulate financial institutions. Consumer reporting agencies or users of consumer reports who willfully fail to comply with any FCRA requirement are liable for actual damages sustained by a consumer, plus any punitive damages, court costs, and attorneys' fees. If a violation is found to result from negligence rather than willfulness, the agency or user may be liable for actual damages, court costs, and fees, but not for punitive damages.

When a consumer initiates a civil lawsuit based on a violation of FCRA rules regarding investigative consumer reports, no liability exists if the defendant can show that it had procedures in place to ensure compliance with those FCRA provisions. Defendants also may defend themselves on the basis that the violation did not result from willfulness or negligence.

Any person who knowingly and willfully obtains information from a consumer reporting agency under false pretenses faces criminal penalties. The same penalties also apply to any agency officer or employee who knowingly and willfully provides information from the agency's files to a person who is not authorized to receive that information.

## FAIR DEBT COLLECTION PROCEDURES ACT

Ever-increasing judicial and legislative attention has focused on abusive practices of creditors and those representing creditors in the collection of overdue debt. On the federal level, consumer complaints about abusive debt collection methods resulted in the Fair Debt Collection Practices Act. There is no regulation implementing this law.

## Coverage

The Fair Debt Collection Practices Act applies only to debt collectors who attempt to collect or succeed in collecting on consumer debts—primarily those for personal, family, or household purposes. The act does not cover the collection of debts for commercial or business purposes.

Under this act, **debt collectors** are persons or entities who regularly collect or attempt to collect debts owed to someone other than the debt collector. Creditors seeking to directly collect debts owed to them are not covered by this law unless they use a name that is not their own in order to make the debtor think that a third party is attempting to collect the debt.

### Example

State Bank instructs its debt collectors (who are employees of the bank) to identify themselves as representing "Debt Collectors Incorporated" when calling bank customers about overdue debts. In this situation, State Bank brings itself within the Fair Debt Collection Practices Act because its employees, in speaking to debtors, are using a name other than that of the bank.

## Requirements

In cases where a bank's debt collection activities come within the scope of the act, the bank must comply with provisions governing communications with debtors and third parties; harassment, abuse, false or misleading representations; unfair practices; validation of debts; legal actions by debt collectors; and debt collection forms.

Even though the Fair Debt Collection Practices Act does not cover most collection activities undertaken by banks, its laundry list of disallowed collection activities provides a helpful guideline for banks in their own debt collection efforts. Many of the state laws that govern debt collection practices apply to banks collecting their own debts and prohibit acts or practices like those listed under the federal act. Practices listed as constituting harassment, abuse, or misrepresentation include

- using or threatening violence or other criminal means to injure the physical person, reputation, or property of anyone
- using obscene language in written or oral communication to the debtor
- publishing a list of consumers who refuse to pay debts, except publication to a consumer reporting agency or other entity meeting certain specific requirements of the Fair Credit Reporting Act
- advertising for sale any debt to coerce its repayment
- causing a telephone to ring or engaging any person in telephone conversation repeatedly or continuously with the intent to annoy, abuse, or harass any person at the number dialed
- placing telephone calls without meaningful disclosure of the caller's identity, except in pursuit of location information
- falsely representing or implying that the debt collector is an attorney or that any communication is from an attorney
- representing or implying that non-payment of any debt will result in arrest, imprisonment, or seizure or sale of any property or wages of any person unless such action is lawful and the debt collector or creditor intends to take such action
- using or distributing a written communication falsely represented to be a court or government document or that creates a false impression as to its source, authorization, or approval

- using the name of any business, company, or organization other than the true name of the debt collector's business, company, or organization
- taking or threatening to take any nonjudicial action to take possession of or disable property if no right to possession exists; no intention to take possession exists; or the property is exempt by law from such action

## CREDIT PRACTICES RULE

Unlike the various acts discussed so far, the Credit Practices Rule did not begin as federal law. Rather, it was created by the Federal Reserve Board in 1986 as Regulation AA.

### Coverage

The Credit Practices Rule applies only to consumers seeking or acquiring goods, services, or money for personal, family, or household use (other than for the purchase of real property). The rule's purpose is threefold: 1) it prohibits the existence or enforcement of certain clauses in loan contracts between creditors and consumers; 2) it provides a prescribed notice to cosigners; and 3) it prohibits the pyramiding of late charges.

### Prohibited Provisions

The Credit Practices Rule prohibits the inclusion of the following provisions in a consumer's credit obligation:

- a clause stating that the consumer gives up certain legal rights in the event of a lawsuit
- a clause assigning the consumer's wages to the lender, unless it is in accordance with a payroll deduction plan or applies only to wages already earned at the time of the assignment
- a clause granting the lender a claim on the consumer's household goods, unless the claim is given in connection with credit given for purchase of the goods

### Cosigners

To ensure that cosigners understand their obligations, a creditor must inform a cosigner of the liability involved before any obligation is assumed. The notice may be either separate from or part of the document evidencing the debt (exhibit 8.4).

For purposes of the rule, a **cosigner** is defined as a natural person who assumes liability for the obligation of a consumer without receiving goods, services, or money in return or, in the case of an open-ended credit obligation, without receiving

---

**Exhibit 8.4    Notice to Cosigners**

You are being asked to guarantee this debt. Think carefully before you do. If the borrower doesn't pay the debt, you will have to. Be sure you can afford to pay it if you have to, and that you want to accept this responsibility.

You may have to pay up to the full amount of the debt if the borrower does not pay. You may also have to pay late fees or collection costs, which increases this amount.

The bank can collect this debt from you without first trying to collect from the borrower. The bank can use the same collection methods against you that can be used against the borrower, such as suing you or garnishing your wages, and so forth. If this debt is ever in default, that fact may become a part of *your* credit record.

This notice is not the contract that makes you liable for the debt.

---

the contractual right to obtain extensions of credit under the account. Cosigners include guarantors and anyone else meeting this definition whether or not they are labeled as such in a credit document.

### Unfair Late Charges

The Credit Practices Rule prohibits banks from pyramiding late charges—that is, charging or collecting any late charge from a borrower when the only reason for the charge is a previous unpaid late charge.

## REAL ESTATE LAWS THAT PROTECT CONSUMERS

Over the years Congress has paid particular attention to real estate lending in financial institutions. One reason for this scrutiny is that real estate loans can be very complex and consumers need a great deal of information in order to intelligently shop for credit. Loans secured by real estate generally are the most costly for consumers to obtain, so Congress has taken steps to ensure that consumers enjoy the maximum amount of protection in these transactions. The following laws apply to consumer real estate loans made by banks:

- Real Estate Settlement Procedures Act
- Fair Housing Act
- Flood Disaster Protection Act

### Real Estate Settlement Procedures Act

The Real Estate Settlement Procedures Act (RESPA) was enacted in 1974 in order to require financial institutions to provide borrowers with accurate information regarding the costs to close real estate loans. RESPA also prohibits unearned referral fees (or kickbacks) between parties involved in the loan process. RESPA is not implemented by a banking regulatory agency; rather, it is governed by Regulation X of the Department of Housing and Urban Development (HUD).

RESPA covers all loans to be secured by a one- to four-family dwelling. Several exemptions from the law exist, including loans to be secured by 25 or more acres, loans to be secured by vacant lots, and interim construction loans.

RESPA has several disclosure requirements. Among these are a servicing disclosure statement, a settlement costs booklet, a good faith estimate of settlement costs, and a HUD-1 settlement statement.

The **servicing disclosure statement** indicates to the applicant whether the institution plans to sell the loan after it is closed. This statement must be provided at the time of the application if the loan will be secured by a first lien. If the application is taken by any means other than a face-to-face interview (for example, by mail or by telephone), this disclosure may be mailed within three business days. This disclosure helps the applicant decide whether to continue the application process based on his or her preference to have the loan serviced by a local institution.

A **settlement costs booklet** must be provided to the applicants within three business days of the institution's receipt of an application for a first lien loan transaction. Refinancings are not covered by this requirement. Prescribed by HUD, this booklet defines the costs the borrower will have to pay at closing.

A **good faith estimate of settlement costs** must also be provided to the consumer on all RESPA-covered loans within three business days of the institution's receipt of the application. The good faith estimate is the bank's best estimate of the costs the borrower will have to pay at closing. On this form the bank must also disclose the service providers (appraisers, title companies, and so on) that the bank requires the borrower to use in the transaction.

A **HUD-1 settlement statement** must be provided to the borrower at closing. This document specifies exactly what the borrower is paying and the person or entity that is receiving the funds. A HUD-1A, which is a simplified version of the form, can be given in situations where there is no seller, such as in home improvement loans.

More information about these documents and sample copies are available on the HUD Web site at http://www.hud.gov:80/fha/sfh/res/resp3500.html.

### Fair Housing Act

The Fair Housing Act was passed as a part of the Civil Rights Act of 1968. The Fair Housing Act prohibits discrimination in all housing-related transactions, including loans, based upon race, religion, color, national origin, sex, familial status, or handicap. This law is very broad; it covers all home-related loans. Few regulations implement the Fair Housing Act. Each agency has an advertising regulation requiring the use of the Fair Housing logo on advertisements, as well as the words "equal housing lender." A Fair Housing poster must be displayed in the lending institution's lobby (exhibit 8.5).

### Flood Disaster Protection Act

Enacted in 1972, this law was intended to help ameliorate flood damage to residences and the resulting cost to the federal government flood insurance program. The Flood Disaster Protection Act requires that banks determine whether any improved real property offered as collateral is in a special flood hazard area as designated by the Federal Emergency Management Agency (FEMA). This determination must be made before making the loan.

If the property is in a flood hazard area and in a community that participates in the National Flood Insurance Program, the bank must make the purchase of flood insurance a requirement of the loan. This requirement applies to all loans over $5,000. If the property is in a flood hazard area, the bank must give the applicant a disclosure of that fact and of the requirement to purchase flood insurance as soon as possible. This disclosure must be acknowledged by the applicant before closing the loan. If flood insurance is required, proof of its purchase must be in the file at closing. If the bank escrows for taxes and insurance it also must collect any required flood insurance premiums and hold them in escrow. Should the flood insurance coverage lapse during the life of the loan, the bank must notify the borrower and must force insurance if the borrower fails to purchase it. (If the borrower fails to purchase flood insurance, the bank will purchase insurance to cover only the bank's interest. The bank then adds the cost of the insurance to the loan or collects from the borrower.)

## CONCLUSION

Federal statutes and regulations governing the relationship between banks and their customers have a pervasive impact on the day-to-day functioning of banks. Laws such as the Truth in Lending Act, the Consumer Leasing Act, RESPA, and the Flood Disaster Protection Act require banks to provide information to borrowers. The Credit Practices Rule, ECOA, Fair Housing Act, and Fair Debt Collection Procedures Act impose responsibilities on banks to treat consumers in a consistent, fair, and respectful way. Many of these regulations undergo continual change as the banking industry continues to face an era of dramatic change. Banks and other creditors must ensure that they keep abreast of and comply with laws and regulations governing their consumer lending activities.

**Exhibit 8.5    Fair Housing Poster**

**U.S. Department of Housing and Urban Development**

**EQUAL HOUSING
OPPORTUNITY**

## We Do Business in Accordance With the Federal Fair Housing Law

(The Fair Housing Amendments Act of 1988)

---

## It is Illegal to Discriminate Against Any Person Because of Race, Color, Religion, Sex, Handicap, Familial Status, or National Origin

---

- In the sale or rental of housing or residential lots

- In advertising the sale or rental of housing

- In the financing of housing

- In the provision of real estate brokerage services

- In the appraisal of housing

- Blockbusting is also illegal

---

Anyone who feels he or she has been discriminated against may file a complaint of housing discrimination:
    1-800-669-9777 (Toll Free)
    1-800-927-9275 (TDD)

**U.S. Department of Housing and
Urban Development
Assistant Secretary for Fair Housing and
Equal Opportunity
Washington, D.C. 20410**

---

Previous editions are obsolete

form HUD-928.1A(8-93)

## QUESTIONS FOR REVIEW AND DISCUSSION

1. What are the main provisions of TILA?
2. What is the main purpose of ECOA? What are the three types of discrimination identified by the Joint Agency Statement on Fair Lending?
3. What is the primary requirement for users of credit reports under FCRA?
4. What are the purpose and scope of the Fair Debt Collection Practices Act?
5. What types of actions are forbidden under the Credit Practices Rule?
6. What are three disclosures required by RESPA?
7. Why does the government require banks to be involved in flood protection?
8. Why is the failure to comply with the right of rescission rules dangerous for a financial institution?

## LEARNING ACTIVITIES FOR CHAPTER 8

### Matching

Match each title with the regulation that implements it.

1. Truth in Lending Act
2. Equal Credit Opportunity Act
3. Consumer Leasing Act
4. Real Estate Settlement Procedures Act
5. Credit Practices Rule

a. Regulation AA
b. Regulation B
c. Regulation X
d. Regulation Z
e. Regulation M

### Multiple Choice

Choose the best answer for each question.

1. The broad consumer protection law that requires financial disclosures on consumer loans is the:

   a. Truth in Lending Act
   b. Fair Credit Billing Act
   c. Consumer Leasing Act
   d. Equal Credit Opportunity Act

2. The notice Regulation B requires to be given to applicants in some situations is:

   a. an initial disclosure statement
   b. a periodic disclosure statement
   c. an adverse action notice
   d. a good faith estimate of settlement costs

3. Credit that consists of repeated credit extensions on a revolving basis is known as:

   a. plastic credit
   b. open-door credit
   c. open-ended credit
   d. closed-ended credit

4. A consumer's ability to cancel a credit transaction without the creditor's consent is known as:

   a. privilege
   b. rescission
   c. authorization
   d. restitution

5. A credit cardholder's liability for unauthorized use of a credit card is either the amount of credit obtained before the cardholder notified the issuer of the unauthorized use or _____, whichever is less.

   a. $25
   b. $50
   c. $75
   d. $100

6. The act that directly governs the content of loan application forms is the:

   a. Truth in Lending Act
   b. Fair Credit Billing Act
   c. Consumer Leasing Act
   d. Equal Credit Opportunity Act

7. The following is not a type of discrimination under the Fair Lending guidelines:

   a. overt evidence of discrimination
   b. evidence of disparate treatment
   c. evidence of intentional harm
   d. evidence of disparate impact

## Short Answer

Write a brief statement describing the major purpose(s) of each of the following laws.

1. Truth in Lending Act

   _____

   _____

   _____

   _____

2. Equal Credit Opportunity Act

   _____

   _____

   _____

   _____

3. Real Estate Settlement Procedures Act

   _____

   _____

   _____

   _____

4. Fair Debt Collection Practices Act

   _____

   _____

   _____

   _____

5. Fair Credit Reporting Act

   _____

   _____

   _____

   _____

# 9

# SECURED TRANSACTIONS

## LEARNING OBJECTIVES

After studying this chapter, you should be able to

- explain how Article 9 of the Uniform Commercial Code establishes the requirements and procedures for secured transactions
- list and describe the three basic components of a valid security agreement and identify additional security agreement provisions that give lenders further rights in the collateral
- describe the procedures necessary to accomplish attachment and perfection of a security interest and explain why properly executing these steps is so important to lenders
- discuss how priority in collateral is established, list the contents and use of the financing statement in this process, and identify the types of interests that compete with a secured lender for priority in collateral
- explain the various repossession and sale options lenders have with regard to collateral in the event of default
- define and use the legal and banking terms that appear in bold in the chapter text

## INTRODUCTION

Bankers know that risk is a part of making loans. With every loan the chance exists that the borrower will not repay it. Still, most borrowers do repay their loans, and lenders often make loans based solely upon the borrower's honesty, solvency, and good credit history. In other cases lenders require that the borrower give the bank some security to ensure repayment. This security comes in the form of an interest in some of the borrower's property. As discussed in earlier chapters, the legal term for property given to secure a loan is *collateral*. The bank's right to the collateral is called a *security interest*.

Security interests are extremely important because if the borrower fails to repay the loan, the lender's valid security interest allows the lender to sell the property and apply the sale proceeds to the loan. If the security interest is not valid the lender has no right to the property.

Article 9 of the Uniform Commercial Code (UCC), which covers secured transactions, sets forth the rules and conditions for security interests in collateral for personal property. This chapter begins by presenting the principal terms and classifications addressed in Article 9. It then goes examines the security agreement and the steps, called **attachment** and **perfection,** that must be taken for the security interest to ensure a bank's right to collateral.

Even if the rules are followed precisely, other creditors may still claim to have priority over a lender's security interest. An awareness of how legal priority is established helps lenders prepare for potential competitors. Finally, the chapter looks at the UCC requirements for foreclosing on collateral in the event of default.

Although UCC Article 9 has been around for many years, it does change from time to time. In 1999 Article 9 was amended by the National Conference of Commissioners of Uniform State Laws.

The revised Article 9 has a uniform effective date of July 1, 2001 in all states where the state legislature has adopted it.

## ARTICLE 9 OF THE UNIFORM COMMERCIAL CODE

Security interests are created under UCC Article 9—Secured Transactions. Article 9 applies *only* to loans secured by personal property; that is, any kind of property except real estate. Certain terms are important to understanding the conditions in Article 9. In addition, the way that collateral is classified has implications for banks who expect to use this collateral if needed to repay a debt. Terms referenced in Article 9 include

- **security interest**—a bank or other creditor's right to collateral for payment of a debt
- **secured party**—the creditor who holds a security interest
- **debtor**—the person who owes payment on a loan or extension of credit
- **collateral**—the property used as security
- **default**—the debtor's failure to pay the loan
- **foreclosure**—the procedure by which the secured party takes the collateral, sells it, and applies the sale proceeds to payment of the debt
- **purchase money security interest**—a security interest in property that was purchased by the loan proceeds

### Example

A dentist wants to purchase new chairs for his expanded office and obtains a loan from State Bank to do so. The dentist (the debtor) pledges the chairs as collateral, meaning that if he defaults on the loan, the bank has the right to take possession of the chairs and sell them (foreclose) to satisfy the debt. State

Bank is now the secured party because it has a security interest in the chairs. More specifically, State Bank has a purchase money security interest, because the loan is secured with the property purchased by the loan proceeds.

Article 9 also defines the different types of personal property used as collateral. The classification of collateral is important because if the collateral is not properly described in the security agreement the bank's security interest might not be good enough to give it legal access to the property to repay the debt.

Property is classified according to its use. **Consumer goods** are items (property) used or purchased for personal, family, or household purposes. **Equipment** is property used or purchased primarily for business use. **Inventory** is property that the borrower holds primarily for sale or lease to others.

Classification is not as straightforward as it would appear. For example, a refrigerator is classified as consumer goods if the borrower uses it for personal purposes. But if the refrigerator is on the sales floor of an appliance store it is inventory. If it is in a doctor's office keeping perishable medicine from spoiling, it is equipment.

Many types of property can be used as collateral. The property may be tangible, such as refrigerators or cars, or it may be intangible. Documents are usually titles to property (such as a car title or warehouse receipts), and are useful when taking physical possession of the tangible property itself would be inconvenient. Instruments include negotiable instruments (see chapter 2) and similar types of writings. Accounts are rights to payment for goods sold or leased or for services rendered. Accounts often are referred to as *accounts receivable*. A general intangible is property that does not fall into any other category. Intellectual property like patents or copyrights would be categorized as general intangibles. No matter what form the collateral takes, its classification is determined by its use.

Revised Article 9 maintains the classifications of property, expands some definitions, and adds some new categories. The definition of accounts is broadened to include health care receivables. The category of general intangibles now includes computer software. Commercial tort claims and deposit accounts are added as a category of collateral.

## THE SECURITY AGREEMENT

A **security agreement** is the contract between a borrower and lender in which the borrower grants a security interest in the collateral to the lender. The quality and accuracy of this agreement can make the difference in a lender's ability to sell collateral to satisfy a debt. The security agreement can grant a lender actual possession of collateral but more commonly describes the interest in the collateral possessed by the debtor. If the lender has actual possession of the collateral, an oral security agreement will suffice. However, if the collateral is not in the lender's possession, the UCC requires a written agreement, signed by the debtor. Under revised Article 9 a secured party no longer needs to have actual possession of certain collateral to have a valid security interest in it. A secured party can have *control* of deposit accounts, investment property, electronic chattel paper, and letters-of-credit rights without having actual physical possession.

### Contents of a Basic Security Agreement

While security agreements can be detailed and complex, a security agreement is valid according to Article 9 if it simply

- grants the security interest
- includes the debtor's signature (in the future, *authentication*)
- contains a description of the collateral

### Grant of Security Interest

A security agreement must state that the debtor (or borrower) grants the security interest in the property to the secured party (the lender). A phrase such as "borrower grants to lender a security interest in the following described collateral" or "debtor grants to secured party a security interest in the following described inventory," is all that is needed. The actual wording may vary. As long as the security interest is expressly granted, this requirement is satisfied.

### Debtor's Signature (or Authentication)

For collateral that will remain in the borrower's possession, the security agreement must contain the borrower's authentication (under the current version of Article 9, the debtor's signature). Authentication provides evidence of the borrower's knowledge and intent to pledge the collateral as security. In this respect, a security agreement is similar to any other instrument that conveys property (for example, a deed). Only the party conveying the property needs to sign. Instead of simply requiring a signature on a security agreement, revised Article 9 will allow it to be otherwise authenticated. This broader term will allow a debtor to adopt or ratify the security agreement without actually signing it. This change anticipates electronic authentication of security agreements, for example.

### Description of Collateral

When lenders extend secured credit, they generally use preprinted security agreements (exhibit 9.1). The use of such forms usually makes compliance with the first two requirements of a valid security agreement (granting the security interest and the debtor's signature) a matter of filling in the blanks. All that needs to be added is the description of the collateral. To be valid, a reasonable person must be able to identify the collateral based on the description in the security agreement. For example, while the word *equipment* would not be a sufficient description, "all equipment owned by Debtor" would adequately describe the property. Proper classification of the collateral is important in the description, such as "all inventory owned by Debtor." Under the revised Article 9 the same rules generally apply; however, a description such as "all personal property" or "all assets" is insufficient. The description should be a specific listing of the property or cite the Article 9 category. Moreover, a description by type is insufficient if the collateral is consumer goods in a consumer transaction, a commercial tort claim, a securities account, or a commodity account.

## Other Security Agreement Provisions

Provisions in security agreements can give additional rights to a secured party, beyond the basic security interest in the collateral.

### Security Interest in Proceeds

A security interest in proceeds gives the lender a security interest in whatever is received if the debtor sells, exchanges, collects on, or otherwise disposes of the collateral during the life of the security agreement. Revised Article 9 expands the definition of proceeds to include whatever is collected on the collateral, distributed on account of the collateral, any rights arising out of the collateral, or any claims arising out of loss of collateral.

#### Example
Mr. Parnell sells one of his table saws for $100 the day before the rest of his equipment is destroyed in a fire for which he was insured. He collects $9,000 from his insurance company for the destroyed equipment. State Bank has a security interest in the table saw

SECURITY AGREEMENT

September 5, 2000

Paula Schmidt of 542 South Huron Street, Cheboygan, Michigan, hereinafter called the Debtor, and First State Bank, Cheboygan, Michigan, hereinafter called the Secured Party, agree as follows:

1. Creation of security interest. The Debtor hereby grants to the Secured Party a security interest in the Collateral described in paragraph 2 to secure the payment of the Debtor's obligation to the Secured Party described in paragraph 3.

2. Collateral. The property that is subject to the security interest created by this agreement consists of equipment, more specifically described as follows: one two-ton Widget, Model 4, Serial #6WYE7, together with any proceeds from the use of such property.

3. Debtor's obligation. The Debtor shall pay to the Secured Party the sum of $9,000 together with interest thereon at the rate of 16 percent per annum, as follows: in monthly installments of $1,000, the first such installment to be paid on November 15, 1995, and each succeeding installment to be paid on the first day of each month thereafter, until the entire principal sum, together with all accrued interest thereon, shall have been paid in full.

4. Default. In the event that the Debtor fails to pay any monthly installment required to be paid under paragraph 3 of this agreement on or before the twentieth day of the month in which such installment is due, all unpaid installments shall, at the Secured Party's option, become immediately due and payable, and in addition to such right of acceleration, the Secured Party shall be entitled to any and all remedies available under the Uniform Commercial Code in force in the State of Michigan on the date of this agreement.

FIRST STATE BANK

BY:

_____          _____

ROBERT CHURCHILL,          PAULA SCHMIDT, Debtor
Vice-President

and other equipment. In this situation, because both the $100 and the insurance money are proceeds, the bank now has a security interest in them.

### Future Advances Provision

This provision is an agreement that the collateral will secure repayment not only of the original loan but of any future loans (future advances) made by the lender to the debtor.

### Example

State Bank grants a $10,000 loan, secured by equipment, to Ms. McFee. One year later, the bank advances an additional $5,000 to Ms. McFee, with the same terms as the original loan agreement. A provision in the original agreement granted the lender a security interest in this collateral to secure the original debt as well as to secure all **future advances** made by the lender to debtor. In this situation, as a result of the future advances clause, Ms. McFee's equipment secures both the $5,000 loan and the original $10,000 loan.

### After-Acquired Property Clause

The **after-acquired property** clause imposes the lender's security interest on any new property acquired by the debtor that is of the same classification as the collateral, except in the case of certain consumer goods purchases.

#### Example

The Johnsons borrow $10,000 from State Bank, secured by the equipment used in their small business. The security agreement contains a clause stating that State Bank's security interest extends to all equipment acquired after the loan date. A year later, the Johnsons pay cash for a new table saw. Because of the after-acquired property clause, the saw becomes collateral subject to State Bank's security interest for the balance still due on the $10,000 loan.

## ATTACHMENT AND PERFECTION

Under Article 9 two steps are necessary to give the lender the right to take the collateral in the event of default. The first step, attachment, establishes the lender's legal right to the property. The second step, perfection, notifies the general public that the lender has this right. To be effective each step requires that certain conditions be met. If one of the conditions is not met, the steps of attachment or perfection may be compromised. If this happens the lender may not be able to take possession of and sell the property if the borrower defaults on the debt.

### Attachment

According to Article 9, **attachment** gives legal right to the property when all three of the following conditions are met:

- the creditor gives value for the security interest
- the debtor has ownership rights in the collateral which he or she can legally convey to a creditor
- the debtor signs (or authenticates) a security agreement that describes the collateral, or the secured party is in possession of the collateral

These conditions do not have to occur in any particular order, but without all three the lender's security interest does not attach and will not be effective.

### Value Must Be Given

Attachment will not occur until the creditor gives value for the security interest. While many nonmonetary items qualify as value, a loan or commitment to loan money from a creditor to a debtor is the most common form of value. For example, if Ms. Greene applies for a loan from State Bank, value is given when the bank commits to grant her the loan or actually gives her the money.

### The Debtor Must Have Ownership Rights

Attachment also does not occur until the debtor has acquired rights in the collateral. This can happen at the time of signing or after signing the security agreement. Revised Article 9 makes it clear that attachment will occur if the debtor has the power to transfer collateral.

#### Example

Ms. Greene applies for a $15,000 loan from State Bank to purchase a tractor for her business. The bank grants the loan request on September 15. On that day Ms. Greene signs a note and security agreement describing the tractor and the bank issues a check payable to the tractor supplier for $15,000. Three days later, on September 18, Ms. Greene uses the check to purchase the tractor. In this situation State Bank's security interest attaches on September 18. Although the security agreement was signed and value given on September 15 (through the commitment), Greene did not actually acquire rights in the collateral (the tractor) until she paid for it on September 18.

### The Debtor Must Sign a Security Agreement

For attachment to occur, the secured party currently must have a valid (and signed) security agreement or be in possession of the collateral. Under revised Article 9 attachment may occur if the secured party has *control* of the collateral, even if the secured party does not have actual possession of the property. Because taking possession or control of the property often is inconvenient, most lenders use the security agreement as the primary way to satisfy this condition.

## Perfection

**Perfection** of a security interest is necessary to give the public notice that property owned by the debtor is subject to the interest of the secured party. Other potential lenders can see the first creditor's interest in the property and know that they would not have first priority on the collateral in the event of the debtor's default. A properly perfected security interest will give the first lender priority over all others who perfect against the collateral at a later time.

### Example

Charles Murray owns a small business. To obtain a loan from State Bank, he offers the machinery, inventory, and accounts receivable of his business as collateral. When considering the loan request, State Bank checks the UCC filing records in the state in which Mr. Murray's business is located. They find that Mr. Murray secured a loan at First National Bank with the same collateral

three months ago. If State Bank makes the loan to Mr. Murray secured by this collateral, State Bank's interest will be subordinate to First National's, because First National has properly perfected its interest by filing first.

### Filing the Financing Statement

To perfect a nonpossessory security interest (one for which the lender does not physically hold or control the collateral), the secured party must **file** notice of the security interest in the public records, alerting other potential lenders that a security interest exists. Although the secured party could file a copy of the actual security agreement, generally lenders file a standard form called a **financing statement.** The financing statement summarizes the information on the security agreement. To file, the secured party registers either the security agreement or the financing statement with the proper state or local authority.

Before its latest revision, Article 9 required that the financing statement summarize the security agreement and, at a minimum

- list the debtor's and secured party's names and addresses (to identify the parties to the transaction)
- describe the collateral (to give a general summary of the property)
- contain the debtor's signature (to confirm the debtor's intent)

### *Identification of the Debtor*

Financing statements are filed under the debtor's name. Improperly identifying the debtor on a financing statement could make the filing useless. Problems with identifying debtors most frequently occur when

- multiple debtors are involved
- the debtor operates under a trade name
- the debtor changes his or her name

If more than one debtor is involved, the financing statement must identify all of them. This requirement permits a third party to search the public records to look for any security interests on the individual debtors' property.

As was discussed in chapter 4, trade or assumed names are common in the business world. For example, Heather Martin may operate her business under the trade name Floral Designs. The lender can identify the debtor on the financing statement as Heather Martin or as Heather Martin dba Floral Designs. However, a filing in a trade name alone does not sufficiently protect the lender's interest. The actual legal name of the debtor must be used.

If a debtor's name changes, the lender has four months to file a new financing statement or the security interest will no longer be perfected in after-acquired property. The old financing statement remains valid for collateral acquired before, and up to four months after, the name change. A financing statement filed for the purpose of changing the debtor's name does not require the signature of the debtor. Revised Article 9 allows the secured party to file an amendment to the original financing statement if the debtor's name changes. A new financing statement need not be filed

### Example

State Bank has a loan to Valley Corporation secured by all of Valley Corporation's inventory. The bank has filed a financing statement that identifies "Valley Corporation" as the debtor. Two years later, Valley Corporation changes its name to Better Products, Inc. Six months after the name change, Better Products acquires more inventory. State Bank is not perfected as to this new inventory. The bank had four months after the name change to file a new financing statement showing "Better Products, Inc." as the debtor. Because State Bank failed to do so, it does not

have a valid security interest in the inventory that Better Products acquired six months after the name change.

### Description of the Collateral

Like a security agreement, a financing statement must contain a description of the collateral. A secured party may copy the description used in the security agreement or may summarize it by simply listing the types of property in which it has the security interest. Article 9 classifications for collateral generally suffice for this purpose. However, the descriptions should not be more generic than those provided by Article 9. A description such as "all equipment owned by Debtor" is sufficient, but a description such as "all assets" or "all personal property" currently is ineffective. This rule changes under Revised Article 9. When the revision becomes effective, an "all assets" description would be sufficient on a financing statement.

The UCC does not require a fanatical adherence to its provisions governing financing statements. It merely attempts to simplify the formal requirements leading to perfection. Consequently, minor errors in financing statements, which are not seriously misleading, do not prevent perfection of the interest.

### Financing Statements Under Revised Article 9

Revised Article 9 minimizes the information required on a financing statement. Revised Article 9 requires

- the debtor's legal name
- the name of the secured party
- an indication of the collateral covered by the financing statement

The financing statement does not have to be signed by the debtor. The deletion of this requirement will facilitate the process of electronic filing. However, in case of a bogus or wrongful filing, revised Article 9 allows a debtor to file a corrective statement that sets forth the facts regarding the wrongful or bogus filing. It is important for lenders to keep abreast of state laws governing their secured transactions so that all filing requirements will be met.

#### Where to File

The most skillfully drafted financing statement will mean little if it is filed in the wrong place. Creditors must check their specific state UCC to determine the proper filing location. Generally, states require that some financing statements be filed centrally and some be filed locally.

Because of the variations of the UCC, no generalization can be made about the proper place to file financing statements for all secured lenders. Note, however, that a secured lender who improperly files a financing statement receives no protection against a third party that properly perfects an interest in the same collateral.

Revised Article 9 changes some of the filing rules. Under the amended article the general guideline is that financing statements must be filed in the jurisdiction where the debtor is located. A corporation, limited partnership, or limited liability company is considered to be located in the state where it is organized. An individual is considered to be located in the state of his or her residence. Revised Article 9 also requires centralized filing for types of collateral other than fixtures and timber to be cut.

In very limited situations, a creditor is not required to file a financing statement to perfect a nonpossessory security interest. In these few situations perfection occurs automatically at the time of attachment. The UCC currently allows for this automatic perfection in the case of a purchase money loan to purchase consumer goods. Revised Article 9 expands the types of collateral eligible for automatic perfection to include the sale of payment intangibles and promissory notes, health-care insurance receivables given as collateral to the health-care provider, and security interests given in favor of an issuer for a draw under a letter of credit. These types of collateral may all be perfected without filing or taking possession or control of the collateral.

#### Other Methods of Perfection

While filing a financing statement usually is the best way to perfect a security interest, other methods exist for notifying third parties of a lender's interest in collateral. These include

- taking physical possession of the collateral
- noting the interest on a certificate of title

### Possession

A lender who perfects a security interest by physical possession does not need to sign a written agreement in order for the interest to attach; however, the lender benefits from the additional provisions in a written agreement. Security interests in collateral that is money or negotiable instruments can be perfected only by possession. If the collateral consists of documents, goods, or letters of credit, the security interest may be perfected by either filing or physical possession.

### Certificates of Title

State certificate of title laws specify certain types of property for which the state issues a certificate of title to property owners. Certificates of title generally supersede the UCC when perfection of collateral is at issue. Motor vehicles are the most common form of property subject to certificate of title laws, but mobile homes, boats, and farm equipment also may be covered. A lender claiming a security interest in titled property generally must put a notation about the interest on the title certificate itself.

Revised Article 9 offers an alternative method of perfection in certain cases. The secured party can perfect its interest in the collateral by taking control of the property. Control is achieved if the party with possession of the collateral will honor instructions from the secured party without consent of the debtor. The types of collateral that can be perfected by control include investment property, deposit accounts, electronic chattel paper, and letter-of-credit rights.

## PRIORITIES ON DEFAULT

**Priority** is the position a secured party has in relation to other lenders. Secured creditors who seek to take possession of collateral can find themselves competing for the property with other parties, such as the defaulting debtor, other secured creditors, unsecured creditors, bankruptcy trustees, and purchasers of the collateral. It is very important that the lender be able to establish the priority of its interests.

### The Debtor

Debtors often resist a bank's effort to repossess collateral upon default. A bank that is able to show it complied with the required procedures for attachment when it took the security interest can overcome this resistance. Attachment alone is all a lender needs to enforce the security interest against a debtor.

### Other Secured Creditors

Attachment alone does not protect a lender who is competing with another secured creditor for the same collateral. A secured lender must perfect the security interest to have priority over another secured lender. Only one perfected lender (the one with priority) will have the right of foreclosure over other creditors.

Many factors influence the priority of claims to collateral. Generally, the secured lender who first perfected its security interest has priority in the collateral, even if another party was first to obtain a signed security agreement and disburse funds. This is known as the *first-to-file rule*. In some circumstances, a purchase money security interest on property other than inventory will have priority over a conflicting security interest in the same collateral.

### Unsecured Creditors

An unsecured creditor is one who loans money or extends credit to a borrower without obtaining an interest in any property as security for payment. A secured lender with a defaulting borrower generally does not need to worry about competing with unsecured creditors for collateral. If other creditors have placed a lien on the borrower's property, the lien may be superior to the secured lender's claim. Liens are legal claims recorded against property as security for the payment of an obligation. A lien can be placed on real property not covered by Article 9. Some types of liens that may affect property serving as loan collateral are possessory liens, judgment liens, and tax liens (see chapter 7).

## Purchasers of Collateral

So that commerce may flow as smoothly as possible, the UCC permits a person to purchase goods free from the claims of third parties (including secured creditors), as long as the purchase is made from a person in the business of selling such goods

- in good faith
- without knowledge that the sale violates any third party's ownership rights or security interest in the goods

A person who buys in this manner is considered a buyer in the ordinary course of business, meaning that he or she purchases goods free and clear from the claims of third parties. Customers who buy products at a store generally meet the criteria for being buyers in the ordinary course of business. If the buyers are aware that the products are collateral for a bank's loan to the store owner, it does not affect their status. However, if the buyers know that sale of the product they are purchasing actually violates someone else's ownership rights or rights under a security agreement, then their purchase is subject to those rights, and the secured party may ultimately be able to reclaim the property.

## Bankruptcy Trustees

In situations of default, secured lenders often compete with bankruptcy trustees for the rights to collateral. A bankruptcy trustee may challenge the secured creditor's interests and try to keep as much collateral as possible for the bankruptcy

estate. Bankruptcy trustees are given specific tools to accomplish this duty. Bankruptcy trustees are considered hypothetical lien creditors and have the ability to set aside as preferences some transfers of property made by the debtor. A bankruptcy trustee has power to set aside preferential property transfers that the debtor has made to any creditors. If a debtor treats a lender preferentially (for example, pays off a loan or grants a security interest immediately before the bankruptcy filing), the trustee can reverse the transaction. Bankruptcy trustee powers are discussed more fully in chapter 10.

## Fixtures

Goods become *fixtures* when they are so attached to and part of a building that they do not remain items of personal property but are considered to be a part of the real property. Items of personal property that may become fixtures include lights, vents and ducts, furnaces, boilers, shelving, and air conditioners. For example, lights owned by a lighting company are personal property. Once they are installed in a building, the lights become real property. While a lender might have a security interest in the lights when they are personal property, this might not be the case once they become real property.

Because the laws governing the use of personal and real property as collateral differ greatly from state to state, creditors that wish to secure debt with personal property that might become a fixture face the problem of maintaining the perfection of their security interest after the property becomes part of the building.

The UCC resolves priority conflicts between creditors that secure debts with goods before they are attached to real property and creditors that secure debts with real property to which goods are attached. Generally, the first creditor to file a financing statement (in the first situation) or to record a mortgage (in the second situation) has priority with regard to the fixtures. The

UCC specifies that procedures for filing include filing a financing statement or mortgage in the real estate records.

# FORECLOSING ON COLLATERAL

The possibility that the debtor will default is the major reason why a lender takes a security interest in collateral. Should the debtor default, a secured creditor has the right to take possession of the collateral, sell or otherwise dispose of it, and use the proceeds to repay all debts the collateral secures according to their respective priorities.

## Default

Default is any failure by the borrower to comply with the terms of a security agreement or the promissory note it secures. The most common default is the borrower's failure to make payments on the loan as agreed. However, depending on the requirements of the promissory note and security agreement, other events may constitute default. For example, the failure to maintain or properly insure collateral, the unauthorized sale or movement of the collateral, or the failure to provide financial statements may be grounds for default if a note or security agreement includes those requirements. The debtor's breach of any term in a promissory note or security agreement can constitute a default.

Many security agreements have what is called an *insecurity clause* that can put the debtor in default if the lender has reason to believe that the repayment of the debt is in doubt or insecure. Some state laws prohibit the use of insecurity clauses in consumer contracts, but courts have upheld them in commercial contracts if the lender acts in good faith.

## Self-Help Repossession

One of the most helpful parts of Article 9 from a lender's perspective is the ability to effect self-help repossession. Under certain circumstances, a secured creditor who cannot obtain full repayment of a debtor's obligation may take possession of the collateral without resorting to expensive legal action. However, a creditor must accomplish a self-help repossession of collateral without a **breach of the peace.** The UCC has not defined exactly what constitutes a breach of the peace, nor have the courts uniformly defined it. In most jurisdictions repossession must at least involve a threat of violence to constitute a breach of the peace. In most cases the use of trickery also is considered a breach of the peace in self-help repossessions. Secured creditors who breach the peace in repossessing collateral expose themselves to liability to the debtor.

Secured lenders should become thoroughly familiar with the definitions for a breach of the peace that have been adopted by their state courts. While self-help repossessions are legal—and secured creditors regularly undertake them—such actions do call for restraint and strict compliance with applicable law.

## Court-Ordered Repossession

If a secured creditor cannot repossess collateral peacefully, its only alternative is court-imposed relief. In most states, courts can grant this only after a hearing. At the hearing, the creditor must prove that the debt exists, that it is in default, and that the creditor has a secured interest in the collateral. If a court grants the relief, it will order a sheriff or other law enforcement officer to take possession of the collateral for the creditor. A court-ordered repossession will be a more expensive undertaking than self-help repossessions are, but the cost of the repossession can be deducted from the sale proceeds.

## Assembling Collateral

If a security agreement so provides, a secured lender may require a defaulting debtor to assemble the collateral at a location convenient for both parties so that the secured party may take possession of it. If the debtor refuses, a court may issue an order to compel assembly of the collateral.

If the collateral is equipment, a secured creditor may take possession of it on the debtor's premises, render it unusable, and dispose of it (by conducting a sale, for example) on those premises. This provision is useful when heavy equipment is involved and its removal is difficult.

## Disposing of Collateral

The UCC permits secured creditors who take possession of collateral either to sell it and apply the proceeds to the debt, or to keep it (under very specific circumstances) in satisfaction of the debt. Secured creditors who decide to sell the collateral must ensure that every aspect of the sale, including its method, manner, time, place, and terms, is performed in a commercially reasonable manner. The UCC strictly controls the method of selling repossessed collateral.

### Sale Procedures

A creditor who intends to sell repossessed collateral must first give notice to the debtor of the time and place of a public sale or, if the sale is to be private, a date after which the sale will take place. A major reason for giving such *notice of sale* is to allow the debtor the chance to exercise his or her right to **redeem** the collateral. The debtor may redeem the collateral by paying the amounts owed plus expenses.

Exceptions to the requirement for notification of sale are allowed when the collateral is perishable (like food), when it threatens to decline rapidly in value (like corporate stock), or when it is customarily sold in a recognized market (like publicly traded securities).

Revised Article 9 also requires a notice of sale. However, it does make some changes. In a commercial transaction

**Case for Discussion**
*The Quick Sale*

Upon default of a loan agreement, Jewel State Bank repossessed computers and other office equipment owned by Gerald Allen. However, the bank failed to notify Allen of its intention to sell the collateral. The sale yielded proceeds of $34,200, which was $11,500 less than the balance owed the bank. After the sale the bank sued Allen for the deficiency of $11,500. Allen's attorney based his client's defense on the fact that the bank had failed to give Mr. Allen notice of the sale of the collateral.

The court ruled in Gerald Allen's favor. Because his attorney was able to demonstrate that the bank's lack of notice had caused his client damages amounting to at least $11,500 in loss of business, Allen was found to be not liable for the deficiency. The attorney also was able to prove to the satisfaction of the court that Allen had been ready and able to redeem the computer and office equipment had he been given adequate notice of the sale.

**Questions for Discussion**
1. What specific evidence could Allen's attorney have provided the court to prove that the bank's lack of notice had damaged his client's business?
2. What procedures should banks take upon a borrower's default to ensure that proper notice of the sale of collateral is given?

10 days' notice of sale is considered reasonable. Notices in commercial transactions must contain at least

- a description of the debtor and the secured party
- a description of the collateral that is the subject of the intended disposition
- the method of intended disposition

- a statement that the debtor is entitled to an accounting of the unpaid indebtedness and that states the charge, if any, for an accounting
- a statement of the time and place of a public sale or the time after which any other disposition is to be made

Notices in consumer transactions must contain all of the information required in commercial notices, *plus*

- a description of any liability for a deficiency of the person to which the notification is sent
- a telephone number from which the amount that must be paid to the secured party to redeem the collateral may be obtained
- a telephone number or mailing address from which additional information concerning the disposition and the obligation secured may be obtained

Article 9 also provides model notice forms for use both in commercial and consumer transactions. Notice must also be sent to secondary obligors like cosigners and guarantors.

In a commercial transaction the secured party has some obligation to notify other secured parties. If the secured party has received, before the notification date, an authenticated notification of a claim of an interest in the collateral, or if the other lien holder has filed a financing statement covering the collateral to be disposed of, the secured party must send a notice of disposition.

### Public or Private Sale

The lender may choose to sell the collateral in a pubic or private sale. In either situation the lender is responsible for ensuring that the sale is commercially reasonable. Generally, the secured party should base the decision on which type of sale will bring the highest price. While public sales generally result in the best price for automobiles, commercial channels generally work best for specialized equipment or inventory.

### Price

Debtors often complain that the creditor's repossession sale did not bring a high enough price and therefore was not commercially reasonable. The UCC takes the position that the fact that a better price could have been obtained is not an issue. Rather, the secured party who sells the collateral in the usual manner in any recognized market, or sells it at the current market price, or has otherwise sold it in conformity with reasonable commercial practices among dealers in the type of property sold, has sold the collateral in a commercially reasonable manner.

### Sale Proceeds

The UCC is specific about distribution of sale proceeds. The UCC requires that proceeds be applied in the following order:

1. reasonable expenses incurred by the secured party in retaking, holding, preparing for sale, and selling the collateral
2. payment of the debt secured by the security interest in the collateral
3. payment of debt secured by any subordinate security interest in the collateral

### Example

Citizens Bank repossesses the inventory of River Corporation, which includes the parts to make 3,000 toys. The parts are valued at $10,000. The value of the assembled toys is expected to be $20,000. Citizens Bank decides to pay for the cost of assembling the toys, which comes to $3,400, and sells them for $20,000. According to the UCC, Citizens Bank is entitled to reimbursement for the $3,400 and repayment of the $11,000 debt balance. The remaining $5,600 ($20,000 less $11,000 less $3,400) is either returned to River Corporation or passed on to other creditors with a security interest in the collateral.

## Keeping Repossessed Collateral

Unless the collateral is consumer goods for which the debtor has paid more than 60 percent of the debt, the secured party may simply choose to keep the collateral to satisfy the obligation. This option is rarely used. If a lender chooses to exercise this option, notice must be given to the debtor and other secured lenders. If any parties object within 21 days, the secured party must sell the collateral.

Revised Article 9 slightly changes the rules regarding the retention of collateral. The notice sent to the debtor by the secured party must be an authenticated notice. This notice must also be sent to other lien holders. If an objection to the secured party's decision to keep the collateral in satisfaction of the debt is raised either by the debtor or by another lien holder, the secured party may not retain the collateral. The period for objections is 21 days. Under the revised code the secured party may retain the collateral in partial satisfaction of the debt in a commercial transaction.

## Penalties for Failure to Comply with Repossession Rules

A secured party who fails to comply with UCC requirements regarding the repossession and sale of collateral is liable for damages to injured debtors or other secured parties. Also, if the lender does not sell the collateral in a commercially reasonable manner, the debtor is entitled to recover the difference between the net amount received and the amount that would have been received had the sale been commercially reasonable.

In the case of consumer goods, the debtor has a right to recover the amount of the finance charges plus 10 percent of the principal amount of the debt. This is the minimum recovery available to consumers whose rights have been violated under the UCC.

Revised Article 9 also makes the secured party liable for improperly enforcing its security interest in the collateral. In cases where the secured party has failed to comply with Article 9 in exercising its enforcement rights, a presumption exists that the value of the collateral was equal to the debt. This presumption effectively eliminates any deficiency claim in such cases.

### Example

John Stewart purchases a car for $25,000. He puts down $5,000 and borrows the remaining $20,000 from State Bank. The loan is for 36 months and the car is pledged against the loan. After making eight monthly payments, and with $18,700 remaining on the loan, Mr. Stewart defaults.

The bank repossesses the car in a peaceful manner and sells it to an employee for $10,000, even though the value of the car has been estimated to be $21,000. After claiming $500 in expenses, the bank applies the $9,500 funds remaining to the loan balance. The bank then sends Mr. Stewart a demand letter for the deficiency remaining.

Mr. Stewart files suit against the bank, claiming that the bank did not sell the car in a commercially responsible manner by not offering it in a public or private sale where it might have sold for closer to its actual value.

## CONCLUSION

UCC Article 9 governs security interests in personal property. As a general rule, for a security interest to be valid and enforceable, it must not only attach but also be perfected. A security interest attaches when value has been given, the debtor has ownership rights in the collateral, and a signed security agreement describes the collateral or the secured party takes possession of the collateral pursuant to an agreement. Perfection occurs when the creditor gives notice to third parties of its security interest. To give this notice, the creditor usually files a financing statement with the appropriate public official. For certain types of collateral, the creditor's possession gives sufficient notice of the interest.

Attachment and perfection give a secured party significant powers over property belonging to a debtor. The strongest of these powers is the ability to sell the debtor's property and apply the proceeds as payment of the debt. Another significant power that perfection gives a creditor is the ability to take first claim on collateral and its value despite valid interests that others may have in the property.

If competing claims exist, only a lender who has perfected its security interest in collateral can benefit upon a debtor's default. Generally, the secured party who perfects first is allowed first claim to the collateral. The principal exception to this rule arises with purchase money security interests. If perfected at or near the time of the purchase money loan, a purchase money security interest will have priority over an existing security interest in the same type of collateral. If the collateral is consumer goods, perfection occurs automatically with attachment. No filing is necessary except if needed to protect the interest against the rights of a consumer buyer from the debtor.

If a debtor defaults on an obligation, the secured party has the right to foreclose the debtor's rights in the collateral by selling it and applying the sale proceeds to pay the debt. When secured parties prepare to sell collateral, they must perform every aspect of the sale in a commercially reasonable manner. A creditor who fails in this obligation may be unable to recover any deficiencies from the debtor.

## QUESTIONS FOR REVIEW AND DISCUSSION

1. What steps are necessary to effectively attach a security interest?
2. Perfection of a security interest is accomplished by several methods. What are two of them?
3. What is the first-to-file rule?
4. What is a purchase money security interest?
5. What aspects of a foreclosure must be commercially reasonable?

## LEARNING ACTIVITIES FOR CHAPTER 9

### Multiple Choice

1. A provision in a security agreement that the collateral will secure repayment not only of the original loan but of any future loans is called:

   a. a future advances provision
   b. an attachment agreement
   c. an after-acquired property clause
   d. a perfection clause

2. Which of the following is *not* a condition leading to the attachment of a security interest?

   a. the creditor gives value for the interest
   b. the debtor has rights in the collateral
   c. the debtor authenticates a security agreement that describes the collateral
   d. a financing statement is filed with the proper authorities

3. The document that summarizes a security agreement for filing purposes is called:

   a. a perfecting agreement
   b. an attachment
   c. a writ profunda
   d. a financing statement

4. A future advances provision is an agreement under which:

   a. the collateral will secure the loan until an unspecified date
   b. future loans by the lender to the debtor are secured by the same collateral
   c. the security interest is extended to new property acquired by the debtor
   d. future loans by the lender to the debtor are ensured

5. A lender of purchase money for consumer goods that are pledged as collateral under a written security agreement acquires a perfected security interest when:

   a. a financing statement is filed by the lender
   b. a security agreement is signed by the debtor
   c. the creditor gives value for the security interest
   d. the goods are purchased

6. When a borrower uses loan money to purchase property that secured the loan, what is the lender's interest in the property called?

   a. a perfected security interest
   b. an unperfected security interest
   c. a collateral-based interest
   d. a purchase money security interest

7. Priority in collateral generally goes to the secured lender:

   a. who is first to perfect the security interest
   b. whose security interest is attached
   c. whose security interest is prioritized
   d. who has a purchase money security interest

8. One who loans money or extends credit to a debtor without obtaining an interest in any property as security for payment is called:

   a. an insecure creditor
   b. an unsecured creditor
   c. a purchase-money creditor
   d. an unconflicted creditor

9. If the sale of collateral yields more than enough money to cover the costs of repossession and sale, cover the debt, and pay any other creditors who have a secured interest in the collateral, the excess funds:

   a. must be divided among creditors
   b. may be kept by the creditor who repossessed and sold the collateral
   c. must be given to the debtor
   d. will be distributed by the court

10. Which of the following circumstances would result in a purchaser of goods *not* being a buyer in the ordinary course of business under the UCC?

   a. both the buyer and the seller are ordinary consumers
   b. the buyer is aware that sale of the products violates a creditor's right to the product
   c. the seller is in the business of selling such goods
   d. the purchase is made in good faith

## Completion

For each of the following situations, decide the appropriate UCC Article 9 classification of collateral.

1. ABC Computers, a local computer store, obtains a loan to remodel its showroom. ABC secures the loan with its stock of computers held for sale.

   The collateral is: _____.

2. Robin Myers purchases a computer system for her use at home. She obtains financing for the purchase and secures the loan with the computer system itself.

   The collateral is: _____.

3. Marty Cook is a CPA who operates as a sole practitioner. She has approximately 30 clients for whom she does work on a regular basis. Most of her customers pay on a regular basis on receipt of invoices Mary sends. Mary needs a short-term business working capital loan to hire extra clerical help. She pledges the amounts her customers owe to her.

   The collateral is: _____.

4. Woodworking Company, Inc. acquires new planing machines to use in manufacturing its products. It obtains a loan to purchase these machines and pledges them as security.

   The collateral is: _____.

5. A local author requests an investment loan and would like to pledge a copyright to a popular book she has written.

   The collateral is: _____.

# 10

# BANKRUPTCY

## LEARNING OBJECTIVES

After studying this chapter, you should be able to

- trace the history of bankruptcy legislation through the Bankruptcy Reform Act of 1978 and explain the goals of liquidation and rehabilitation
- distinguish between voluntary and involuntary liquidation and list the powers and responsibilities of a bankruptcy trustee
- describe what is included in a bankruptcy estate and explain the trustee's powers regarding the estate
- describe the rights of creditors in bankruptcy proceedings and the options available to the debtors
- explain other provisions of Chapter 7 bankruptcy, including distribution of the estate, discharge, and nondischargeable debts
- differentiate between Chapter 7, Chapter 13, and Chapter 11 of the Bankruptcy Code and explain the conditions of each
- define and use the legal and banking terms that appear in bold in the chapter text

## INTRODUCTION

Society in the United States is based on individual liberties and the processes of a free economic market. An important part of the free market system is the availability of credit to grow businesses and to fuel the demand for consumer goods. However, in such a system there are times when individuals and businesses become financially over-extended and are unable to pay their debts on time. This situation can arise from poor financial planning, unforeseen circumstances such as health problems or an unexpected job loss, or a downturn in the economy. Long ago, Congress saw fit to provide relief to debtors in dire circumstances by giving them a fresh start through the bankruptcy process.

Bankruptcy is the legal process by which debtors—who may face wage garnishment or foreclosures of assets pledged against loans—can seek protection from their creditors. Bankruptcy laws also allow for an orderly liquidation or reorganization of the debtor's property and thereby afford creditors some protection. Creditors want to recover something of value for the funds they extended to the debtor and they want the court to protect the property pledged as collateral against their loans.

Bankruptcy court is the forum for these competing interests to find the most equitable solution. In general, in a bankruptcy proceeding, the debtor's property is gathered up and assigned to a bankruptcy estate. The bankruptcy estate is evaluated and administered under the direction of the court with the goal of repaying creditors in an organized fashion. In bankruptcy an individual debtor can choose either to sell his or her assets and divide the proceeds among the creditors or to work out a plan to pay creditors over a period of years to keep and use the property instead of selling it. When the bankruptcy estate is sold (or the payment plan completed), the creditors are paid what is available and the debtor's debts are discharged.

## BANKRUPTCY LAW

The U.S. Constitution gives Congress the power to enact bankruptcy legislation. By 1898 Congress had passed three federal statutes on bankruptcy, none of which was in effect for very long.

Under the first bankruptcy law, passed in 1800, debtors could not seek relief from their debts. The law was designed to provide creditors with a method of seizing the debtor's property. The second bankruptcy statute, enacted in 1841, allowed debtors to file a bankruptcy petition for their own relief. Passage of this statute introduced the concept of a fresh start for honest but overburdened debtors.

Over time, individual states also passed laws relating to persons unable to pay their debts. These state laws were used during periods when federal bankruptcy laws did not exist. Some states still allow debtors to achieve some relief by making an assignment for the benefit of their creditors.

The third federal bankruptcy law was enacted in 1867 and came to an end in 1878. Thereafter efforts to promote a long-term national law resurfaced as part of an overall push by business for national and uniform state laws. After much debate, Congress passed a fourth bankruptcy law in 1898—the National Bankruptcy Act. The National Bankruptcy Act survived for 80 years with very few amendments. The most important change occurred in 1938 when Congress added an amendment that gave debtors an alternative to straight bankruptcy. This alternative was rehabilitation—a chance for debtors to recover from their condition of indebtedness and reestablish themselves. In 1978 Congress entirely rewrote the Bankruptcy Act.

### Bankruptcy Reform Act of 1978

By far the biggest change to the nation's bankruptcy law in the twentieth century occurred in 1978 with the Bankruptcy Reform Act. This act became effective on October 1, 1979 and was most significant because it organized all provisions of U.S. bankruptcy laws into a **Bankruptcy Code.** This act has been revised and amended several times since its enactment, most recently by the Bankruptcy Reform Act of 1994. The Bankruptcy Code provides for both straight bankruptcy, most commonly called **liquidation,** and for debtor rehabilitation. The 1978 change to the bankruptcy laws preceded a tremendous increase in the number of debtors who filed bankruptcy petitions. In 1978, before the effective date of the new law, there were a total of 172,000 consumer bankruptcy filings. Twelve years later, in 1990, there were 718,000 consumer filings. In 1998 there were nearly 1.4 million consumer filings.

## CHAPTER 7—LIQUIDATION

Typically, liquidation is considered to be the primary relief provided by bankruptcy. **Liquidation** involves collecting all of a debtor's assets, converting the assets to cash, and distributing the cash among the creditors according to the type and amount of their claims. The debtor is then discharged from indebtedness. Chapter 7 of the Bankruptcy Code presents the liquidation provisions.

---

### Critical Terms

*Liquidation* Converting property into cash. Liquidation usually involves selling the property to obtain the cash.

*Priorities* Rank order in the exercise of legal rights (in this case, the right to be paid for a debt).

---

### Voluntary and Involuntary Liquidation

Under **Chapter 7** a debtor may file a petition to begin a liquidation proceeding. When the debtor files a Chapter 7 petition on his or her own accord it is called a *voluntary liquidation.* Individuals, partnerships, corporations, and unincorporated organizations may file under Chapter 7.

Governmental units (such as cities and counties), insurance companies, banking institutions, and credit unions may not file Chapter 7 bankruptcy petitions. However, Municipalities may seek bankruptcy relief under other chapters of the code.

Creditors may file a Chapter 7 petition against the debtor to force an *involuntary liquidation.* One reason creditors might want to force a debtor into bankruptcy is to assure themselves that the debtor's assets are liquidated and distributed according to **priorities** stated in the Bankruptcy Code.

Involuntary bankruptcies differ from voluntary ones only in the way the proceeding begins. If a required number of creditors with a certain minimum debt owed to them can establish that a debtor generally is not paying debts as they come due, the court will usually grant their petition for involuntary bankruptcy of the debtor. Once permitted, the bankruptcy will proceed as do voluntary proceedings.

To initiate a voluntary liquidation, the debtor files a petition with the clerk of a federal bankruptcy court. The petition must include

- a schedule (list) of the debtor's assets and debts
- a statement of the debtor's financial affairs with a list of questions answered by the debtor
- a schedule of the debtor's current income and expenses

Attached to this petition must be a list of all the debtor's creditors. The court uses this list to notify creditors of the bankruptcy proceeding. The creditors also receive a notice of the requirement that they file proof of their claims as part of the proceeding. The proof of claim is important if the creditor wants to establish the debt in the bankruptcy proceeding.

### Automatic Stay

Once a bankruptcy petition has been filed, an **automatic stay** against further debt collection is in place. This means that creditors must halt any efforts to obtain payment of their claims from the debtor or to foreclose or sell collateral. Creditors may not contact the debtor at all for the purpose of collecting the debt. Once the debtor's affairs are in the hands of a bankruptcy court, a creditor's only means of obtaining payment for pre-petition debts is through the court. The stay preserves the status quo and gives the debtor a breathing spell.

## Trustees

When a Chapter 7 petition for bankruptcy is filed, the Office of the U.S. Trustee names a temporary **trustee** to administer the debtor's property in the bankruptcy proceedings. The temporary trustee functions until the first meeting of the debtor's creditors, which usually takes place 20 to 40 days after the filing of the petition. The debtor must appear at the meeting, submit to examination under oath, and respond to questioning by creditors, their attorneys, and the trustee about assets, transfers of assets, and other financial matters. At the meeting, the creditors may also select a permanent trustee, although it is customary to name the temporary trustee to that position.

# BANKRUPTCY ESTATE

The **bankruptcy estate** is composed of all the debtor's property and property interests as of the day the case was filed. The debtor must surrender all property belonging to the estate to the appointed trustee except for property the debtor is allowed by law to exempt from the estate. All property that debtors want to exempt is described in a list of assets given to the bankruptcy court. The trustee and creditors may object to the items on this list but must do so promptly. If no objections are made when the deadline for objections has passed, all the exemptions on the list will be allowed.

Both state law and the Bankruptcy Code list certain kinds of property to be exempt. Depending on state law a debtor may be able to choose between the code exemptions or state exemptions. Some states do not allow a debtor to choose the federal exemption. Depending on the generosity of state exemptions, a debtor might prefer the exemptions allowed by federal law. Exemptions allowed by the Bankruptcy Code include

- up to $15,000 interest in the value of property used as a residence by the debtor or a dependent, or in a burial plot for the debtor or dependent
- up to $2,400 interest in one motor vehicle
- up to $8,000 interest in all household goods and furnishings, wearing apparel, appliances, books, animals, crops, or musical instruments held primarily for personal or family use by the debtor or a dependent (this exemption may not exceed $400 in value in any particular item)
- up to $1,000 in jewelry used for personal or family use
- in addition to all other exemptions, the debtor may claim as exempt an interest in any property not to exceed $800 in value plus up to $7,500 of any unused portion of the residence and burial plot exemption (this catch-all provision allows the debtor to claim a total of $8,300 in property without restriction as to its type)
- up to $1,500 in value in implements, tools, or professional books used in the trade of the debtor or a dependent
- professionally prescribed health aids for the debtor or a dependent
- rights to certain types of income and life insurance benefits

### Example
Joe Conroy has $5,000 in a savings account at First State Bank. Conroy files a bankruptcy petition listing this account. The trustee is entitled to these funds unless Conroy claims the account

balance as exempt. He would have to use the catchall exemption, because none of the specific exemptions is for savings account funds.

Sometimes an analysis of a debtor's property and the various exemptions allowed by state and federal law is required to determine which exemptions are in the debtor's best interest.

### Example

Katherine Willis has a large amount of credit card debt, a car loan, and a mortgage. Her home is worth approximately $80,000; her car is worth $14,000. The balance on her mortgage is $55,000 and the balance on her car loan is $12,000. Facing unexpected medical expenses, she files a bankruptcy petition. Her state allows debtors to choose between the state and federal exemptions. State law allows an exemption of up to $100,000 on an individual's principal dwelling, unlimited exemptions on up to two automobiles, and $40,000 of other personal property. Should she choose her state exemptions or the federal exemptions? In this case, because she has more than a $15,000 interest in her home, she should probably choose the state exemptions.

## Trustee Powers Over the Estate

Once the bankruptcy estate is created, the trustee acquires all rights in the debtor's property. Serving as an officer of the bankruptcy court, the trustee determines the extent and value of the estate and converts the estate to cash for distribution to creditors. To perform these duties, the trustee has broad powers of investigation and the right to sue third parties to collect assets of the debtor for inclusion in the estate.

The Bankruptcy Code has complicated rules concerning when property that has been given away, sold, or pledged as security for loans can be considered to belong to the debtor and thus to be within the trustee's jurisdiction. In some cases, if the debtor transferred property in the time period immediately before filing for bankruptcy, the trustee has the right to reach back to reclaim property for the estate. In certain cases, the trustee can reach back as far as a year before the filing and reclaim property. These powers help the trustee to obtain additional cash for the estate with which to repay creditors.

### Trustee as Lien Creditor

The bankruptcy trustee may have the power to invalidate certain property transfers made by the debtor. For example, property held by a bank as collateral for a loan may be seized by the trustee if the bank's interest is unperfected (see chapter 9). That is, if the security interest was not recorded according to procedures required under UCC Article 9, the bank may lose its rights to the collateral. Because trustees are required to assemble as much estate property as possible, they frequently will try to establish the priority of their claim to property over that of a bank holding title to the property as collateral. To protect their claims to property, banks must be sure to perfect their security interests.

### Example

On July 1, Second State Bank loans Mr. Everett $50,000 and accepts a security interest in his inventory as collateral. However, the bank fails to file a financing statement to perfect its security interest in this collateral according to Article 9. Thus, the bank's security interest is unperfected. On September 15, Everett files a petition for bankruptcy. In this situation, the trustee's claim will have priority over the bank's unperfected security interest. The trustee can take possession of Everett's inventory, sell it, and use the proceeds to pay the creditors. The bank's claim for $50,000 will be that of an unsecured creditor.

### Trustee as Bona Fide Purchaser of Real Estate

The trustee acquires the rights of a bona fide purchaser of the debtor's real estate on the date of the bankruptcy petition. Therefore, if the debtor has transferred any interest in real estate and evidence of the transfer has not been perfected (usually by recording it in the real estate records) by the date of the bankruptcy petition, the trustee may claim such real estate without regard to the holder of the unperfected interest.

#### Example

On June 8, Peoples' National Bank lends Ms. Hay $80,000, secured by real estate. The bank's mortgage is left on the loan officer's desk while she takes a two-week vacation. On June 15, Ms. Hay's creditors file a petition for involuntary bankruptcy. The bank's mortgage is recorded on June 22. State laws provide that a bona fide purchaser can take real estate free of any prior unrecorded interests. In this situation, the bank's unrecorded mortgage is worthless. The bank's status is that of an unsecured creditor.

### Trustee as Successor to Actual Creditors

The trustee stands in the place of the debtor's general creditors and has power to take any action that the debtor's creditors could take under state law. Trustees usually use this power to set aside certain transfers that were made by debtors before bankruptcy. These transfers often are the types that the creditors themselves could have set aside under the state's fraudulent-transfer laws.

### Trustee's Preferences

The concept of **preferences** is important in bankruptcy. A preference occurs when someone transfers property to a creditor in payment of a debt within 90 days before filing for bankruptcy. This type of transfer may enable the particular creditor to receive more than would be awarded by the bankruptcy court under Chapter 7, so trustees have the power to cancel these preferences and reclaim the transferred property for the estate. Preferences can include many types of transfers.

#### Example

Marcus Rand realizes he is insolvent and considers bankruptcy. One of his debts is to his father for $20,000, so Marcus pays that debt with the last of his cash and a deed to vacant land he owns. Two months later, he files for bankruptcy and lists several other creditors on the schedule. In this situation Marcus has preferred one creditor, his father, over the other creditors.

Because the definition of preference includes the transfer of *any* interest in property, it can have damaging effects even on **secured creditors,** such as banks. Consider the following:

#### Example

On August 1, Perry Lee executes a mortgage to secure an already-existing debt to Citizens' State Bank that he has been unable to pay. The bank's mortgage is recorded immediately. On October 10, Perry files for bankruptcy. The mortgage constitutes a transfer of an interest in property under the definition of preference. Because it was made to secure a prior debt within 90 days of the filing, the trustee may cancel the transfer. This will make the bank an unsecured creditor in the bankruptcy proceeding. Had the mortgage not been given to secure a prior debt (that is, had the mortgage secured a new loan made August 1), the trustee could not set it aside.

The definition of preference is that it is a transfer made by an insolvent debtor. Under the code, debtors are insolvent when the sum of their debts is greater than the value of their nonexempt assets. All bankruptcy debtors are presumed to be insolvent during the 90 days immediately preceding the filing of the bankruptcy petition. To avoid a transfer within those 90 days being set aside as a preference, the creditor must disprove the presumption of insolvency.

Another type of preference involves transferring property or funds to insiders. Insiders to an individual debtor are

- relatives of the debtor
- general partners of the debtor
- a general partnership in which the debtor is a general partner
- a corporation if the debtor is an officer or director of the corporation

If the debtor is a general partnership, any of the general partners and their relatives will be considered insiders. If the debtor is a corporation, any of the officers, directors, or principal shareholders will be considered insiders. In any case, anyone controlling the debtor is an insider.

A transfer occurring between the 91st day to one year before filing of the bankruptcy petition is a preference if the transferee was an insider.

### Example

On April 22, an insolvent corporation pays off a $50,000 note to its president. On March 15 the next year, the corporation files its petition for bankruptcy. Because the president is an insider and the insolvent debtor has made the transfer within one year of bankruptcy, the trustee may claim the $50,000 for the estate.

Payments made in the ordinary course of the debtor's business are not considered to be preferential transfers.

### Example

On October 7, New Town Products, Inc. pays its bolt supplier $5,000 pursuant to a "net 30 days" invoice dated September 15, for bolts delivered on August 14. This payment is not a preference because New Town Products, Inc. has incurred the debt and made the payment in the ordinary course of the business of both parties.

### Code Provisions on Fraudulent Transfers

The Bankruptcy Code gives a trustee the right to stand in the shoes of the debtor's actual creditors and bring into the estate property that was fraudulently transferred out of it. By its own definitions, the Bankruptcy Code characterizes certain transfers as fraudulent if they are made within one year before the filing of a bankruptcy petition. If a trustee can establish intent to defraud, the debtor's solvency or insolvency at the time of transfer is irrelevant.

### Example

Sharon Mills gives $10,000 to her friend to place it beyond the reach of her creditors. Six months later, she files for bankruptcy. If the trustee can prove that she intended to defraud creditors by making this transfer, the transfer can be invalidated and the friend must turn the money over to the estate.

Under the code, the transfer of property for less than its value is considered to be fraudulent if the debtor is insolvent at the time of the transfer or became insolvent because of it.

### Example

To get money for overdue bills, Fred Franks sells his Cadillac to his neighbor for $6,000 when its market value is $20,000. Five months later, Franks files a bankruptcy petition. A trustee can undo this transfer and retrieve the Cadillac for inclusion in the estate.

Once the court determines that an invalid transfer has occurred, the trustee may seek return of the money, property, or value of the property from the transferee.

If necessary, the trustee may bring a lawsuit in the estate's name to get the property returned.

### Executory Contracts

Executory contracts are those in which neither of the parties has yet completed performance. If a debtor is a party to an executory contract at the time of bankruptcy, the contract becomes a part of the estate. The trustee can decide to either perform or reject executory contracts, subject to court approval.

### Example

When Denise Eppler files her petition for bankruptcy, she is in the process of buying property under a land contract. The balance left on the contract is $20,000 and the market value of the property is $50,000. To protect the $30,000 in equity, the trustee in this situation would choose to perform the contract by paying from estate funds the amount due. In this way the trustee gains a $50,000 asset for the estate.

## Secured Creditors

As discussed in chapter 9, **secured creditors** hold claims that are secured by an interest in collateral (some property of the debtor). On receiving notice of a debtor's bankruptcy petition, secured creditors are barred by the automatic stay from suing the debtor or trying to take possession of the collateral. To obtain their collateral, secured creditors must deal with the bankruptcy court and the trustee.

### Abandonment

Bankruptcy trustees have the ability to simply **abandon** property in the estate if the debtor has no equity in it or its value is inconsequential. A secured creditor can ask to have its collateral abandoned through informal discussions with the trustee, or the trustee can initiate the abandonment without the secured creditor's request. The secured creditor also may file a motion to compel abandonment. The trustee must give notice of intended abandonment to all interested parties. If any objections are filed, the court will hold a hearing. If the property is abandoned, the secured party with a valid security interest may take possession of it.

While trustees may voluntarily abandon collateral, creditors often find that filing a motion with the court for relief from the automatic stay is a quicker procedure. If the collateral is worth less than the amount owed on the debt, the court (or trustee) may decide that it has no value for the estate. The court is required to hold a preliminary hearing on the creditor's motion within 30 days of filing.

### Example

Third State Bank has a security interest in Sue Thorpe's vehicle. The vehicle has a value of $10,000 and secures a debt of $18,000. After Thorpe files the petition for bankruptcy, she surrenders the vehicle to the trustee. The bank then contacts the trustee and requests an abandonment. The trustee says he is too busy to deal with the request and tells the bank to wait a few months. The bank then files a motion for relief from the stay. Thirty days pass and neither the trustee nor any other person files an objection and the court does not hold a hearing. Under the code, the stay is lifted as to the vehicle, and the bank can proceed to take possession of it under applicable state law. On sale of the vehicle, the bank will recover $10,000 and still has a claim against the estate for the $8,000 remaining on the debt.

If secured creditors do not move to obtain their collateral, the trustee can sell, use, or lease bankruptcy estate property, including property that is collateral. If collateral is worth more than the debt it secures, the trustee will pay the creditor its value when the trustee sells it. Before using or leasing collateral the trustee must notify the secured creditor, who can request a hearing to object to such use or seek adequate protection. A court order always is required before a trustee may use cash collateral. Protection is particularly important for a creditor who fears that use of the collateral will lower its value. Adequate protection can be cash payment to the secured creditor equaling the collateral's loss of value, a regular monthly payment, or a lien on other property belonging to the estate.

## Options Available Under Liquidation

During liquidation certain procedures are available to help resolve the situation. These include redemption of personal property, reaffirmation, setoff, and discharge.

---

### Critical Terms

*Redemption* A debtor's right to reclaim personal property seized when he or she was unable to pay debts by repaying the remaining debt or the value of the seized property, whichever is less.

*Reaffirmation* Obtaining the right to use personal property by promising to repay debt remaining on the property at some time in the future.

*Setoff* A procedure whereby, in situations involving mutual debts between a bankruptcy debtor and a creditor, the creditor may offset the amount he or she owes against the amount owed to him or her by the debtor.

*Discharge* Obtaining release from the legal obligation to pay certain debts.

---

### Redemption

If the trustee abandons collateral that is personal property, individual debtors have the right to **redeem** the collateral if it secures a consumer debt and is primarily for personal, family, or household use. The debtor may redeem the collateral by paying either the amount remaining on the debt or the value of the collateral, whichever is less.

### Example

Albion National Bank has a purchase money security interest in Larry Hoop's auto, which Hoop bought to provide transportation for his family. The debt that the auto secures is $15,000 and the auto is worth $12,000. By paying the bank $12,000, Hoop can redeem the auto.

To request a **redemption,** a debtor must file a motion in the bankruptcy court. Secured creditors and others designated by the court must have an opportunity for a hearing. Typically, if there is a dispute at such a hearing, it is likely to be about the value of the collateral. A debtor's right to redeem applies to exempt as well as abandoned property.

### Reaffirmation

Debtors who cannot afford to redeem their property securing debt may reaffirm their debt and thereby keep possession of collateral. In a **reaffirmation** the debtor agrees to pay the entire debt owed to the creditor, even if it is greater than the value of the collateral. Unlike redemption, reaffirmation cannot be forced on a creditor. The creditor must agree to the plan for repaying the debt. Reaffirmation agreements relating to consumer debts must meet certain requirements. For example, the debtor must be given a 60-day period in which to cancel the agreement. If the debtor has no lawyer, a hearing before the bankruptcy judge must occur to ensure that the debtor is fully informed of the consequences of reaffirmation.

### Setoff

The Bankruptcy Code recognizes the creditor's right of setoff. **Setoff** is a procedure often used when two parties are in debt to each other. One party simply credits the amount due to it against the amount it owes to the other party. This right can be extremely beneficial in bankruptcy. Banks that are involved in taking deposits from and making loans to a debtor may, with authorization from the bankruptcy court, exercise the right of setoff. The deposit account represents debt owed by the bank to the debtor, while a loan represents debt owed to the bank.

### Example

When Rob Wills files his petition for bankruptcy, he has $400 on deposit in a checking account with First National and owes the bank $1,000 on a loan. In this situation, the bank may claim a setoff of the amount it owes the debtor ($400) against the amount the debtor owes the bank ($1,000). After setoff, the bank's claim against the estate would be for the $600 remaining on the loan.

Setoff has been held not to extend to individual retirement accounts (IRAs) on the theory that an IRA is not a bank's debt to the account holder. Rather, an IRA is a bank's obligation as trustee to the account holder.

## Distribution of the Estate

Once the trustee has given secured creditors their collateral or its value and converted the debtor's estate into cash, the liquidation is complete. The trustee then distributes payments according to the code's provisions.

All priority claims must be paid first. Priority claims include administrative expenses of the estate, wage claims by a business debtor's employees, certain unpaid contributions to the debtor's employee benefit plans, reimbursements to individual customers of the debtor for deposits on consumer goods or services that were never received, and tax claims. In addition, priority claims can exist for money owed to certain business creditors who extend credit after an involuntary liquidation petition has been filed against the debtor.

After payment of priority claims, the trustee divides the estate's remaining assets among the general unsecured creditors who have filed a proof of claim.

## Discharge

The primary benefit obtained by debtors in a bankruptcy proceeding is discharge of their indebtedness. **Discharge** is the legal release of a debtor from further obligation to pay the bankruptcy creditors. Discharge of debt is available only to individuals. Corporations declaring Chapter 7 bankruptcy cannot have their debts discharged. Thus, corporations legally continue to owe debt after distribution of their estates. However, most liquidated corporations do not stay in business, so their creditors have little hope of repayment even without a formal discharge.

Because having one's debts discharged is a privilege, only those debtors who are honest and cooperative with the bankruptcy system may receive a discharge. Procedures to deny discharge to debtors can be initiated by the court, trustees, creditors, or other interested parties. The code provides the following reasons for denying discharge to a debtor:

- fraudulently concealing or transferring property of the debtor within one year before filing a petition, or of property of the estate since filing
- failing to maintain financial records, or the concealment, destruction, or falsification of such records
- intentionally and fraudulently committing a bankruptcy crime, including making a false oath or account in the course of a bankruptcy proceeding, participating in a false claim, giving or receiving a bribe, or withholding records

- failing to satisfactorily explain a loss of assets
- refusing to answer questions or obey orders of the bankruptcy court

## Nondischargeable Debts

For reasons of public policy, certain types of debt will not be discharged even when a debtor complies with the requirements for a discharge under the Bankruptcy Code. These debts are

- taxes (with some exceptions)
- debt incurred by fraud, including obtaining credit, property, or services by use of false financial statements
- debts intentionally not listed in the schedules filed with the bankruptcy petition
- debts resulting from the debtor's embezzlement or larceny, or from fraud while acting in a fiduciary capacity
- debts to a spouse, former spouse, or child for alimony, maintenance, or support arising out of a divorce decree, separation agreement, or property settlement
- debts for willful and malicious injuries caused by the debtor
- fines or penalties imposed on a debtor by the government
- certain student loans
- debts arising from civil judgments for damages done by debtors while driving drunk
- certain debts to condominium associations

When banks object to discharge of a debt, it is most often based on the fact that the person or company has provided false financial statements when applying for a loan. Banks and other creditors must file a complaint based on fraudulently incurred debt within 60 days after the first meeting of creditors. Once the complaint is filed, the court will hold a hearing at which the creditor can present evidence of fraud.

A bank whose objections to discharge are based on fraudulent financial statements must demonstrate three facts to prove fraud. The three facts are

- that the financial statement used to induce the bank to make a loan was materially false
- that the debtor prepared the statement with the intent to deceive the bank
- that the bank relied on the statement in making its loan decision

### Example

On October 3, John Stapleton files a petition for bankruptcy and lists on his schedule an unsecured debt to South State Bank for $200,000. The bank's objection to discharge of this debt is based on a financial statement Stapleton had submitted along with his loan application. The statement lists a parcel of real estate valued at $25,000 which in fact he had sold two months earlier. Under questioning by Stapleton's lawyer, the bank's loan officer admits that his chief reasons for approving the loan were Stapleton's good credit history and the cash he had on deposit at the bank. The loan would have been made even if the real estate had not been listed on the financial statement. In this situation, because the bank cannot show that it relied on the false information contained in the financial statement in making the loan, the court rejects the bank's objection to discharge of the debt.

Creditors have long objected to abuse of bankruptcy relief by debtors who, on the eve of filing their petitions, engage in spending sprees and then seek discharge of the debts. Thus, within the category of debts incurred by fraud a presumption exists that certain consumer debts were fraudulently obtained. These include

- consumer debts of more than $1,000 owed to a single creditor for

luxuries purchased within 60 days of filing for bankruptcy
- cash advances under an open-ended consumer credit plan totaling more than $1,000 within 60 days of filing

Creditors who charge fraud when objecting to the discharge of consumer debt must pay the debtor's expenses and attorney fees in defending the discharge if the creditor's position is found to be not substantially justified.

All the debts to be discharged must be listed in the required schedule. All creditors will be notified of the bankruptcy proceedings and given a deadline for filing any objections to discharge. Debts to creditors not listed in the schedule typically will still be discharged unless it can be shown that the debtor was seeking to conceal the bankruptcy from the creditor.

### Example

In the course of contacting Ms. Foley about a delinquent payment, Detroit State Bank learns that she has filed a petition for bankruptcy. The bank confirms the filing with the court and discovers that the petition does not list the bank as a creditor. The bank, believing its debt will not be discharged, elects not to file a proof of claim. The bank later attempts to collect the debt. However, because the bank had knowledge of Ms. Foley's bankruptcy petition, her debt to the bank was discharged. By not filing a proof of claim, the bank has deprived itself of any distribution from the estate.

### Discrimination Based on Discharge

Federal, state, or other governmental agencies cannot discriminate against an individual whose debts have been discharged in a bankruptcy proceeding. Therefore, drivers who do not pay discharged judgments arising out of traffic accidents cannot be denied licenses nor can students in state schools be prohibited from registering for classes when their unpaid tuition debt has been dis-

charged. In addition, no government or private employer may discriminate against an individual in hiring, firing, or other employment decisions solely because of bankruptcy. However, nothing within the Bankruptcy Code prohibits banks or others from refusing to extend credit to individuals who have had their debts discharged. Banks may legitimately deny a loan application solely because, in the past, the applicant's debts were discharged.

## CHAPTER 13 AND CHAPTER 11—REHABILITATION

The Bankruptcy Code offers an alternative to liquidation for debtors who have regular sources of income. These are debtors who do not need the discharge of their debts or who do not want to lose all their nonexempt property. Individuals may seek this type of relief under Chapter 11 or Chapter 13 of the code while businesses use Chapter 11. The goals of debtor **rehabilitation** (also referred to as **reorganization**) are to conserve assets and restore the insolvent debtor to a condition of solvency. Exhibit 10.1 presents a brief comparison of Chapters 7, 13, and 11.

### Chapter 13—Adjustment of Debts

**Chapter 13** permits insolvent individuals to repay existing debt according to a payment plan, or wage-earner plan, that the debtor proposes and files with the court. Any individual with a stable and regular income may qualify for adjustment of debts under Chapter 13. Allowed indebtedness for an individual or married couple seeking this relief is $250,000 of unsecured debt, and secured debt of $750,000.

### Automatic Stay

As with other chapters of the Bankruptcy Code, filing a petition under Chapter 13 results in an automatic stay that halts creditor collection efforts. This automatic stay continues during the three- to five-year period that the wage-earner plan is in

## Exhibit 10.1 Comparison of Bankruptcy Chapters

| Bankruptcy Chapter | Who Can File | Automatic Stay in Effect | Trustee Distributes Debtor's Assets | Treatment of Secured Creditors |
|---|---|---|---|---|
| Chapter 7 | Individuals, partnerships, and corporations | Yes | Yes | Secured creditors can take back their collateral or receive the value of the collateral in cash. |
| Chapter 11 | Corporations and individuals with large amounts of debt | Yes | No | Secured creditors receive payments equal to the value of their collateral plus the same percentage on any unsecured debt as the other (unsecured) creditors receive. |
| Chapter 13 | Individuals | Yes | No | Secured creditors receive payments equal to the value of their collateral plus the same percentage on any unsecured debt as the other (unsecured) creditors receive. |

effect. Creditors can take no collection action during this time. The stay provisions of Chapter 13 also apply to the debtor's cosigners and guarantors on those debts. Creditors may seek relief from stays of actions against the debtor and co-debtors.

### Example

On April 2, Ms. Hayes files a petition for bankruptcy under Chapter 13. Her father had guaranteed one of her consumer debts and had also put up property to secure the guaranty. While the stay exists, the creditor cannot pursue Hayes, her father, or the property.

### Trustees

In a Chapter 13 proceeding the trustee does not take possession of the debtor's assets. Rather, assets remain in possession of the debtor as property of the estate. The trustee's duties are to review the debt payment plan to determine whether it is workable, investigate the debtor's financial affairs, examine the creditors' proofs of claim, and make reports on the status of the estate. The trustee must also administer the plan as approved by the court and ensure that the debtor makes the required payments.

### The Plan

The Chapter 13 wage-earner plan must provide for a method to pay off creditors within three years, unless the court approves a longer period (up to five years). The plan may propose to make payments from income or from liquidation of estate assets. It may modify the amount of interest or monthly payments required under the contracts with most creditors; however, the requirements of the debt secured by the debtor's home cannot be different from those required by the original debt instrument. The plan must also provide for making up any defaulted payments within a reasonable time.

Secured creditors must approve the Chapter 13 plan. The plan must provide either that secured creditors keep the lien securing their claim and get payments at least equal to the claim, or that they receive the collateral. Unsecured creditors must receive in the plan at least as much as they would receive in a liquidation. The plan may propose assumption or rejection of executory contracts and unexpired leases.

### Example

Joe Hanson files a Chapter 13 wage-earner plan. The court approves the following actions for his plan:

- His car loan balance is $19,500, but the car securing the loan is worth only $12,500 according to the industry valuation guides. Joe's plan provides for payments to his car lender based on the $12,500 value of the collateral, not the $19,500 balance. The remaining $7,000 is an unsecured claim and under the plan only 50 percent of unsecured claims are paid.

- Joe's credit card balance accrues interest at a rate of 16 percent per annum before the bankruptcy filing. The plan lowers this rate to 7 percent.

- One of Joe's obligations arises out of a health club membership that

### Case for Discussion
*Monroe v. Quality Loan & Trust Co.*

On January 13, 2000, the Monroes filed for voluntary bankruptcy. The court appointed a trustee and on March 11, 2000, the creditors met. At that time Quality Loan & Trust Co. filed objections to discharge of the Monroes' debt and alleged that on December 23, 1999, the parties disposed of their home for $500 when their equity in it was $3,466. Quality Loan further charged that the parties took this action to "secrete and hide" assets from the bank's and other creditors' lawful claims.

In their voluntary petition for bankruptcy, the Monroes stated that they sold their home for $500 plus an assumption of a $7,800 mortgage. However, the bank contended that the Monroes sold their home at a time when the value of the real estate was at least $11,000, subject to a mortgage of $7,534, with a resultant net equity of $3,466.

The trustee found in this case that the Monroes had numerous debts when they sold their home and that they were hard pressed by their creditors. The couple owed $250 to the purchaser of the house and they were behind in their mortgage payments. Before the purchaser, a Mr. Grieves, bought the house, the Monroes had asked him to try to sell it for $10,100. When Grieves was unsuccessful in selling the house, he offered to purchase it. The Monroes agreed to sell the house and continued to live in it for two months, paying $100 in rent per month.

Finding the evidence insufficient to sustain a denial of a discharge in bankruptcy and that the Monroes did not convey their house to defraud their creditors, the court ruled in favor of the Monroes. According to the trustee, the facts did not indicate that the Monroes were hiding assets from creditors. The

Monroes revealed the conveyance of their home to Grieves, and for the court to infer secret dealings would be to indulge in speculation and surmise about the Monroes' intentions.

This case reinforces the well-accepted principle that the Bankruptcy Code was intended to allow the honest debtor a new start in life, free from debt and objections by creditors. The court ruled that the Bankruptcy Code had to be construed strictly against the objectors and liberally in favor of the bankrupt parties.

**Questions for Discussion**

1. What rules address a debtor's sale and transfer of property before the debtor files a petition for bankruptcy?
2. Who qualifies as an *insider,* and when does the distinction matter?

requires a monthly payment. The debtor's plan rejects this executory contract and thereby relieves Hanson of this burden.

After the debtor submits the plan, the court schedules a hearing at which the trustee, creditors, and other interested parties may present objections. Generally, creditor objections must be filed with the court in advance of the hearing. To confirm the plan, the court must find that the plan meets six requirements. The six requirements are

- The plan must comply with the Bankruptcy Code.
- The plan must provide for payment of prescribed fees and charges before confirmation.
- The plan must be proposed in good faith. (Courts have interpreted this requirement to mean that proposed payments must not abuse the purpose of Chapter 13, a flexible standard that results in case-by-case analysis.)

- Unsecured creditors must receive at least what they would be paid under a Chapter 7 proceeding.
- Secured creditors must accept the proposed payment scheme, under which either they retain their liens and receive payments or property the value of which will be no less than the amount of the claim, or the debtor surrenders the collateral to the secured creditor.
- The plan must establish a payment scheme that the debtor will be able to meet and that is otherwise workable.

If the trustee or an unsecured creditor objects to the plan, the court may not confirm the plan unless the value of money or property planned for payment of an objector's claim is no less than the claim, or the plan provides that all the debtor's available income during the time the plan is in effect will be applied to make the payments.

### Discharge

Once confirmed, the plan binds both debtor and creditors. When the plan is completed, the debtor is entitled to a discharge of indebtedness to the creditors. A debtor who does not complete the plan may receive a hardship discharge if certain requirements are met, but such a discharge relates only to unsecured claims.

### Chapter 11—Reorganization

Chapter 13 rehabilitation is available only to individuals and sole proprietorships with a limited amount of debt. Any entity eligible for a liquidation of assets under Chapter 7 qualifies for reorganization under Chapter 11. If certain criteria are met, creditors may initiate the Chapter 11 proceedings.

**Chapter 11** gives a business suffering financial hardship a break from its creditors to reestablish itself on a solid footing. As with other relief under the Bankruptcy Code, a Chapter 11 proceeding begins with the filing of a petition. In addition to the petition, the debtor must submit the same documents required in a Chapter 7 proceeding, plus a list of equity security holders (such as stockholders), if applicable, and a list of its 20 largest unsecured creditors.

### Automatic Stay

For a debtor operating a business to effectively rehabilitate the business, the debtor must be able to continue in operation without fear that its creditors will take action against its assets. In addition, suppliers and banks with which the debtor does business must be assured that the business will continue to operate. Thus, an automatic stay goes into effect when a corporate debtor files a Chapter 11 bankruptcy petition. In a Chapter 11 proceeding, secured creditors are in a different position from that of Chapter 7 creditors. The availability and use of their collateral for the continued operation of the business is considered an integral part of rehabilitation under Chapter 11. Over the years the courts have carefully developed rules to assure adequate protection for secured creditors whose collateral remains with the debtor for use in its business.

### Debtor in Possession

Usually no trustee is appointed in Chapter 11 proceedings. Instead, the business debtor itself takes on a trustee's rights and powers as a **debtor in possession.** However, on an interested party's request and after a hearing, a trustee can be appointed in a Chapter 11 proceeding. At the hearing, the requesting party must demonstrate dishonesty, incompetence, fraud, or mismanagement on the part of the debtor, or must show that the appointment of a trustee is otherwise in the best interests of the creditors and the estate.

Once the petition is filed, a first meeting of the creditors is scheduled, which the debtor must attend to answer questions about its financial status. The meet-

### Case for Discussion
*Oregon State Bank & Trust Co. v. Lindell*

Mr. Lindell filed a petition for relief under Chapter 11 of the Bankruptcy Code. At that time, Lindell owed the Oregon State Bank & Trust Co. approximately $249,000. Lindell came from a wealthy family and was for many years an outside director of the bank. In the course of his business affairs with the bank, Lindell filed periodic financial statements, including one on May 23, 1993, and one on November 9, 1993. The May 23 statement reported a net worth of $3,711,311 and the November 9 statement reported a net worth of $32,386.

The bank objected to Lindell's discharge from liability for his debt, contending that the May 23 report was false, fraudulent, and made with the intent to deceive the bank. The bank also claimed that it relied on the May 23 statement in renewing loans to Lindell on October 1, 1993. In addition, the bank argued that Lindell was acting in a fiduciary capacity as a director when he incurred debts to the bank by fraud, embezzlement, or misappropriation. If these allegations were true, the court could not discharge Lindell from his debts under the Bankruptcy Code's exceptions to discharge.

Lindell's financial reverses between May 23 and November 9, 1993, were brought about by unexpected losses in real estate ventures. Those losses accounted for the discrepancies in the two financial statements. Lindell prepared the November financial statement with the assistance of his attorney, who knew of the real estate losses. Lindell claimed that he informed the bank of this matter and yet they still agreed to renew his loan. The bank countered by claiming that it renewed the loans based solely on Lindell's relationship with the bank as a director and in reliance on his written financial statement, which the bank believed was published with intent to deceive.

In determining whether sufficient evidence existed to deny a discharge of Lindell's debt, the bankruptcy court noted that the primary purpose of the Bankruptcy Code is to discharge debts of an honest debtor and offer him or her a fresh start. The court found untrue the bank's charge that Lindell intended to deceive the bank with the May 23 statement because the evidence showed that Lindell suffered subsequent serious financial reverses and informed the bank of his problems. The court thus decided that Lindell did not intentionally make false statements or intend to deceive the bank. Furthermore, the court held that in this situation Lindell was simply a borrower of the bank and could not be held to a higher standard because he was a director.

**Questions for Discussion**

1. What rules address a bankrupt party's giving false information?
2. Why would the bank want to disallow the discharge of this debt, particularly if Lindell had no assets or sources of revenue?
3. Should the court in this case have held Lindell to a higher standard because he was an outside director of the bank?

ing gives the parties an opportunity to discuss the debtor's cash requirements, plans for loans, and repayment of any new debt incurred to keep the debtor's business operating.

### Continued Operation of the Business

The debtor in possession is authorized to continue operating the business and, aided by the automatic stay, to retain possession of assets sufficient to continue in business. The debtor in possession must report periodically to the court regarding its financial condition. The debtor may make decisions and take actions without the court's approval so long as the decisions and actions are in the **ordinary course of business.** The debtor may not take action outside the ordinary course of business unless it first notifies interested parties and provides them with the opportunity for a hearing.

**Example**

Right Bilt Manufacturing Co. is operating under a Chapter 11 proceeding. Right Bilt continues to manufacture and sell its products, buy raw materials, and enter into contracts. So long as these functions are in the ordinary course of business, the company may continue them without court approval. However, if Right Bilt wants to sell one of its three plants, it must provide its creditors an opportunity to be heard.

**New Debts**

Once a debtor files a petition under Chapter 11, money in the debtor's accounts becomes the property of the estate, for which the debtor in possession usually will open new banking accounts. In addition to needing banks as depository institutions, Chapter 11 debtors also need banks for loans. The debtor in possession may obtain unsecured credit in the ordinary course of business, including loans and purchases on credit. To encourage creditors to deal with Chapter 11 businesses, the code provides that new debts be paid in the ordinary course of business. If the reorganization is unsuccessful, the code provides that the administrative costs of the Chapter 11 proceeding will have priority over unsecured, old (prior to petition) debts. Most debts incurred after a Chapter 11 petition is filed are considered administrative costs.

### Committees

Many interested parties have a stake in the success of a Chapter 11 reorganization. These parties include the debtor, the creditors, the debtor's shareholders, and other equity security holders. The code provides for interested parties to be represented by committees. The committees monitor the debtor in possession, negotiate with the debtor in possession in preparing a reorganization plan, and, if necessary, draft their own plan. Committees may engage the services of attorneys, accountants, and other professionals to assist them. All committee members represent their class of interested parties, not themselves personally; that is, they have obligations to the individuals and entities that their committees are formed to protect.

### Reorganization Plan

Within 120 days of filing a petition for bankruptcy under Chapter 11, a debtor must submit a reorganization plan. After that time, any party in interest may also propose a plan. Once the debtor's plan has been filed, the debtor has 60 days in which to have creditors and equity security holders accept the plan.

The code requires that the plan include certain provisions. It must identify the various classes of claimants, such as creditors who have security interests in the same property, unsecured creditors, shareholders, and bondholders.

The plan also must list claimants or interested parties who will be disadvantaged, or impaired, by the plan; the extent of the impairment; and the proposed treatment of their claims. In addition, the plan must state how its goals will be achieved, describing what steps the debtor will take to place the business in a position to pay the creditors, equity security holders, and others.

Once the debtor has formulated a plan, it must provide copies to interested parties. With the plan, the debtor must include a court-approved disclosure statement that provides enough information about the debtor's history and present financial condition to enable the parties to make an informed judgment about the plan.

Once the plan is filed and the court approves the disclosure statement, the debtor seeks its acceptance from parties who are impaired by it. The plan may be modified to overcome any objections. The code has detailed procedures regarding the identity and number of interested parties who must agree to the plan before it is confirmed.

A plan can be confirmed only on acceptance by every impaired class or by a *cram down*. A cram down involves the court's forcing the plan on dissenting classes of creditors—based on at least one impaired class consenting to it—if the court finds that the plan does not discriminate and is fair with respect to each impaired class that opposes the plan. Either method of confirmation is subject to detailed rules in the code.

On confirmation, the plan fixes the legal rights and obligations of the various parties. The debtor and interested parties must perform their obligations according to the plan requirements.

## CONCLUSION

Over time bankruptcy has evolved from serving principally as a creditor's tool for collection to providing relief to debtors as well. Two concepts within the Bankruptcy Code, liquidation and rehabilitation, help to provide that relief to debtors. Those seeking complete relief from their debts submit to liquidation under Chapter 7, while those wishing to retain their nonexempt assets and repay some if not all of their indebtedness can seek rehabilitation under Chapter 11 or Chapter 13 of the code. Because, as creditors, banks continually confront the actual or threatened bankruptcies of borrowers and depositors, bank employees must be aware of the many choices that bankruptcy proceedings present to creditors.

## QUESTIONS FOR REVIEW AND DISCUSSION

1.  Compare the goals of a Chapter 7 bankruptcy with those of a Chapter 11 or Chapter 13 bankruptcy.
2.  How does a debtor initiate a bankruptcy proceeding under Chapter 7?
3.  What prevents a creditor from collecting from a debtor or liquidating collateral once the debtor has filed a bankruptcy petition?
4.  Who is the trustee in a bankruptcy proceeding? What is the duty of the trustee?
5.  What are exemptions? Give some examples.
6.  What is a preference?
7.  What happens to a secured creditor's collateral in a Chapter 7 bankruptcy?
8.  What are two types of nondischargeable debts?
9.  What is a plan in Chapter 11 and Chapter 13 proceedings?

## LEARNING ACTIVITIES FOR CHAPTER 10

### Multiple Choice

Choose the best answer for each question.

1.  Liquidation refers to:

    a.  converting a debtor's assets to cash for distribution to creditors
    b.  an action taken by creditors to force repayment in full of debts owed
    c.  a petition by a debtor requesting a hearing for relief from all debt obligations
    d.  a proceeding to prevent creditors from collecting on debts

2.  Once a debtor's affairs have been placed in the hands of a bankruptcy court, creditors:

    a.  should attempt to become named trustee
    b.  should proceed to collect all debts owed
    c.  have lost all hope of collecting debts
    d.  can only receive payment through the court

3.  The debtor's property and property interests as of the day of filing a bankruptcy petition:

    a.  are placed in the care of a trustee
    b.  are known as the bankruptcy estate
    c.  are protected from creditors by a stay
    d.  all of the above

4.  Involuntary bankruptcies differ from voluntary ones:

    a.  in that only involuntary bankruptcies involve a trustee
    b.  in that only voluntary bankruptcies involve a trustee
    c.  only in the way the proceeding begins
    d.  in that involuntary proceedings are more likely to end in full repayment to creditors

5.  Setoff is:

    a.  a means by which a debtor may keep possession of collateral
    b.  a means by which a creditor may claim possession of collateral
    c.  a procedure used when two parties are in debt to one another
    d.  seldom useful in bankruptcy proceedings

6. When a Chapter 7 bankruptcy petition is filed, a temporary trustee is named by:

    a.  the debtor in the case
    b.  the creditor(s) in the case
    c.  the judge in the case
    d.  the Office of the U.S. Trustee

7. Which of the following would be a priority claim in a bankruptcy?

    a.  a wage claim
    b.  an unpaid bill
    c.  an unsecured debt
    d.  a doctor's bill

8. All of the following types of debts are nondischargeable *except:*

    a.  taxes
    b.  debts incurred by fraud
    c.  alimony
    d.  hospital bills

9. Which of the following would be grounds for denial of discharge?

    a.  debts not listed in schedules filed with the bankruptcy petition
    b.  failure of the debtor to maintain financial records
    c.  failure of the debtor to maintain a consistent employment history
    d.  both *a* and *b*

10. Reorganization plans are filed by corporations under:

    a.  Chapter 7
    b.  Chapter 9
    c.  Chapter 11
    d.  Chapter 13

11. Debtors in Chapter 11 proceedings typically are referred to as:

    a.  bankrupts
    b.  debtors in possession
    c.  debtors in rehabilitation
    d.  dischargees

## Completion

Fill in the blanks with the word or words that best complete the sentences.

1. Contracts in which neither of the parties has yet completed performance are known as _____ contracts.

2. For secured creditors desiring return of their collateral, _____ is the simplest way to obtain it.

3. In a _____ the debtor agrees to pay the entire debt owed to the creditor, even if it is greater than the value of the collateral.

4. If the trustee abandons collateral that is personal property, individual debtors have the right to _____ the collateral under some circumstances.

5. _____ is the legal release of a debtor from obligation to pay bankruptcy creditors.

6. When banks object to the discharge of a debt, it is usually because the person or company has committed _____ when applying for a loan.

7. _____ permits insolvent individuals to repay existing debt according to a payment plan that the debtor proposed and files with the court.

8. Interested parties in a Chapter 11 reorganization are represented by _____.

## Short Answer

Briefly answer each of the following questions.

1. What is the goal of bankruptcy?

    _____

    _____

    _____

    _____

2. How is a bankruptcy proceeding initiated?

_____

_____

_____

_____

3. What is an automatic stay?

_____

_____

_____

_____

4. What is a bankruptcy trustee?

_____

_____

_____

_____

5. What is the trustee's function as a lien creditor?

_____

_____

_____

_____

6. What is the effect of a discharge?

_____

_____

_____

_____

7. Who may seek rehabilitation under Chapter 13?

_____

_____

_____

_____

8. May a bank refuse to extend credit to an individual whose debts have been discharged?

_____

_____

_____

_____

9. What is a debtor in possession?

_____

_____

_____

_____

## True/False

Indicate whether each of the following statements is true or false.

T  F  1.  The U.S. Constitution gives Congress the power to enact bankruptcy legislation.

T  F  2.  The Bankruptcy Code, which sets forth all the basic provisions of U.S. bankruptcy law today, is part of the National Bankruptcy Act of 1898.

T  F  3.  Both state law and the Bankruptcy Code allow certain kinds of property to be exempt from bankruptcy proceedings, so debtors may sometimes choose between the federal or state exemptions.

T  F  4.  Preferences can have damaging effects on both secured and unsecured creditors.

T  F  5.  Executory contracts to which the debtor is a party when a bankruptcy petition is filed become part of the estate.

T  F  6.  Discharge of debt is available only to individuals; corporations declaring bankruptcy cannot have their debts discharged.

T  F  7.  Certain types of debts cannot be discharged.

T  F  8.  Filing a petition under Chapter 13 results in an automatic stay that halts creditor collection efforts.

T  F  9.  A trustee is usually appointed to oversee Chapter 11 bankruptcy proceedings.

T  F  10.  Adequate protection refers to rules developed to protect all creditors in a Chapter 11 proceeding.

T  F  11.  Chapter 11 rehabilitation is available only to individuals and sole proprietorships with a limited amount of debt.

T  F  12.  Once confirmed, a Chapter 13 wage-earner plan is binding for both debtor and creditor.

# GLOSSARY

**abandonment** A procedure in bankruptcy whereby collateral worth less than the debt it secures may be released to the secured creditor. Abandonment may be undertaken on the trustee's initiative or in response to a motion filed by the secured creditor; in either case, the trustee must give notice to all interested parties, who may file objections with the bankruptcy court.

**acceptance** Agreement by the offeree to the terms and promises to meet the obligations spelled out in the contract.

**access device** A debit card, personal identification number (PIN), telephone bill-payment code, or other such means of access to account funds, used by an account holder to complete an electronic funds transfer.

**ACH operator** The central clearing facility for Automated Clearing House transfers. The ACH operator receives entries from originating depository financial institutions, distributes the entries to the appropriate receiving depository financial institutions, and performs settlement functions for the participating financial institutions.

**actual authority** Such authority as a principal definitely and intentionally confers on an agent; includes both express and implied authority.

**Administrative Procedure Act** A statute passed by Congress in 1946 that specifies the procedures government agencies must follow in promulgating new regulations and provides guidelines for courts to follow in reviewing agency regulations.

Many jurisdictions have enacted similar laws at the state level.

**adverse action notice** The notice required to be sent to an applicant by the Equal Credit Opportunity Act (ECOA) when the creditor does not approve the applicant's application on the terms and conditions requested.

**adverse possession** The act of taking possession of the real property of another (using or living on the property) and acting as an owner (paying taxes, putting up fences, making improvements, and so forth). If these actions are done openly, are obvious to everyone, continue without interruption for the required number of years under state law, and the true owner never asserts a claim against the possessor for the entire time, the possessor acquires ownership and the owner loses it.

**advising bank** A bank that agrees on behalf of an issuing bank to send notice to the beneficiary that a letter of credit has been issued. An advising bank may agree to receive and forward documents relating to a letter of credit but, unlike a confirming bank, does not assume any responsibility for paying under the terms of the letter of credit.

**after-acquired property** property obtained by a debtor after incurring a debt and that has been pledged in advance to a secured party as collateral for the debt.

**agency relationship** A relationship in which one person acts for another in a representative capacity.

**agent** A person or other legal entity who has authority to transact business or otherwise act on behalf of another.

**annual percentage rate** The expression of the interest and other finance charges on a loan as an annual rate.

**apparent authority** As distinguished from actual authority, such authority as a third party reasonably believes an agent has because conduct on the part of the principal creates the appearance that the agent has such authority.

**appellate courts** Courts that review trial court decisions. Also referred to as *courts of appeals.*

**articles of incorporation** The document that must be filed with the appropriate state agency in order to establish a corporation. Articles of incorporation ordinarily must include the name of the corporation, the name and address of each incorporator, the broad purposes of the corporation, the address of the corporation's principal office, and the name and address of the corporation's agent on whom a summons can be served if the corporation is sued, the length of time the corporation is to last, the number of shares of stock the corporation is authorized to issue, and the par value of the stock.

**assignment** The transfer in writing by one person to another of rights, title to property, or other interests.

**attachment** The process by which property owned by a debtor is pledged to a secured party. In the attachment process the secured party obtains a right to the property.

**attorney-in-fact** A person designated by a power-of-attorney to serve as an agent.

**automated teller machine (ATM)** A machine, activated by a magnetically encoded card or by keyboard transmission of a code, that allows customers to perform routine banking transactions such as withdrawal and deposit of funds, transfer of funds between accounts, and certain payments.

**Automated Clearing House (ACH)** A nationwide funds transfer system established in the 1970s to process recurring payments electronically for financial institutions. In many ways, ACH transfers are similar to wire transfers. Both are payment systems through which funds are transferred electronically, and both are generally subject to Uniform Commercial Code Article 4A except to the extent that the funds transfers involved are governed by the Electronic Funds Transfer Act or are debit, rather than credit, transfers.

**automatic stay** In bankruptcy law, the legal requirement that, once the bankruptcy petition is filed, all creditors halt any efforts to obtain payment of their claims from the debtor except through the procedures of the bankruptcy court.

**B**

**bailment** The delivery of goods or other personal property into someone else's possession for a specific purpose. In a bailment relationship, ownership of the property is in one person (the bailor) while another (the bailee) has the right to possess the property for the specific purpose. Bailees have a duty of care with respect to the property in their possession and must redeliver it to the bailor or otherwise dispose of it in accordance with the bailor's instructions when the bailment ends.

**bank charter** A document, issued by a state or federal bank regulatory agency, granting the right to provide banking services.

**bank deposit** Funds (cash, checks, and so on) placed in a bank account for safekeeping. Because funds deposited in these accounts can be withdrawn at any time with no advance notice, they are generally referred to as *demand deposit accounts.* Checking accounts are the most common type of demand deposit account.

**bank examinations** Detailed examinations conducted on a regular basis by state and federal regulatory agencies to ensure that banks are operating in accordance with the banking laws and regulations, that their financial reports are accurate, and that they are financially sound.

**bank examiners** Officials from state and federal regulatory agencies who conduct regular examinations of commercial banks. State-chartered banks are examined by state officials, typically from the state banking commission or state superintendent of banks. The Federal Deposit Insurance Corporation is the federal agency responsible for conducting examinations of all state-chartered banks that are not members of the Federal Reserve System. Bank examinations for state-chartered banks that are members of the Federal Reserve System are conducted by employees of that agency, and examinations of national banks are conducted by agents of the Office of the Comptroller of the Currency.

**banking day** That part of a business day during which a bank is open to the public for carrying on substantially all its services. See *business day.*

**bank officers** Persons appointed by the board of directors of a bank to be responsible for the day-to-day management of the bank. Bank officers typically include a president, cashier, auditor, trust officer, and vice-presidents.

**Bank Bribery Act** A federal law that makes it a felony for a bank employee to receive gifts, money, or favors for any bank-related decision or activity.

**bankruptcy estate** The assets of a debtor in bankruptcy assigned to a trustee in bankruptcy who may sell or otherwise administer the assets with the goal of paying off creditors in an organized fashion.

**Bankruptcy Code** The basic provisions of U.S. bankruptcy law, enacted under the Bankruptcy Reform Act of 1978 (as amended).

**Bank Secrecy Act** A term commonly used to refer to the Currency and Foreign Transaction Reporting Act. Passed by Congress in 1970, this act is designed to facilitate detection of money laundering and similar kinds of criminal activity involving the use of banking services.

**beneficiary** A person for whose benefit property in trust is managed. Also, the party entitled to demand payment under the terms of a letter of credit. In the context of electronic funds transfers, the term used in Article 4A of the Uniform Commercial Code to refer to the person to be paid under the payment order.

**beneficiary's bank** The term used in Article 4A of the Uniform Commercial Code to refer to the bank identified in a payment order at which an account of the beneficiary is to be credited, or which is to make payment otherwise if the order does not provide for payment to an account.

**bilateral contract** A contract in which the offeror makes a promise in return for a promise by the offeree. Acceptance of a bilateral contract occurs when the offeree agrees to the contract terms and makes the specified promise in return.

**bill** A proposed law introduced by a member of the U.S. Congress or a member of a state legislature.

**bill of lading** A transport document, issued by a shipping company or its agent, which serves as a receipt for goods, as a contract to deliver goods to a specific destination, and as title to the goods when used in negotiable form.

**binding/bound** Bringing or placing under legal obligation; to be legally obligated

**board of directors** A committee of persons appointed or elected to oversee the management of a corporation. The responsibilities of a board of directors include establishing corporate policy, approving major corporate transactions, and appointing and supervising corporate officers who have the day-to-day management responsibilities.

**bona fide purchaser** Someone who, in good faith and for valuable consideration, acquires an interest in property without having notice of any outstanding or prior interests. Purchasers are deemed to be on notice of all interests which, at the time of purchase, are properly recorded. The ownership rights of a bona fide purchaser without notice will be superior to all other claims against the property of which he or she had no notice.

**breach of contract** The unexcused failure to perform an action promised in a contract.

**business day** Under Regulation CC implementing the Expedited Funds Availability Act (EFAA), any calendar day except Saturday, Sunday, and legal holidays. See *banking day*.

## C

**certificate of deposit** A transferable receipt issued by a commercial bank in return for a customer's deposit of funds. The bank agrees to pay the amount deposited plus interest to the bearer on a specified future date.

**certiorari** The name of a petition that must be filed with the U.S. Supreme Court in order to seek review of a case that the Court has discretion to accept or reject. By contrast, in a case the Court has no option to reject, the parties seek review by filing an appeal.

**Chapter 7** The chapter of the Bankruptcy Code that contains the provisions on liquidation.

**Chapter 11** A chapter of the Bankruptcy Code that provides a means whereby individuals or businesses may, under reorganization procedures somewhat different from the procedures under Chapter 13, retain possession of their assets and continue in business while repaying all or most of their debts. As in the case of a wage earner plan under Chapter 13, a reorganization plan under Chapter 11 will be approved by the Bankruptcy Court only if it is found to give adequate protection to creditors.

**Chapter 13** A chapter of the Bankruptcy Code that permits insolvent individuals and sole proprietorships with a limited amount of debt to retain possession of their assets and, under the supervision of a trustee, repay their existing debt according to a payment plan (called a *wage earner plan*) that the debtor proposes and files with the court. The court will approve a wage earner plan only if it provides adequate protection to creditors.

**charter** See *bank charter*.

**check** A demand instrument (a draft) signed by the drawer (or maker) and payable to a person or bearer upon presentation to the bank on which it is drawn. What distinguishes a check from other drafts is that it is always drawn on a bank and is payable on demand.

**check routing symbol** The first four digits of a nine-digit routing number form that generally appear as a fraction in the upper right-hand corner of a check and in a magnetic ink strip at the bottom of the check. The routing symbol identifies the Federal Reserve bank in whose check-processing region the payor bank on which the check is drawn is located. If the routing symbols of both the depositary bank and the payor bank are listed in the same district, the deposited item is considered a local item; otherwise, it is considered a nonlocal item. This ready reference for ascertaining whether a check is a local or nonlocal item assists banks in determining when funds deposited by means of a check must be made available in the customer's account.

**class action** A court action brought on behalf of a group of individuals.

**close corporation** A corporation whose stock is not generally traded in the public securities markets. Close corporations usually are owned by a limited number of persons.

**closed-ended credit** According to Regulation Z, credit that is not open-ended credit.

**collateral** Property in which a security interest is granted to a creditor for the purposes of securing a debt.

**collecting bank** A general term that describes any bank that handles an item for collection, except the payor bank.

**collection** Presenting a check or other negotiable instrument for payment and receiving cash or credit in return. Receiving checks from their customers for collection from other banks is one of the most important services provided by banks. The rules governing the collection process are contained in Article 4 of the Uniform Commercial Code.

**commercial letter of credit** A written agreement issued by a bank promising to pay a specified amount at some future time when the conditions specified in the letter of credit have been satisfied. Generally used in transactions for the sale of goods to pay the seller or his agent upon presentment of the seller's draft, along with an invoice, an inspection certificate, an insurance policy, a bill of lading, or other documents.

**common law** Law derived from the ancient, unwritten law of England that has been reflected in judges' rulings over the years. Common law usually is based on prevailing moral standards.

**concurrent jurisdiction** A term used to describe a situation in which different courts (for example, a federal district court and a state trial court) each have jurisdiction to hear a particular case.

**confirming bank** A bank that agrees to assume responsibility, along with the issuing bank, for paying under the terms of a letter of credit.

**consideration** Something of value (an act or forbearance, or promise thereof) that must be exchanged by each party in order to form an enforceable contract. Consideration is said to be the price each party pays for the right to enforce the contract. Consideration need not be monetary. However, doing (or promising to do) something that one is already under a legal obligation to do does not constitute consideration. See *legal detriment.*

**consumer goods** Property that is used for personal, family, or household purposes.

**consumer lease** According to the Consumer Leasing Act, a lease for the use of personal property entered into primarily for personal, family, or household purposes, for a period exceeding four months and for a total obligation not exceeding $25,000.

**consumer reports** Information that consumer reporting agencies communicate by written, oral, or other methods regarding a consumer's creditworthiness, credit standing, credit capacity, character, general reputation, personal characteristics, or mode of living.

**contract performance** The fulfillment or accomplishment of a contract according to its terms.

**corporation** A legal entity formed for the purpose of conducting business that is regarded as being distinct from its owners. Owners of a corporation are not personally liable for the corporation's debts, obligations, or liabilities, and a corporation is vested with perpetual existence that remains unaffected by the death of any director, officer, or shareholder. Also, ownership of corporate stock may be transferred freely by sale or by gift.

**cosign** Typically used to refer to the requirement that a surety sign the original promissory note or other debt instrument signed by the borrower, thus making the surety equally liable with the borrower for repayment of the loan. This situation is distinguished from the situation where a guarantor signs a separate document guaranteeing repayment of the loan only if the borrower cannot pay.

**credit advertisement** Any commercial message in any medium that directly or indirectly promotes a credit transaction.

**credit card** Any card, plate, coupon book, or other device that may be presented to obtain money, property, labor, or services on credit.

**creditor** A person to whom a debt is owed by another person (the *debtor*).

**credit reporting agency** An organization or company that assembles or evaluates the credit histories of consumers for purposes of furnishing consumer reports to third parties.

**crime** An offense against the community at large in violation of a criminal statute.

**currency transaction report (CTR)** A report (Form 4789) that, under the Bank Secrecy Act, banks are required to file with the Internal Revenue Service whenever cash transactions with a customer involve more than $10,000 in one day.

**customer** The term used in Article 4A of the Uniform Commercial Code to refer to a person, including a bank, having an account with a bank or from whom a bank has agreed to receive payment orders.

## D

**damages** The amount of money awarded by a court to a person because of a breach of contract or other legal wrong done to him by another. Statutes and case law generally divide damages into six categories: compensatory, consequential (special), punitive (exemplary), incidental, nominal, and liquidated.

**debit card** A plastic card that enables the cardholder to make purchases or withdraw cash, the cost of which is immediately charged to the cardholder's bank account. Debit cards are used to activate point-of-sale terminals in supermarkets, gas stations, and stores. Together with credit cards, they are commonly referred to as *bank cards.*

**debt collectors** Persons or companies who regularly collect or attempt to collect debts owed by a borrower to a third party.

**debtor** A person or entity who, in exchange for value, agrees to pay to a creditor amounts owing under a promissory note or other debt instrument.

**debtor in possession** A bankruptcy debtor who, under Chapter 11 or Chapter 13 of the Bankruptcy Code, is permitted to retain possession of nonexempt assets that, under Chapter 7, would be assigned to the bankruptcy estate and liquidated.

**deed** A written document that the owner of real property must sign and give to the new owner in all transfers of real property. The deed contains a legal description of the property and declares that all right, title, and interest in it now belong to the new owner. When the new owner receives the deed, the transfer of ownership is accomplished.

**defamation** A tort that involves making an untrue statement that causes injury to someone's reputation by exposing a person to hatred, contempt, or ridicule, or by injuring that person's reputation in his or her position or business. (See also *slander* and *libel.)* For example, it is defamatory to spread a false rumor that a person or business is on the brink of bankruptcy, as that would tend to injure their reputation and their business.

**default** The failure to pay a financial obligation when due.

**delegation** Authorizing someone to perform an action on behalf of another person.

**demand deposit account** An account of funds, maintained at a bank, which can be withdrawn at any time with no advance notice.

**deposit account** a demand account, savings account, or certificate of deposit at a bank in which the bank becomes the owner of the customer's deposited funds and the customer receives a credit on the bank's books that may be withdrawn according to predetermined terms.

**depositary bank** The first bank to which an item is transferred in the collection process.

**director** See *board of directors.*

**disaffirm** The lawful act of repudiating a voidable contract; for example, minors who lack legal capacity to enter into a contract may disaffirm their obligations under a contract.

**discharge** Obtaining release from the legal obligation to pay certain debts. In bankruptcy proceedings, discharge of debts is available only to individuals, not to corporations.

**disclosure** A notice to a consumer borrower pertaining to the credit terms and containing other facts relevant to a loan.

**dishonor** Refusal to pay an instrument that has been presented for payment. A transferee who knows that an instrument has been presented for payment and dishonored cannot become a holder in due course.

**dividends** That portion of a corporation's profits or surplus paid to its shareholders.

**documentary draft** The demand for payment that the seller must submit to the issuing bank in order to receive payment under a commercial letter of credit.

**donee** The person to whom a gift is given.

**donor** A person who gives a gift.

**draft** A negotiable instrument containing an order to pay. Drafts are similar in purpose to checks.

**drawee** The person or bank on whom a draft is drawn and who is directed to pay the sum specified.

**drawer** The person or company who instructs the drawee in writing to pay funds. A drawer is also referred to as a *maker.*

**duty of due care** The level of care required of corporate directors in exercising their corporate responsibilities. This duty has been defined as the level of care that a reasonable and prudent person would exercise in a similar situation.

## E

**element of a crime** A part of a crime that must be proved in court if an accused person is to be found guilty.

**embezzlement** A crime involving the fraudulent use or keeping of money or other property that has been entrusted to one's care. When money is embezzled from banks, this crime is also referred to as misappropriation of funds.

**enact** The process of making a new law is called *enactment.* When the Congress enacts or passes a bill, it is sent to the president of the United States to be signed. The bill becomes a law when the president signs it. Bills enacted by state legislatures become laws when the governor of the state signs them.

**enjoin/injunction** To prohibit or forbid. A court enjoins payment under a letter of credit by issuing an injunction against the issuing bank.

**equipment** Property that is used or purchased for use in a business.

**escheat** The process by which property becomes owned by the state. This happens when a decedent has no heirs at all or when the owner abandons property (like a bank account).

**established customer** The term used in regulations issued under the Bank Secrecy Act to refer to a person who has an account at the bank, or whose name, address, and taxpayer identification number (TIN) the bank has and maintains on file, and to whom it provides financial services in reliance upon that information.

**estate** The property of a decedent.

**examination** See *bank examinations.*

**executor** A person nominated in a will to manage a decedent's estate.

**express authority** Permission specifically given, either orally or in writing, for an agent to do something.

## F

**failure of consideration** Consideration, a critical element of a contract, requires something of value to be exchanged. Failure of consideration occurs when goods are defective or never delivered.

**federal courts of appeals** Appellate courts in the federal judicial system (also referred to as federal circuit courts of appeals). These courts have jurisdiction to review decisions by U.S. district courts and certain actions by federal agencies.

**federal district courts** See *U.S. district courts.*

**Federal Deposit Insurance Corporation (FDIC)** The agency of the federal government that insures accounts in commercial banks up to a certain amount. Currently, this amount is $100,000. The FDIC must insure all commercial banks that are members of the Federal Reserve System. Although most state-chartered banks participate in the FDIC, they are not required to do so by state law. The FDIC is also responsible for conducting examinations of all state-chartered banks that are not members of the Federal Reserve System.

**Federal Reserve** The central banking system that regulates the nation's money supply. The Fed, as it is popularly known, includes 12 regional banks and their branches. The Fed also supervises state-chartered banks that choose to be members of the Federal Reserve System. All commercial banks that are members of the Federal Reserve System have direct access to the Fed's check-clearing system and must be insured by the Federal Deposit Insurance Corporation.

**federal tax lien** A means for the federal government to collect delinquent taxes, including by the seizure and sale of taxpayer property.

**Fedwire** A payment service operated by the Federal Reserve System for the electronic transfer of funds between banks that have reserve or clearing accounts at Federal Reserve banks.

**fee** The most extensive interest that can be enjoyed in real property, a fee (or fee simple) comprises unconditional rights of ownership which, unless transferred to another, last as long as the property itself and may pass from one generation to the next.

**felony** A serious offense punishable by death or imprisonment for a term exceeding one year.

**fiduciary** A relationship existing between two persons, founded on confidence and trust, requiring that each person exercise a corresponding degree of loyalty and good faith; for example, the relationship between an agent and principal. Also refers more specifically to the person who manages money or property on behalf of another and who is obligated to exercise a high standard of care in performing this duty for example, a guardian serves as a fiduciary for a ward.

**filing** The process by which a secured party gives notice to the public concerning its rights in a debtor's property by placing a notice in the public records.

**finance charge** The consumer' cost for a loan in dollars and cents.

**financing statement** A document that contains the basic information about the collateral pledged by a debtor on a loan, including the debtor's name and address, the creditor's name and address, and a description of the collateral. A financing statement is filed in the public records to give notice to third parties of the creditor's security interest in the property described in the statement.

**fixed amount in money** A definite amount of money. An instrument must state that it is payable in a definite amount in money in order for it to be negotiable.

**foreclosure** The legal process by which a lender enforces repayment of a debt secured by a mortgage, by taking and selling the mortgaged property.

**four-day test** See *two-day test.*

**fraud** A tort, also referred to as *deceit* or *misrepresentation,* that involves: 1) a false statement of fact made by one person to another; 2) knowledge by the maker of the statement that it is false; 3) making the statement with the intent that the other person

will believe and act upon it; 4) justifiable reliance by the other person on the truth of the statement; and 5) damage to the other person from relying and acting on the false statement.

**freehold** When the right to possess and use real property is held by an owner, the interest is called a *freehold.* Freehold means that no one else has superior rights in the property and there is no fixed or definite time at which the interest must come to an end. Distinguished from a tenant's conditional (and time-limited) right to possess and use real property.

**future advances** Disbursements of loan poceeds, made after the initial funding of the loan, which also are secured by the same collateral as the first advance.

**G**

**gift** Something of value voluntarily given by one person to another.

**good faith estimate of settlement costs** The disclosure statement provided to an applicant for a mortgage loan within three business days of the application, describing the types and amounts of charges that will be payable at the closing of the loan.

**goods** Defined by the Uniform Commercial Code as things that are movable.

**gratuitous promise** A promise to do something with no request for something in exchange. Lacking consideration, a gratuitous promise is not enforceable as a contract.

**guarantor** One who makes a legally enforceable promise to pay money or perform any other act originally promised by a promisor, if the promisor defaults or otherwise fails to perform its obligations under the contract.

**guardian** A person appointed by a court to care for someone who because of age, mental illness, or other condition is unable to care for himself or herself.

**H**

**heir** A person who inherits or is entitled by law or by the terms of a will to inherit the estate of another.

**holder** A person or company in possession of an instrument and entitled to payment.

**holder in due course** A holder who takes a negotiable instrument for value, in good faith, and without notice. A holder in due course may enforce payment of an instrument even though the drawer may have a defense against payment to the original payee. The law provides this protection against loss to holders in due course, because if the protection did not exist, there would be extreme reluctance to exchange cash or goods for a written instrument.

**home banking services** A variety of arrangements that allow customers to check balances, confirm deposits, and transact other banking business by telephone or computer link.

**HUD-1 settlement statement** The settlement statement provided to all parties to a residential real estate transaction, describing the amounts paid at the closing of the transaction and the parties to whom each amount is disbursed.

## I

**implied authority** Authority that is necessary in order to accomplish the things for which an agent has been given express authority. This type of permission is not actually stated.

**indemnify** reimburse for losses.

**initial disclosure statement** Required by Regulation Z, a written notification of the credit terms and other facts about a consumer loan that must be given to the consumer(s) before the closing of their loan.

**intermediary bank** The bank to which an item is transferred during collection, other than the depositary or payor bank.

**Internet** a worldwide information system created by the linking of computers.

**inter vivos trust** A trust that becomes effective during the lifetime of the person establishing the trust.

**intestate succession** The transfer of property ownership after the death of a person, by operation of law, to the person's heirs. The process occurs when the property owner dies without leaving a proper will.

**inventory** Goods that are held by a person for sale or lease, including raw materials that are used or consumed in the business itself.

**irrevocable letter of credit** A letter of credit that, once it is established, cannot be canceled by the issuer without the consent of the other parties.

**issuer/issuing bank** The bank that issues a letter of credit.

**item** A check or draft that has entered the bank collection process.

## J

**joint tenancy** Ownership of real property where two or more people each have one and the same undivided interest in the property. After the death of one of the owners, under the right of survivorship the others continue to own the property and to have the right to use it.

**judicial/judgment lien** A lien that attaches to an owner's property as a result of a court judgment against the owner in a lawsuit. If the owner has been found liable to pay damages to the other party and cannot pay, the judgment allows the party to claim a lien on the owner's property to secure payment.

**judicial review** The term used to describe a situation in which a party (such as a bank or association of banks) appeals an order or decision of a regulatory agency, seeking to have it reviewed and reversed by a court.

**jurisdiction** The power of a court to interpret the law in relation to a particular matter. The jurisdiction of federal courts is established under the U.S. Constitution and in legislation enacted by Congress. Similarly, the jurisdiction of state courts is established under each state constitution and in laws enacted by most state legislatures.

## L

**larceny** The crime of taking and carrying away personal property from the lawful possession of another without consent and with intent to steal it. If the property taken has a sufficiently high value, the crime will be defined as grand larceny, a felony. If the property is of lesser value, the crime is petty larceny, a misdemeanor.

**law** That which must be obeyed and followed by citizens, subject to sanctions or legal consequences. The law may be found in the common law, statutes enacted by legislatures, state and federal constitutions, and agency regulations.

**lease/leasehold** A contract in which the owner of property grants to another the right to possess and use the property for a specified time in return for payment. An owner who leases property is called a *lessor;* the party with the right to possess the property under a lease is the *lessee.* If the lease concerns real property, these parties are also known as landlord and tenant. The lessor owns the property but does not have the right to use or possess it during the time the lease is in effect, as the right to possession has been transferred to the lessee.

**legal capacity** The capacity to represent or protect one's own interests; the capacity to enter into and be held accountable for contract obligations, such as the repayment of a loan. Persons lacking legal capacity include minors and persons who are mentally incompetent at the time of the transaction.

**legal detriment** A type of valid consideration for a contract, other than a payment or other thing of value given, that involves giving up a legal right that one is entitled to exercise, refraining from doing what one has a legal right to do, doing something one has a right not to do, or giving up something one has a right to keep.

**legal obligation** Any obligation that is enforceable under the law, such as a contract obligation.

**legally adequate consideration** Consideration that is at least reasonably proportioned to the value of that for which it is given. Although the law is not concerned with whether the price paid as consideration is fair in the marketplace, in instances where the consideration exchanged is grossly inadequate, and thus not reasonably just and equitable under the circumstances, the contract may be held to be invalid and unenforceable for lack of consideration.

**legislature** A group of elected officials with the authority to enact new laws. The United States Congress is an example of a legislature. All 50 states have state legislatures.

**liability** The legal obligation to pay a debt or a money judgment for damages.

**libel** A false written statement that damages a person's reputation. Such a statement is libelous.

**lien** A legal claim against a piece of property to be used to obtain repayment if a debt is not paid as promised.

**life estate** A property interest consisting of the right to possess real property for life. A person possessing a life estate in property has no right to sell the property, nor is a life estate inheritable.

**limited liability company** A form of business organization recently introduced in the United States that combines various features of both corporations and partnerships. As in the case of corporate shareholders, owners of an LLC (called *members)* are not personally liable for the obligations of the business. For tax purposes, however, LLCs are treated as partnerships, and thus are not subject to income tax; instead, all income and losses of the business are passed through to the members. Also, unlike limited partnerships, all members may manage the company without losing liability protection.

**limited partnership** A partnership that includes at least one limited partner, whose liability is limited to the amount he or she invested in the partnership, provided the limited partner does not actively participate in the management of the business.

**liquidation** Converting property into cash. Also, the term used to refer to the specific legal procedures under Chapter 7 of the Bankruptcy Code for collecting a debtor's assets, selling the assets, and then distributing the proceeds among the creditors according to the type and amount of their claims. Following liquidation, the debtor is discharged from indebtedness. (Also called *straight bankruptcy.)*

## M

**maker** The person who is primarily obligated to pay a promissory note.

**managers** Persons whom members may delegate to be responsible for managing a limited liability company.

**mechanic's lien** A lien created by operation of law (rather than by contractual agreement) that secures payment for work performed and materials furnished in the construction or repair of a building, and that attaches to the land as well as the buildings and other improvements erected thereon.

**members** Owners of a limited liability company.

**misdemeanor** Criminal offenses less serious than felonies, generally punishable by a fine and/or imprisonment for less than one year.

**mitigation of damages** A legal doctrine that, in situations where one party has breached a contract, requires the nonbreaching party to do all that is reasonable to minimize the resulting damages. The doctrine requiring mitigation of damages was not developed to favor breaching parties, but rather to prevent unnecessary economic waste.

**money laundering** A crime involving transferring cash acquired in criminal activities from one bank account to another as a means of concealing the true source of the cash.

**mortgage** A legal document, which varies from state to state, in which a borrower gives the lender a lien on property as security for the repayment of the loan. Mortgages usually are issued in conjunction with loans for purchasing or improving real property. In return for the loan, the mortgage gives the lender (mortgagee) the legal right to take possession, acquire the fee, and sell the property if the borrower (mortgagor) fails to pay on time.

**mutual assent** The agreement of each contracting party to contract terms in the same sense and with the same meaning. Also called a *meeting of the minds.*

## N

**national bank** A commercial bank chartered and supervised by the Office of the Comptroller of the Currency (OCC). The words *national* or *National Association* or the initials *N.A.* must appear in the bank's name. A national bank must belong to the Federal Reserve System.

**National Automated Clearing House Association (NACHA)** An association that has issued rules governing all funds transfers using the Automated Clearing House system.

**negligence** A tort involving carelessness in conducting one's affairs that results in injury to someone else. Unlike conversion and some other torts, wrongful intent is not a necessary element of negligence. Rather, negligence is based on a failure to satisfy the duty of care, which is defined as the degree of care that a reasonable person would exercise under similar circumstances. Acts done without that degree of care and that cause injury to others are legally negligent.

**negotiable instrument** A document recognized as a substitute for cash and that can be transferred from one person or business to another. Checks, drafts, notes, and certificates of deposit are examples of negotiable instruments.

**note** An instrument containing a promise to pay a specified amount, either on demand or at a future date.

## O

**offer, offeror, offeree** A proposal in which one person (the offeror) promises to do something if another person (the offeree) does something in return.

**Office of the Comptroller of the Currency (OCC)** An agency of the U.S. Treasury Department that is responsible for chartering and supervising all national banks. Officials from the OCC conduct regular examinations of national banks to ensure that all banking regulations are followed.

**Office of Thrift Supervision (OTS)** The regulatory agency that is responsible for governing thrift institutions, like savings and loan associations. The OTS is an agency of the U.S. Treasury Department.

**officers** Persons appointed by the board of directors of a corporation to be responsible for the day-to-day management of the corporation.

**open-ended credit** Repeated consumer credit extensions on a revolving basis. Credit extended to a consumer under an arrangement in which the parties contemplate repeated transactions, the creditor may impose a finance charge, and the amount of the credit extended to the consumer is made available to the extent that any outstanding balance is repaid.

**ordinary care** According to the Uniform Commercial Code, the exercise of reasonable commercial standards prevailing in the area where the bank is located and pertaining to the business in which the bank is engaged.

**ordinary course of business** The transaction of business according to the usual customs of the commercial world generally, of the particular community, or (in some cases) of the particular individual whose acts are under consideration. In bankruptcy proceedings, a debtor in possession may continue to make decisions concerning the operation of his or her business without notifying interested parties and without the bankruptcy court's approval, so long as the actions he or she takes are in the ordinary course of business.

**original jurisdiction** The United States Supreme Court's jurisdiction to act, in a very limited class of cases, as the trial court in a matter. Such a case exists, for example, when one state sues another state. Original jurisdiction is distinguished from appellate jurisdiction.

**originating depository financial institution (ODFI)** The term adopted by the National Automated Clearing House Association to refer to the bank that receives payment instructions from the originator and forwards those instructions (entries) to the Automated Clearing House operator.

**originator** The term used in Article 4A of the Uniform Commercial Code to refer to the sender of the first payment order in a funds transfer. Also, the term adopted by the National Automated Clearing House Association to refer to the person or entity that initiates an Automated Clearing House entry into the payment system pursuant to an arrangement with a receiver.

**originator's bank** The term used in Article 4A of the Uniform Commercial Code to refer to the bank that first receives the originator's payment order.

# P

**parol evidence rule** A rule of common law, adopted by statute in many states, which holds that once parties have entered into a written contract that reflects a complete statement of their agreement, outside evidence (parol evidence) of earlier understandings or negotiations between the parties may not be introduced to contradict or vary the terms of the written agreement. Parol evidence may be introduced, however, to show that a written contract was induced by fraud or mistake, is illegal, or is voidable due to one party's lack of legal capacity.

**parties** Persons who reach agreement and form a contract are called *parties* to the contract.

**partnership** An unincorporated business entity owned by two or more persons who agree to contribute money, labor, property, or skill to the business and share the business profits and losses.

**payee** The person or company named on a draft as the recipient of the sum specified.

**payment order** The term used in Article 4A of the Uniform Commercial Code to refer to an unconditional (except for time of payment) instruction of a sender to a receiving bank, to pay, or to cause another bank to pay, a certain amount of money to a beneficiary named by the sender.

**payor bank** The bank at which an item is payable as drawn that is, the drawee bank.

**perfected interest** An interest in the property of another that is protected against claims of third parties who may also acquire interests in the same collateral.

**perfecting an interest** Taking the appropriate steps (for example, recording a security interest with the recorder of deeds office) to give public notice of a secured creditor's interest in certain property owned by the debtor.

**perfection** The process by which a secured party protects its security interest from third parties by filing or recording documentation of the security interest in the public records.

**periodic disclosures** Disclosures that reflect transactions in the account during each billing cycle.

**personal liability** Individual liability of partners for losses incurred by the partnership.

**personal defenses** Defenses that might be valid if the seller were suing the buyer, but that are not good against the holder who can prove his or her status as a holder in due course.

**personal property** Anything that is not real property, including tangible and movable objects as well as intangible rights, such as those represented by a stock certificate or an I.O.U.

**plaintiff** A person who initiates a lawsuit by filing a complaint.

**point of sale (POS)/point-of-sale transaction** A system that permits bank customers to transfer funds from their bank accounts and perform other financial transactions at a retail point of sale.

**posting** The process by which the bookkeeping department of a drawee bank makes debit entries, or a depositary bank makes credit entries, in a customer's account. For example, the bookkeeping department first examines the check for form and signature, then ensures that sufficient funds are on deposit to cover the amount of the check, and finally posts the check to (debits) the drawer's account.

**power of attorney** A document that appoints an agent to perform specific acts on behalf of an individual. The agent under a power of attorney is called an *attorney-in-fact*. The authority of the attorney-in-fact may be limited to a particular transaction or may be very broad.

**preauthorized credit transaction** An electronic funds transfer involving a third-party direct deposit into a customer's asset account made under the terms of a separate agreement between the third party and account holder; for example, the federal government's direct deposit of Social Security payments into payees' bank accounts.

**preauthorized debit transaction** An account feature in which an individual authorizes recurring debits from his or her personal account.

**preference** A debtor's transfer of property to a creditor in payment of a debt within 90 days before filing for bankruptcy. Under Chapter 7 of the Bankruptcy Code, trustees have the power to cancel these preferences and reclaim the transferred property for the bankruptcy estate.

**presenting bank** Any bank that presents an item to the payor bank for payment.

**primary rule of interpretation** A rule of law governing the interpretation of contracts that provides that words in a contract shall be given their plain and usual meaning. This rule has three exceptions: 1) technical words (terms of art) must be given their technical meaning; 2) the usual meaning of words may vary according to their usage within the particular trade or locality; and 3) words may not be given their plain meaning if that would contradict the intentions of the parties.

**principal** 1) The person who authorizes another (agent) to act on his or her behalf. 2) The actual amount of a deposit, loan, or investment, exclusive of interest. 3) The primary borrower on a loan, as opposed to the guarantor.

**priority/priorities** Priorities are the rank order in the exercise of legal rights. Thus, when two parties hold similar rights in respect of the same subject matter (for example, mortgages on the same real property) but one party is entitled to exercise his or her rights before the other, he or she is said to have priority.

**probate** A judicial procedure whereby the validity of a will is proved and a decedent's estate (in accordance with the terms of a will, if one exists) is administered.

**proceeds** Anything that is received when collateral is sold, exchanged, or otherwise disposed of.

**prohibited basis** Characteristics of a person that cannot be considered when a creditor makes a decision on a consumer credit application. Prohibited bases include race, color, religion, national origin, age, sex, marital status, the receipt of public assistance income, or the exercise of rights under the Consumer Credit Protection Act.

**promisee** A person to whom a promise is made.

**promisor** A person who promises to do something for someone else.

**property interests** Legal rights or shares that, taken all together, make up ownership of property. The right to possess property, and the right to use or control property, are property interests.

**publicly held corporation** A corporation whose stock is traded publicly.

**punitive damages** An amount of money ordered by a court to be paid as punishment for a serious and willful violation of a civil law.

**purchase money security interest** A security interest used primarily in connection with the purchase of personal property on credit.

**Q**

**quasi contract** In situations where no contract exists, but one party has received a benefit and would be unjustly enriched if allowed to keep the benefit without paying, the principle of quasi contract imposes a legal obligation to pay for the value of the benefit received.

**R**

**ratification** A bank defense against liability on a forged signature claim, ratification of an instrument occurs when a drawer adopts a forged or unauthorized signature as his or her own. Ratification may also refer to the principal's approval of the unauthorized acts of his or her agent.

**reaffirmation** A procedure whereby, on the consent of the secured creditor, a bankruptcy debtor may retain possession of personal property pledged as collateral by promising to repay the underlying debt at some time in the future, even if the debt is greater than the value of the collateral.

**real defense** A defense that, it proven, will enable a party to get out of paying an instrument.

**real property** Land and anything attached to land such as buildings, trees, or growing plants.

**receiver** The term adopted by the National Automated Clearing House Association to refer to a person or entity that authorizes an originator to initiate an Automated Clearing House entry to the receiver's account.

**receiving bank** The term used in Article 4A of the Uniform Commercial Code to refer to the bank to which a sender's instruction is addressed.

**receiving depository financial institution (RDFI)** The term adopted by the National Automated Clearing House Association to refer to the bank that receives Automated Clearing House entries from the ACH operator and posts them (either as credits or debits) to the accounts of its depositors, the receivers.

**recording** The procedure for officially registering, in the office of public land records or other appropriate office of the county or other jurisdiction in which property is located, deeds, mortgages, liens, and other documents reflecting security interests affecting title to said property. Recording serves the purpose of perfecting an interest in property by giving notice of its existence and establishing its priority against other interests.

**redeem** To buy back. In many states, a mortgagor whose loan is in default may redeem his or her property within a specified period and thus escape foreclosure.

**redemption** Under the Bankruptcy Code, redemption is the right of an debtor to recover collateral that has been abandoned by the trustee (provided the collateral is personal property that secures a consumer debt and is primarily for personal, family, or household use), by paying either the amount remaining on the debt or the value of the collateral, whichever is less.

**regulation** An official rule or set of rules having the force of law. Regulations are issued by government agencies and are based on, and designed to implement, laws enacted by legislatures. For example, the Federal Reserve Board's Regulation C is a set of rules based on the Home Mortgage Disclosure Act of 1975.

**regulatory agencies** Government entities responsible for issuing regulations and for enforcing those regulations. The federal government and the state governments have many of these agencies. The Office of the Comptroller of the Currency and a state banking commission are examples of regulatory agencies.

**rehabilitation/debtor rehabilitation** The goal of Chapter 11 and Chapter 13 of the Bankruptcy Code, which permit a debtor to continue business operations and retain the use of creditors' collateral while repaying existing debt, and thus ultimately to be restored to a condition of solvency.

**remedy** A legal means to enforce a right or correct a wrong.

**removal** The right of a defendant to have a case that has been filed in a state court but that involves federal law transferred from state court to federal court. The purpose of the removal power is to allow defendants some control over where claims filed against them will be heard, rather than leaving that choice solely to the plaintiff.

**restitution powers** The power of regulatory agencies to order creditors to return overcharges to consumers.

**returning bank** Any bank handling a returned check except the payor bank and the depositary bank.

**right of rescission** The right of a customer to cancel a contract or legally binding agreement within a specified period of time.

**routing symbol** See *check routing symbol*.

## S

**secondary rules of interpretation** The following rules, which are used to interpret the meaning of a contract if the meaning remains unclear after the primary rules of interpretation have been applied: 1) an interpretation that gives a reasonable meaning to all of the main provisions of the contract is preferred; 2) a specific clause in the contract will prevail over a conflicting general clause; 3) an interpretation that makes a contract valid and reasonable will be preferred over an interpretation that makes the contract unenforceable or harsh; 4) if a conflict exists between handwritten or typed provisions and provisions printed on a form, the handwritten or typed provisions will prevail; 5) related writings may be interpreted together.

**secured party** A creditor possessing a security interest.

**securities** Evidences of contracts under which a corporation agrees to make certain payments or give certain rights to the holders of such securities. Bonds (debt securities) and stock certificates are types of securities. Laws that regulate the issuing and selling of securities are referred to as *securities laws*.

**security agreement** An agreement in which a debtor grants to a secured party rights in certain of the debtor's property, creating a security interest.

**security interest** A claim to property that secures repayment of a debt by allowing the creditor to take the property, sell it, and retain the proceeds (up to the amount of the indebtedness) if the debt is not repaid as promised.

**sender** The term used in Article 4A of the Uniform Commercial Code to refer to the person giving an instruction to a receiving bank to issue a payment order.

**setoff** A procedure whereby, in situations involving mutual debts between a bankruptcy debtor and a creditor, the creditor may offset the amount he owes against the amount owed to him by the debtor.

**settlor** The person who establishes a trust.

**slander** A false statement made orally that damages a person's reputation. Such a statement is slanderous.

**smart card** A card that contains a computer chip that stores a dollar value and a variety of other financial, medical, and security information.

**sole proprietorship** A business that is owned and operated by a single individual and is not incorporated. (The term *sole proprietor* means single owner, while *proprietorship* refers to the business itself.) A sole proprietorship is perhaps the simplest form of business organization.

**specific performance** A remedy for breach of contract whereby a court compels the breaching party to perform the contract according to the precise terms agreed upon.

**standby letter of credit** A letter of credit established to guarantee the customer's performance of an obligation owed to the beneficiary. It does not deal with financing the purchase of goods, but is used for such purposes as ensuring the completion of a construction project, ensuring payment of a court judgment should the losing party's appeal of the judgment fail, and so forth.

**state banking authority** The agency in every state—typically a state banking commission or superintendent of banks—that is responsible for enforcing state laws pertaining to the operation of state-chartered banks.

**state-chartered bank** A bank that is chartered by a state banking authority, as opposed to being chartered at the federal level by the Office of the Comptroller of the Currency.

**statute** A law that specifies actions that are not allowed or actions that must be taken. Some statutes apply to everyone. Others statutes apply only to certain types of people or organizations. For example, many laws apply only to banks.

**Statute of Frauds** A statute originally enacted three centuries ago in England, and adopted in varying forms throughout the United States, that provides that certain kinds of contracts are unenforceable unless they are in writing. Contracts subject to the Statute of Frauds include contracts for the sale of land, contracts for the sale of goods above a certain price, contracts that by their own terms cannot be performed within one year from the date of the contract, and promises to be responsible for someone else's debts. The Statute of Frauds is designed to prevent fraud and false testimony regarding oral contracts.

**stock** An ownership interest in a corporation. This term is also used to refer to the stock certificates that evidence such ownership.

**substantial performance** A doctrine that holds that where a contract has been substantially performed—that is, the failure to perform involves only technical or unimportant omissions or defects—the party who substantially performed is entitled to receive the compensation he or she bargained for, minus an adjustment to cover the costs of correcting or completing those items not performed. In certain circumstances courts may not apply the doctrine of substantial performance if the failure to perform completely is willful or negligent.

**supreme court** A court of final appeal (or court of last resort). In the federal system, this is the U.S. Supreme Court. The states' highest courts also are generally called supreme courts, but this is not so in every state.

**surety** A person who, under the original contract signed by the promisor, agrees to pay money or do any other act promised by the promisor. A surety is primarily liable under the contract—that is, a promisee need not wait until the promisor is in default to enforce payment or performance by the surety.

**T**

**tenancy by the entirety** Essentially a form of joint tenancy involving ownership by a husband and wife. The characteristic that distinguishes it from a joint tenancy is that neither spouse in a tenancy by the entirety has the right to transfer his or her share except with the agreement of the other; they must both join in a deed or other conveyance for the transfer to be effective. By contrast, a joint tenancy may be terminated by one tenant's conveyance of his or her interest. In many states, tenancy by the entirety has been abolished in favor of husband and wife holding their property simply as joint tenants.

**tenancy in common** Common ownership of real property by two or more persons, each of whom can leave his or her interest in the property to someone else when he or she dies.

**terms** Propositions stated or promises made which, when assented to or accepted by another, settle the contract and bind the parties.

**testamentary trust** A trust that becomes effective after the person establishing the trust dies.

**third-party beneficiary** A person who is intended to be provided a benefit under a contract to which he or she is not a party.

**time deposit account** A deposit account with a specific maturity date.

**title** The term used to indicate that one is the legal owner of property. A legal owner has title to property; the property is titled in the owner's name.

**tort** A noncriminal interference with the rights of an individual member of society, causing harm, damage, or other injury to that person, the person's property, or the person's reputation.

**tortfeasor** A person who is found liable for a tort in a civil proceeding.

**transfer agent** A bank or other person retained by a corporation to handle stock transfers, which involves receiving the transferor's stock certificate, canceling it, and issuing a new certificate in the name of the new owner.

**transfer/transferor/transferee** A change of ownership whereby one person (the transferor) conveys his or her ownership to another (the transferee).

**trust** An arrangement in which one person or institution (the trustee) holds legal title to property and administers it for the benefit of another (the beneficiary).

**trustee** A person who is granted legal title to property with a duty to see that it is used for the benefit of another.

**trustee in bankruptcy** The person selected by creditors under Chapter 7 of the Bankruptcy Code to administer the debtor's property in the bankruptcy proceedings, subject to the supervision of the Bankruptcy Court. Usually, creditors select as trustee the temporary trustee appointed by the Office of the U.S. Trustee.

**two-day/four-day test** Tests for determining under Regulation CC whether a check return has been expedited in compliance with the Expedited Funds Availability Act. Under the two-day test, which applies to payor banks that are local with respect to the depositary bank, a local payor bank expedites the return of a check if it sends the check so that it would normally be received by the depositary bank no later than 4:00 p.m. (local time of the depositary bank) of the second business day following the banking day on which the check was presented to the payor bank. Under the four-day test, which applies to payor banks that are nonlocal with respect to the depositary bank, a nonlocal payor bank expedites the return of a check if it sends the check so that it would normally be received by the depositary bank not later than 4:00 p.m. (local time of the depositary bank) of the fourth business day following the banking day on which the check was presented to the payor bank.

**U**

**unauthorized transfer** An electronic funds transfer made by someone without authority to do so and from which the account holder receives no benefit.

**unauthorized use** Use of a credit card by a person who has no permission to do so.

**Uniform Commercial Code (UCC)** A model law proposed by the National Conference of Commissioners on Uniform State Laws that governs banking and other kinds of commercial transactions. The UCC in its entirety, or some version of the UCC, is now effective in 49 states, the District of Columbia, and the Virgin Islands.

**unilateral contract** A contract that requires the offeree to perform an act in return for the offeror's promise to pay when performance is complete. In a unilateral contract, acceptance of the offer occurs only upon performance of the act.

**unsecured creditor** A creditor whose loans are not secured by a mortgage, lien, or other means.

**U.S. district courts** Trial courts in the federal judicial system. There are currently 91 federal districts, with at least one in each state. U.S. district courts, which also are referred to as federal district courts, conduct trials in civil and criminal cases under their jurisdiction, which includes cases involving the federal Constitution, federal laws, treaties with other nations, controversies between states, and certain controversies between persons who reside in different states.

**usury/usurious** The collection of interest in an amount greater than what is permitted by federal or state law. A loan agreement or other contract that charges a rate of interest that is higher than the law permits is a usurious contract.

# V

**void contract** A contract that never had any legal existence or effect and thus creates no legal rights; for example, contracts that have an illegal purpose.

**voidable contract** A contract that may be avoided or declared void and thus made unenforceable—for example, a contract with someone lacking legal capacity.

# W

**ward** A person who because of age, mental illness, or other condition is unable to care for himself and is under the protection of a court-appointed guardian.

# ADDITIONAL RESOURCES

## Internet Web Sites

| Name | Address | Description |
|------|---------|-------------|
| *Name* | *Address* | *Description* |
| ABA Banking | banking.com/aba | An online comprehensive banking journal covering a variety of banking-related topics and including a compliance clinic feature. |
| American Bankruptcy Institute | abiworld.org | A site containing a great deal of information about current bankruptcy law and about legislative efforts to amend the law. |
| Bankinfo.com | bankinfo.com | A daily financial services magazine operated by Thomas Financial Publishing and containing regulatory compliance information and links to regulations. |
| Code of Federal Regulations | access.gpo.gov/nara/cfr/ index/html | The entire Code of Federal Regulations along with a search engine for research. |
| Cornell Legal Information | law.cornell.edu/ statutes.html#state | A valuable link to all state laws online, including individual state, commercial, and banking laws. |
| Cornell Legal Information Institute | law.cornell.edu/topics/ banking.html | A source for banking laws of all varieties; includes links to federal laws, regulations, and judicial decisions, as well as some state laws. |
| Federal Cross Reference | fedcrossref.com | A valuable search tool for locating information in the federal register and the Code of Federal Regulations. |

*(continued)*

## Internet Web Sites

| Name | Address | Description |
| --- | --- | --- |
| Federal Deposit Insurance Corporation (FDIC) | fdic.gov | The official FDIC Web site, containing regulatory issuances (including Financial Institution Letters), regulatory manuals, directives, policies, laws, regulations, consumer information (including how to determine if an online bank is a member of the FDIC), and an Electronic Deposit Insurance Estimator (to determine how much of a consumer's deposits are insured by the FDIC). |
| Federal Financial Institutions Examination Council | ffiec.gov | The official FFIEC Web site, containing press releases, updates to reports, a link to the FFIEC Appraisal Subcommittee (which ensures that real estate appraisers are properly trained and certified), and HMDA information, including a HMDA geocoder that converts U.S. addresses into HMDA-reportable data (census tract, metropolitan statistical area, and so forth). |
| *Federal Register* | access.gpo.gov/su_doc/ aces140.html | A source for the *Federal Register* from 1995 to the present; you can search the *Federal Register* at this site using keywords, dates, or page numbers. |
| Federal Reserve Banks | | Individual Web sites maintained by each Federal Reserve bank, with links to the Federal Reserve Board; many of the banks also have their own publications, which are referenced on their sites. |
|   Atlanta | frbatlanta.org | |
|   Boston | std.com/frbbos/ | |
|   Chicago | frbchi.org | |
|   Cleveland | clev.frb.org | |
|   Dallas | dallasfed.org | |
|   Kansas City | kc.frb.org | |
|   Minneapolis | woodrow.mpls.frb.fed.us | |
|   New York | nyfrb.org | |
|   Philadelphia | phil.frb.org | |
|   Richmond | rich.frb.org | |
|   San Francisco | frbsf.org | |
|   St. Louis | stls.frb.org | |

## Internet Web Sites

| Name | Address | Description |
|---|---|---|
| Federal Reserve System | federalreserve.gov | The official site of the Board of Governors of the Federal Reserve, containing all the Fed's issuances, including press releases, monetary policy publications, research information, and data, as well as Fed regulatory information (including supervisory letters and manuals). |
| FedWorld | fedworld.gov | A central access point for searching, locating, and acquiring government documents maintained by the U.S. Department of Commerce, this site allows searching through a large network of U.S. government-related Web sites. |
| Financial Crimes Enforcement Network (FinCEN) | ustreas.gov/fincen | The official FinCEN Web site, containing all FinCEN issuances, advisories, and Bank Secrecy Act forms and publications. |
| Financial Net | financial-net.com | A list with hyperlinks to government, regulatory, and legal Web sites relevant to banking. |
| Financial Services Internet Network | financialsnet.com | A directory of financial services providers with links to their sites. |
| FindLaw Internet Legal Sources | findlaw.com | A legal search engine capable of searching several legal databases, including legal organizations, law review journals, state and federal statutes, and state and federal judicial cases by subject matter. |
| Government Printing Office Superintendent of Documents | access.gpo/su_docs/ | The government printing office site, providing access to legislative, regulatory, judicial, and administrative documents. |
| House Committee on Banking and Financial Services | house.gov/banking/ | A site containing all documents published by the Committee on Banking and Financial Services of the U.S. House of Representatives, searchable by topic. |

*(continued)*

## Internet Web Sites

| Name | Address | Description |
| --- | --- | --- |
| Laws Online | lawsonline.com | A comprehensive list of links to federal and state law databases, legal directories, and legal resources (such as law libraries). |
| National Conference of Commissioners on Uniform State Laws | nccusl.org | The official NCCUSL site, containing model acts and drafts of model acts proposed by the NCCUSL, and lists of the states that have adopted the model acts. |
| National Consumer Law Center | consumerlaw.org | A pro-consumer Web site run by the National Consumer Law Center, Inc., containing information on consumer credit laws and advice for consumer attorneys. |
| National Consumer's League | fraud.org | A site dedicated to preventing consumer fraud (particularly Internet scams) and containing a business fraud prevention section. |
| Office of the Comptroller of the Currency | occ.treas.gov | The main OCC site, containing all regulations published by the OCC, all new issuances (including bulletins and advisory letters), all OCC CRA information, and an OCC directory. |
| Office of Thrift Supervision | ots.treas.gov | The official OTS Web site, containing all of the OTS laws, regulations, policies, and publications. |
| Self-Help Law Center | nolo.com | A consumer-oriented site containing a debt and credit section with some useful legal information. |
| Thomas Legislative Information | thomas.loc.gov/home/thomas2.html | A site maintained by the Library of Congress containing legislative information, including all current bills, public laws, the *Congressional Record,* House and Senate committee information, and links to other congressional Web sites. |

## Internet Web Sites

| Name | Address | Description |
| --- | --- | --- |
| U.S. Department of the Treasury | treas.gov | The official U.S. Treasury Web site, containing information on Treasury publications, bureaus, agencies, and offices. |
| U.S. House of Representatives | house.gov | The official U.S. House of Representatives site, containing the schedule of the full House, committee schedules, records of roll-call votes, and house reports. |
| U.S. Securities and Exchange Commission | sec.gov | The official SEC Web site, containing SEC press releases, current rulemaking issuances, access to SEC digest, and the EDGAR database. |
| U.S. Senate | senate.gov | The official U.S. Senate Web site, containing a Senate calendar, committee membership and activities, and roll-call vote information; searchable and allows for tracking of bills. |

# INDEX

Beneficiaries, 27, 28, 79
    bank of, 27, 28
    donee, 98
    third-party, 98
Benefits, given in emergency, 105
Bilateral contract, 85
Bill, 7
Billing errors, 130
Binding, 55
Blue Sky laws, 70
Board of directors, 72–73
Bona fide purchaser, 120
Bound, 55
Breach of contract, 100
    remedies for, 102–5
Breach of the peace, 160
Bribery, 41–42

# C

Capacity, legal, 90
Certificates of deposit (CDs), 20, 21
Certificates of title, 158
Chapter 7, liquidation, 169–70
Chapter 11, reorganization, 181–85
Chapter 13, adjustment of debts, 178, 179–81
Check, 21
Class action, 131
Clearing House Interbank Payments Systems (CHIPS), 27
Close corporations, 70
Closed-ended credit, 125
Collateral, 150
    assembling, 160–61
    description of, 152, 156–57
    disposing of, 161
    foreclosing on, 160–63
    keeping repossessed, 163
    purchasers of, 159
Collecting bank, 24
Collection, 24–25
Commercial letters of credit, 28
Committees, 184
Common law, 7
Community Reinvestment Act (1977), 5
Compensatory damages, 103
Comptroller of the Currency, Office of (OCC), 3, 9–10, 12
Concurrent jurisdiction, 14
Conditions
    express, 102
    implied, 102
Congress, U.S., 7, 9
Consequential damages, 103
Consideration, 88
    adequacy of, 89
Construction liens, 119
Consumer Credit Protection Act, 4
Consumer goods, 151
Consumer lease, 137
Consumer Leasing Act (1977), 5, 136–37
Consumer lending, 124–44
    Consumer Leasing Act (1977), 136–37
    Credit Practices Rule, 142–43

Equal Credit Opportunity Act (ECOA) (1975), 132–36
    Fair Credit Reporting Act (FCRA) (1971), 137–40
    Fair Debt Collection Practices Act (1977), 140–42
    Truth in Lending Act (TILA) (1968), 124–32
Consumer Protection Act, 132
Consumer reporting agencies, 138
Consumer reports, 138
    content of, 138–39
    disputing accuracy of, 139–40
    furnishing of, 139
    investigative, 139
    right to review, 139
    users of, 140
Consumers, real estate laws that protect, 143–44
Contracts, 84–106
    bilateral, 85
    breach of, 100
        remedies for, 102–5
    defined, 84
    elements of, 84–89
    enforcing, 100–102
    executory, 174
    interpreting, 99–100
    involving third parties, 96–98
    quasi, 104–5
    for sale of goods above certain price, 95
    for sale of land, 95
    unilateral, 85
    void, 90
    voidable, 90
Contractual promises, addressed by Statute of Frauds, 94–95
Conversion, 36
Corporate officers, 74
Corporations
    board of directors, 72–73
    close, 70
    organization of, 68, 70
    publicly held, 72
    stock, 70
    stock transfers, 71
Cosigners, 142–43
Court-ordered repossession, 160
Cram down, 184
Credit
    closed-ended, 125
    open-ended, 125, 127
Credit advertisement, 129
Credit cards, 128–29
Creditors, 132
    secured, 172
    unsecured, 158–59
Credit Practices Rule, 142–43
Crimes, 36, 37
    bribery, 41–42
    embezzlement, 41
    larceny, 41
    money laundering, 42, 45
*Crowne Bank* v. *Tri-State Airport Authority,* 96–97
Cumulative voting, 73
Currency transaction report (CTR), 42
Customer, responsibilities of bank to, 26
Cut-off time, 27–28